Scottish SECONDARY MATHEMATICS

Tom Sanaghan

Jim Pennel

Carol Munro

Carole Ford

David Finnemore

John Dalton

James Cairns

heinemann.co.uk
✓ Free online support
✓ Useful weblinks
✓ 24 hour online ordering

01865 888058

Heinemann

Inspiring generations

Heinemann is an imprint of Pearson Education Limited,
a company incorporated in England and Wales, having
its registered office at Edinburgh Gate, Harlow, Essex, CM20 2JE.
Registered company number: 872828

Heinemann is a registered trademark of Pearson Education Limited

© Tom Sanaghan, Jim Pennel, Carol Munro, Carole Ford, John Dalton, David Finnemore,
James Cairns, 2004

First published 2005

11
10 9 8 7

British Library Cataloguing in Publication Data is available
from the British Library on request.

ISBN 978 0 435040 15 4

Illustrations by Gustavo Mazali
Cover design by mcc design ltd.
Printed and bound in China (CTPS/07)
Cover photo: Stock Scotland

Acknowledgements
The authors and publishers would like to thank the following for permission to
use photographs:

p15: Photolibrary.com; pp 20, 75: Science Photo Library; pp 19, 26, 27, 58, 101 top, 110,
133, 134 middle left, 141, bottom, 143 top, 145 bottom: Getty Images; p40 top: iStock
Photo/Nicola Stratford; pp 40 bottom, 128, 156, 187: Corbis; p41 top: Harcourt
Education Ltd/Gareth Boden; p41 bottom left: iStock Photo/Geoff Delderfield; pp 41
bottom middle, 141 top, 154: Harcourt Education Ltd/Peter Evans; pp 41 bottom right,
134 bottom left: Brand X Photos; p56: Stock Scotland/Hugh Webster; p74: Ardea/John
Daniels; p78: Alamy Images; p96: Nature PL/Dave Watts; pp 98, 101 bottom: Empics;
pp 134 top, 134 middle right: Dynamic Graphics; p134 bottom right: Creatas;
p143 bottom: Stock Scotland/John MacPherson; p145 top: Rex Features/Richard
Sowersby; p146: iStock Photo/Giles Dumoulin

The Census at School data on p97 reproduced by permission of the Royal Statistical
Society Centre for Statistical Education.

The authors and publishers would also like to thank Alex McKee for assistance with the
manuscript.

Contents

How to use this book

Every chapter is divided into sections.

Each section begins with a list of key points:

1.1 Rounding

> Our numbers were developed from the Arabic system giving the digits 0–9.

An exercise follows:

Exercise 1.1

1 Round the following numbers to the nearest: (**i**) ten   (**ii**) hundred   (**iii**) thousand
  (**a**) 6172   (**b**) 18 776   (**c**) 5217

At the end of the chapter is a review exercise and a summary of all the key points.

Special instructions are shown by these symbols:

 Use a calculator to answer these questions.

1 Sets of numbers

In this chapter you will learn more about different types of number and their properties.

1.1 Sets of numbers

Some sets of numbers are commonly used in mathematics.

N = natural numbers $\{1, 2, 3, 4 \ldots\}$

W = whole numbers $\{0, 1, 2, 3, 4 \ldots\}$

Z = integers $\{\ldots, -3, -2, -1, 0, 1, 2, 3 \ldots\}$

Q = rational numbers – any number which can be written as a fraction $\{\ldots, -4, 1.5, 6\frac{1}{2} \ldots\}$

To describe a number as a member of a set, use $\in$ meaning 'belongs to'.

$8 \in$ **N**   8 belongs to the set of natural numbers

$-2 \in$ **Z** $0 \in$ **W** $\frac{3}{8} \in$ **Q**

> Numbers may belong to more than one set.
> $5 \in$ **N, W, Z, Q**
> $-5 \in$ **Z, Q**

Example 1

Write the whole numbers between 3 and 5, inclusive.

$\{3, 4, 5\}$

Example 2

List the values of x where $x \geqslant -3, x \in$ **Z**

$\{-3, -2, -1, 0, 1, 2 \ldots\}$

Exercise 1.1

1 Write the

(**a**) whole numbers between 1 and 5 inclusive

(**b**) integers between -2 and 4

(**c**) natural numbers between -5 and 6

(**d**) integers between -10 and -3

2 Copy and complete the table for the given numbers.

	Natural N	Whole W	Integer Z	Rational Q
7	✓	✓	✓	✓
6·3				
12				
-6				
0·7				
$\frac{1}{4}$				
0				

3 List the following values of x:

(a) $x \leqslant 5, x \in \mathbf{N}$ (b) $x \leqslant 5, x \in \mathbf{Z}$ (c) $x > 3, x \in \mathbf{W}$

(d) $x \leqslant 4, x \in \mathbf{W}$ (e) $x < 7, x \in \mathbf{N}$ (f) $x \geqslant -2, x \in \mathbf{Z}$

1.2 Adding and subtracting integers

Remember
- Adding a negative number is the same as subtracting the positive number.
- Subtracting a negative number is the same as adding the positive number.

Example

Calculate (a) $(-5) + (-7)$ (b) $6 - (-8)$ (c) $(-4) - (-7) + (-9)$

(a) $(-5) + (-7)$ (b) $6 - (-8)$ (c) $(-4) - (-7) + (-9)$

$= (-5) - 7$ $= 6 + 8$ $= (-4) + 7 + (-9)$

$= -12$ $= 14$ $= 3 - 9$

$= -6$

Exercise 1.2

1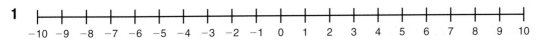

Use the number line to find:

(a) $3 - 7$ (b) $(-2) - 3$ (c) $(-2) + 6$ (d) $(-3) - 5$ (e) $5 - 8$

(f) $(-8) + 2$ (g) $(-10) + 13$ (h) $(-4) - 5$ (i) $(-4) + 1$ (j) $(-3) + 3$

2 Calculate:

(a) $3 + (-4)$ (b) $6 - (-2)$ (c) $10 + (-7)$ (d) $25 + (-14)$

(e) $16 - (-5)$ (f) $(-6) + 23$ (g) $(-12) - 10$ (h) $(-4) + (-9)$

(i) $(-7) + (-15)$ (j) $(-16) - (-14)$ (k) $(-25) - (-20)$ (l) $(-20) + 30$

3 Calculate:

(a) $4 + 6 + (-3)$ (b) $8 - 7 + (-2)$ (c) $-10 - 6 + (-5)$

(d) $24 - 6 - (-8)$ (e) $16 - (-5) + 3$ (f) $-9 + (-4) - (-12)$

(g) $-14 - (-12) - (-7)$ (h) $51 + (-32) + 8$ (i) $(-34) - 45 - (-16)$

4 The temperature in Oldmeldrum was measured at 10 a.m. every day for one week in November. The temperatures were $-2\,°C$, $1\,°C$, $3\,°C$, $3°C$, $5\,°C$, $-1\,°C$, $-2\,°C$. Find the average mean temperature.

5 The coordinates A(0, 10), B(2, 8), C(-1, 5) and D(-3, 7) form a square. Find its new coordinates if:

(a) the square is moved 12 places to the left

(b) the square is moved 5 places to the right

(c) the square is moved 11 places down

(d) the square is moved 14 places up.

1.3 Multiplying integers

$(-2) + (-2) + (-2) + (-2) + (-2)$ can also be written as $(-2) \times 5$ or $5 \times (-2)$
$= (-2) - 2 - 2 - 2 - 2$ $= -10$ $= -10$
$= -10$

Exercise 1.3

1 Copy and complete:

$(-3) + (-3) + (-3) + (-3)$ $= (-3) \times \quad = \quad \times (-3) =$
$(-5) + (-5) + (-5) + (-5) + (-5) + (-5) = (-5) \times \quad =$
$(-8) + (-8) + (-8)$ $= (-8) \times \quad =$
$(-4) + (-4) + (-4)$ $= (-4) \times \quad =$
$(-7) + (-7) + (-7) + (-7) + (-7)$ $= (-7) \times \quad =$

2 Copy and complete:
Multiplying a positive number by a negative number gives a _____ number.

3 Find:

(**a**) $5 \times (-7)$ (**b**) $6 \times (-3)$ (**c**) $10 \times (-9)$ (**d**) $(-4) \times 7$ (**e**) $(-5) \times 8$
(**f**) $(-12) \times 8$ (**g**) $(-6) \times 20$ (**h**) $13 \times (-10)$ (**i**) $4 \times (-9)$ (**j**) $(-12) \times 12$

4 For each number pattern copy and complete:

(**a**) $(-2) \times 3 =$ (**b**) $(-3) \times 3 =$ (**c**) $(-4) \times 3 =$
  $(-2) \times 2 =$ $(-3) \times 2 =$ $(-4) \times 2 =$
  $(-2) \times 1 =$ $(-3) \times 1 =$ $(-4) \times 1 =$
  $(-2) \times 0 =$ $(-3) \times 0 =$ $(-4) \times 0 =$
  $(-2) \times (-1) =$ $(-3) \times (-1) =$ $(-4) \times (-1) =$
  $(-2) \times (-2) =$ $(-3) \times (-2) =$ $(-4) \times (-2) =$
  $(-2) \times (-3) =$ $(-3) \times (-3) =$ $(-4) \times (-3) =$

5 Copy and complete:
Multiplying a negative number by a negative number gives a _____ number.

6 Calculate:

(**a**) $(-4) \times (-5)$ (**b**) $(-6) \times (-3)$ (**c**) $(-2) \times (-9)$
(**d**) $(-8) \times (-7)$ (**e**) $(-10) \times (-8)$ (**f**) $(-13) \times (-12)$
(**g**) $(-3) \times (-11)$ (**h**) $(-4) \times (-4)$ (**i**) $(-8) \times (-6)$
(**j**) $(-4.5) \times (-4)$ (**k**) $(-7.5) \times (-3)$ (**l**) $(-15) \times (-10)$

7 Calculate:

(**a**) $(-7) \times 12$ (**b**) $6 \times (-7)$ (**c**) $(-9) \times (-7)$ (**d**) $(-11) \times 6$
(**e**) $(-16) \times 5$ (**f**) $(-13) \times 8$ (**g**) $(-12) \times (-10)$ (**h**) $(-5) \times (-15)$
(**i**) $(-2.5) \times 5$ (**j**) $(-1.2) \times (-5)$ (**k**) $(-3.2) \times (-4)$ (**l**) $40 \times (-6)$

8 On 3rd January the temperature in Edinburgh was $-2\,°C$.
The temperature in Wick was three times lower and the temperature
in the Faroe Islands was six times lower.
Calculate the temperatures in Wick and the Faroe Islands.

9 On 2nd January the temperature in Dundee was $-3\,°C$.
The temperature in Vladivostock was nine times lower.
Calculate the temperature in Vladivostock.

1.4 Dividing integers

- Multiplying a positive number by a negative number gives a negative number
- Multiplying a negative number by a negative number gives a positive number

$(-4) \times 3 = -12 \longrightarrow \dfrac{-12}{3} = -4$ or $\dfrac{-12}{-4} = 3$

$(-5) \times (-2) = 10 \longrightarrow \dfrac{10}{-2} = -5$ or $\dfrac{10}{-5} = -2$

- Dividing a positive number by a negative number gives a negative number
- Dividing a negative number by a positive number gives a negative number
- Dividing a negative number by a negative number gives a positive number

> If the signs are the same the answer is positive.
> If the signs are different the answer is negative.

Exercise 1.4

1 Rearrange these multiplications to show divisions.

(a) $(-7) \times 5 = -35 \longrightarrow \dfrac{\blacksquare}{5} = -7$ or $\dfrac{-35}{\blacksquare} = 5$

(b) $6 \times (-7) = -42$ (c) $(-3) \times (-8) = 24$ (d) $(-4) \times (-9) = 36$

2 Calculate:

(a) $\dfrac{(-20)}{4}$ (b) $\dfrac{50}{(-10)}$ (c) $\dfrac{(-15)}{5}$ (d) $\dfrac{24}{(-8)}$ (e) $\dfrac{51}{(-17)}$

3 Calculate:

(a) $\dfrac{(-48)}{(-6)}$ (b) $\dfrac{(-72)}{(-9)}$ (c) $\dfrac{(-55)}{(-11)}$ (d) $\dfrac{(-123)}{(-3)}$ (e) $\dfrac{(-120)}{(-10)}$

4 Calculate:

(a) $\dfrac{18}{(-6)}$ (b) $\dfrac{(-51)}{(-3)}$ (c) $\dfrac{(-60)}{12}$ (d) $\dfrac{(-64)}{8}$ (e) $\dfrac{(-80)}{(-20)}$

5 The balance on the bank statement for Kaye's Cakes is overdrawn and shows −£620. The four owners decide to repay it equally.

How much does each person owe?

1.5 Using integers

Example 1

Calculate: **(a)** $(-3) \times 4 \times (-2)$ **(b)** $\dfrac{3 \times (-8)}{-4}$

(a) $(-3) \times 4 \times (-2)$

$\quad = (-12) \times (-2)$

$\quad = 24$

(b) $\dfrac{3 \times (-8)}{-4}$

$\quad = \dfrac{-24}{-4}$

$\quad = 6$

Example 2

If $T = c + ab$ find T when $a = 3, b = -4$ and $c = -2$.

$T = c + ab$

$T = (-2) + 3 \times (-4)$

$\quad = (-2) + (-12)$

$\quad = -14$

> Remember to multiply before you add.

Exercise 1.5

1 Calculate:

(a) $5 \times 6 \times (-3)$

(b) $3 \times (-4) \times 6$

(c) $(-4) \times (-4) \times 5$

(d) $(-6) \times (-5) \times 4$

(e) $7 \times (-2) \times 5$

(f) $(-5) \times 8 \times (-3)$

(g) $(-2) \times (-9) \times (-7)$

(h) $(-10) \times (-20) \times (-8)$

(i) $15 \times (-10) \times 9$

2 Calculate:

(a) $\dfrac{4 \times (-9)}{3}$

(b) $\dfrac{(-6) \times (-9)}{2}$

(c) $\dfrac{(-8) \times (-3)}{12}$

(d) $\dfrac{9 \times 8}{(-3)}$

(e) $\dfrac{(-5) \times 8}{10}$

(f) $\dfrac{(-6) \times 12}{(-8)}$

(g) $\dfrac{(-7) \times (-8)}{(-2)}$

(h) $\dfrac{(-10) \times (-7)}{(-5)}$

(i) $\dfrac{(-27) \times 6}{4}$

(j) $\dfrac{(-8) \times (-14)}{10}$

(k) $\dfrac{32 \times 9}{(-6)}$

(l) $\dfrac{18 \times (-9)}{(-6)}$

3 Calculate: > **Remember** BODMAS

(a) $4 + (-20) \div 2$

(b) $15 - 3 \times (-2)$

(c) $(-4) \times 7 + 3$

(d) $(3 - 7) \times (6 - 8)$

(e) $(9 + 23) \div (5 - 9)$

(f) $5 + 16 \div ((-10) + 2)$

(g) $((-9) - 27) \div ((-2) + 11)$

(h) $(-12) \times 6 - 10$

(i) $20 - 18 \div ((-4) - 2)$

4 Use each formula to calculate the missing values.

(a) $K = 3T$ — Find K when $T = -5$

(b) $F = 2c - 3$ — Find F when $c = -15$

(c) $P = ab + c$ — Find P when $a = 5$, $b = -6$ and $c = 1.2$

(d) $V = x - y$ — Find V when $x = 4.5$ and $y = -7$

(e) $T = abc$ — Find T when $a = -2$, $b = -7$ and $c = 3$

(f) $S = abc - 2a$ — Find S when $a = -5$, $b = 6$ and $c = -2$

(g) $X = \dfrac{wy}{z}$ — Find X when $w = 4$, $y = -6$ and $z = -2$

1.6 Squares and square roots

Remember

$4^2 = 4 \times 4 = 16$

16 is called a square number.

4

4

Working backwards, if the area of the square is 16 square centimetres then the length of each side is 4 centimetres.

$A = 16\,cm^2$

It is said that the **square root** of 16 is 4.

The symbol $\sqrt{}$ is used to represent the positive square root.

$\sqrt{16} = \mathbf{4}$ $\sqrt{49} = \mathbf{7}$ $\sqrt{121} = \mathbf{11}$ $\sqrt{4\,000\,000} = \mathbf{2000}$

Exercise 1.6

1 Calculate:

(a) 8^2 (b) 5^2 (c) 6^2 (d) 10^2 (e) 1^2

(f) 12^2 (g) 11^2 (h) 20^2 (i) 9^2 (j) 30^2

2 Calculate:

(a) 15^2 (b) 18^2 (c) 600^2 (d) 1.2^2 (e) 5.5^2

(f) 2.3^2 (g) 0.1^2 (h) 34^2 (i) 6.8^2 (j) 0.5^2

3 (a) How many square centimetres are in a square metre?

(b) How many square metres are in a square kilometre?

100 cm

100 cm

4 Find the edge length of each square.

(a)

$A = 25\,mm^2$

(b)

$A = 169\,cm^2$

(c)

$A = 400\,cm^2$

5 Find the square root of:

(**a**) 16   (**b**) 81   (**c**) 100   (**d**) 144   (**e**) 196

6 Find:

(**a**) $\sqrt{25}$ (**b**) $\sqrt{36}$ (**c**) $\sqrt{400}$ (**d**) $\sqrt{169}$ (**e**) $\sqrt{100}$

(**f**) $\sqrt{10000}$ (**g**) $\sqrt{1}$ (**h**) $\sqrt{90000}$ (**i**) $\sqrt{144}$ (**j**) $\sqrt{1\,000\,000}$

7 Copy and complete the table below.

n	1	2	3	4	5	6	7	8	9	10	11	12	13	14	15
n^2	1	4	9												

8 Without using a calculator, match each number to its square root.

Number

1024	361	625
1089	1681	784
576	1600	729
1296		

Square root

24	36	41	25
32	40	33	27
28	19		

9 Tom thinks of a number and adds 4. The square root of his answer is 6. What was the original number?

10 Arthur thinks of a number and divides by 7. The square root of his answer is 3. What was the original number?

11 Rolf thinks of a number, square roots it and adds 7. His answer is 11. What was his original number?

12 Liz thinks of a number and adds 5. She squares her number. The answer is 144. What was the original number?

13 (**a**) Calculate: (**i**) $3^2 + 4^2$ (**ii**) $5^2 + 12^2$ (**iii**) $6^2 + 8^2$.

(**b**) What do you notice about your answers?

 14 Find all the natural numbers between 1200 and 1300 which have exact square roots.

15 Write all the natural numbers less than 200 with exact square roots.

1.7 Estimating square roots

Example

Between which two whole numbers does the square root lie?

(a) $\sqrt{20}$ (b) $\sqrt{38}$

(a) $\sqrt{16} = 4$ and $\sqrt{25} = 5$ so $\sqrt{20}$ lies between **4 and 5**
     Calculator check: $\sqrt{20} = 4.5$ to 1 d.p.

(b) $\sqrt{36} = 6$ and $\sqrt{49} = 7$ so $\sqrt{38}$ lies between **6 and 7**
     Calculator check: $\sqrt{38} = 6.2$ to 1 d.p.

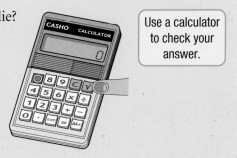

Use a calculator to check your answer.

Exercise 1.7

1 Between which two whole numbers does the square root lie?
Check using a calculator.

(a) $\sqrt{17}$ (b) $\sqrt{24}$ (c) $\sqrt{6}$ (d) $\sqrt{19}$ (e) $\sqrt{26}$
(f) $\sqrt{54}$ (g) $\sqrt{123}$ (h) $\sqrt{105}$ (i) $\sqrt{8}$ (j) $\sqrt{83}$

2 Use a calculator to find the following square roots correct to 1 decimal place.

(a) $\sqrt{27}$ (b) $\sqrt{83}$ (c) $\sqrt{119}$ (d) $\sqrt{272}$ (e) $\sqrt{1050}$
(f) $\sqrt{850}$ (g) $\sqrt{320}$ (h) $\sqrt{2000}$ (i) $\sqrt{3766}$ (j) $\sqrt{2460}$

3 Find the length of side of each square to 1 decimal place.

(a)

Area = 70 cm²

(b)

Area = 240 mm²

(c)

Area = 54 cm²

4 ABCD is a square with area 80 m².
APQR is a square with area 17 m².
Find the length of DR correct to 2 decimal places.

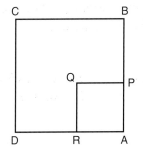

Find AD and AR first.

5 GHJK is a square with area 130 m².
JLMN is a square with area 84 m².
Find KL correct to 2 decimal places.

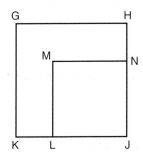

6 ABJH is a square with area 46 square metres..
JDEF is a square with area 152 square metres.

(**a**) Find the length of AC.

(**b**) Find the area of the square ACEG.

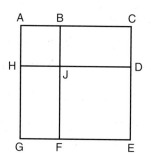

1.8 Powers

This number is called the index.

$2^1 = 2$
$2^2 = 2 \times 2 = 4$
$2^3 = 2 \times 2 \times 2 = 8$ For 2^3 say 'two cubed'
$2^4 = 2 \times 2 \times 2 \times 2 = 16$ For 2^4 say 'two to the power of four'
$2^5 = 2 \times 2 \times 2 \times 2 \times 2 = 32$

Similarly, $7 \times 7 \times 7 \times 7 \times 7 \times 7 = 7^6$ Seven to the power six

Example

Evaluate:

(**a**) 10^4 (**b**) 1^3 (**c**) $(-2)^3$ (**d**) $(-3)^4$

(**a**) $10 \times 10 \times 10 \times 10$ (**b**) $1 \times 1 \times 1$ (**c**) $(-2) \times (-2) \times (-2)$ (**d**) $(-3) \times (-3) \times (-3) \times (-3)$
     $= 10\,000$ $= 1$ $= 4 \times (-2)$ $= 9 \times 9$
                                    $= -8$ $= 81$

Exercise 1.8

1 Write using powers:

(**a**) $4 \times 4 \times 4$ (**b**) $(-9) \times (-9)$ (**c**) $5 \times 5 \times 5 \times 5 \times 5 \times 5$

(**d**) $15 \times 15 \times 15$ (**e**) $1 \times 1 \times 1$ (**f**) $3 \times 3 \times 3 \times 3 \times 3 \times 3 \times 3 \times 3$

(**g**) $(-10) \times (-10) \times (-10)$ (**h**) $(-5) \times (-5)$ (**i**) $(-1) \times (-1) \times (-1) \times (-1) \times (-1)$

2 Evaluate:

(**a**) 2^3 (**b**) 4^3 (**c**) 3^4 (**d**) 2^6 (**e**) 1^9

(**f**) 3^5 (**g**) 1^5 (**h**) 12^1 (**i**) 10^5 (**j**) 20^3

(**k**) $(-1)^2$ (**l**) $(-1)^3$ (**m**) $(-2)^4$ (**n**) $(-3)^3$ (**o**) $(-10)^5$

3 Write these numbers as powers of 2.

(**a**) 8   (**b**) 2   (**c**) 32   (**d**) 128   (**e**) 256

4 Write these numbers as powers of 3.

(**a**) 27   (**b**) 9   (**c**) 81   (**d**) 3   (**e**) 243

5 Write these numbers as powers of 10.

(**a**) 100   (**b**) 1000   (**c**) 100 000   (**d**) 1 000 000   (**e**) 1 000 000 000

6 Copy and complete

(a) $2^{\square} = 32$ (b) $5^{\square} = 125$ (c) $3^{\square} = 729$

(d) $4^{\square} = 1024$ (e) $2^{\square} = 1024$ (f) $10^{\square} = 1\,000\,000$

7 Write $4 \times 4 \times 4 \times 4 \times 16$ as a power of 4.

8 A population of rabbits doubles every month. If there are 2 at the beginning of March, how many will there be at the beginning of September?

9 Find the units digit in 2^{65}.

$2^1 = 2$	$2^5 = 32$
$2^2 = 4$	$2^6 = 64$
$2^3 = 8$	$2^7 = 128$
$2^4 = 16$	$2^8 =$

10 The diagram shows part of Pascal's triangle.
Copy and continue the pattern until you have
8 rows. Add up the numbers in each row and
write your answer at the end of the row.
What do you notice about your answers?

```
        1   1
      1   2   1
    1   3   3   1
  1   4   6   4   1
1   5   10   10   5   1
```

11 (a) Find:

(i) $2^3 \times 2^2$ (ii) $2^3 \times 2^1$ (iii) $2^6 \times 2^2$ (iv) $2^4 \times 2^3$ (v) $2^1 \times 2^1$

(b) What do you notice about your answers?

> Write the powers in full.

1.9 Prime numbers and prime factors

Prime numbers are often used in cryptography, a branch of mathematics involved with codes and security.
In 2004 the largest known prime number was $2^{24036583} - 1$.

Remember

20 is divisible by 1, 2, 4, 5, 10 and 20. These are the **factors** of 20.

A **prime** number is a number which has exactly two factors.
The set of prime numbers = {2, 3, 5, 7, 11, 13 ...}

> $3 = 3 \times 1$
> $17 = 17 \times 1$

To split a number into its **prime factors** use the following method.

Example

Find the prime factors of   (a) 350   (b) 45   (c) 100

(a)
```
2 | 350
5 | 175
5 |  35
7 |   7
  |   1
```

(b)
```
3 | 45
3 | 15
5 |  5
  |  1
```

(c)
```
2 | 100
2 |  50
5 |  25
5 |   5
  |   1
```

> Divide by the prime factors in order, starting with the smallest, and end when you reach 1.

$350 = 2 \times 5 \times 5 \times 7$
$\quad\quad = 2 \times 5^2 \times 7$

$45 = 3 \times 3 \times 5$
$\quad\quad = 3^2 \times 5$

$100 = 2 \times 2 \times 5 \times 5$
$\quad\quad\, = 2^2 \times 5^2$

Exercise 1.9

1 Which of the following numbers are prime?

51		2	9		15
	100		17	29	37
1		73	1124	99	

2 Find the prime factors of:

(**a**) 10   (**b**) 16   (**c**) 48   (**d**) 36   (**e**) 182

(**f**) 150   (**g**) 30   (**h**) 87   (**i**) 1800   (**j**) 6300

3 In 1742, in a letter to Leonard Euler, Christian Goldbach stated that every even integer greater than 2 is the sum of two prime numbers. This became known as Goldbach's Conjecture.
Show how this can be achieved for:

(**a**) 8   (**b**) 20   (**c**) 38   (**d**) 50   (**e**) 46

4 In 1772 Euler discovered a formula

$$n^2 - n + 41$$

which gives prime numbers for the forty consecutive integers from $n = 0$ to $n = 39$.
Copy and complete this table for $n = 0$ to $n = 15$.

n	$n^2 - n + 41$	Prime number
0	$0^2 - 0 + 41$	41
1	$1^2 - 1 + 41$	41
2	$2^2 - 2 + 41$	43

1.10 Divisibility

To check that a number is divisible by:			Check
2 – the last digit will be an even number	936		$\dfrac{468}{2\overline{)936}}$
3 – the digit sum of a number is divisible by 3	225	2 + 2 + 5 = 9 9 is divisible by 3	$\dfrac{75}{3\overline{)225}}$
4 – the last two digits are 00 or divisible by 4	1328	28 is divisible by 4	$\dfrac{332}{4\overline{)1328}}$
5 – the last digit is 5 or 0	65 1050		$\dfrac{13}{5\overline{)65}}$ $\dfrac{210}{5\overline{)1050}}$
6 – divisible by 2 and 3. The last digit is even and the digit sum of the number is divisible by 3	3552	3 + 5 + 5 + 2 = 15 15 is divisible by 3	$\dfrac{592}{6\overline{)3552}}$
8 – the last digit is even and the last three digits are divisible by 8	53616	616 ÷ 8 = 77	$\dfrac{6702}{8\overline{)53616}}$
9 – the sum of the digits is divisible by 9	423	4 + 2 + 3 = 9 9 is divisible by 9	$\dfrac{47}{9\overline{)423}}$
10 – the units digit is 0	60 200		$\dfrac{6}{10\overline{)60}}$ $\dfrac{20}{10\overline{)200}}$

Exercise 1.10

1

143   235   3465   1072   756   57   404   1002

Which of these numbers are divisible by:

(**a**) 2   (**b**) 3   (**c**) 4   (**d**) 9?

2 Find the two possible numbers in the units column which will make 357▢ divisible by 4.

3 Find the missing numbers if:

(**a**) 346▢ is divisible by 5

(**b**) 8701▢ is divisible by 10

(**c**) 35▢71 is divisible by 9

(**d**) 91▢6 is divisible by 4

(**e**) 413▢ is divisible by 6

(**f**) 60▢2 is divisible by 9

(**g**) 562▢6 is divisible by 8

(**h**) 413▢ is divisible by 3

4 A **perfect number** is a number which is equal to the sum of all its factors excluding itself.

For example, 6 is a perfect number because 1 + 2 + 3 = 6.

Find another perfect number.

> There is another perfect number less than 30.

5 Using the digits 1 to 3 (without using any digit more than once) it is possible to make two three digit numbers represented by ABC such that:

ABC is divisible by 3
AB is divisible by 2
A is divisible by 1

The only two possible solutions which satisfy the above condition are:

123   123 is divisible by 3   321   321 is divisible by 3
           12 is divisible by 2   32 is divisible by 2
           1 is divisible by 1   3 is divisible by 1

Using the digits 1 to 6 (without using any digit more than once) investigate whether there are six digit numbers represented by ABCDEF such that:

ABCDEF   is divisible by 6
ABCDE   is divisible by 5
ABCD   is divisible by 4
ABC   is divisible by 3
AB   is divisible by 2
A   is divisible by 1

1.11 Scientific notation – large numbers

When dealing with very large numbers it is easy to make a mistake by missing out a digit, for example writing 25000000000000 instead of 2500000000000. Numbers may be written using **scientific notation** or **standard form**.

> Numbers in scientific notation must be written in the form
> $a \times 10^n$ where $1 \leqslant a < 10$ and $n \in \mathbf{Z}$.

Example 1

Write the following numbers using scientific notation:
(a) 300 000   **(b)** 72 000 000   **(c)** 46·3

(a) 300 000   **(b)** 72 000 000   **(c)** 46·3
    $= 3 \times 10 \times 10 \times 10 \times 10 \times 10$ $= 7.2 \times 10 \times 10 \times 10 \times 10 \times 10 \times 10 \times 10$ $= 4.63 \times 10$
    $\mathbf{= 3 \times 10^5}$ $\mathbf{= = 7.2 \times 10^7}$ $\mathbf{= 4.63 \times 10^1}$

Example 2

Write the following numbers in full:
(a) The radius of the earth is 5×10^6 km   **(b)** The distance from earth to the sun is $1 \cdot 5 \times 10^8$ km

(a) 5×10^6 **(b)** 1.5×10^8 km
    $= 5 \times 10 \times 10 \times 10 \times 10 \times 10 \times 10$ $1.5 \times 10 \times 10 \times 10 \times 10 \times 10 \times 10 \times 10 \times 10$
    $\mathbf{= 5\,000\,000}$ $\mathbf{= 150\,000\,000}$

Exercise 1.11

1 Write the following numbers using scientific notation:

(a) 40 000   (b) 6000   (c) 200 000   (d) 50 000 000

(e) 600   (f) 1 000 000   (g) 80   (h) 90 000 000 000

2 Write the following numbers using scientific notation:

(a) 230   (b) 1600   (c) 78 000   (d) 150 000 000

(e) 960 000   (f) 55 000   (g) 45   (h) 34 000 000 000

3 Write the following numbers using scientific notation:

(a) 258 000   (b) 33 200   (c) 405   (d) 9010

(e) 28·4   (f) 146·23   (g) 2060·2   (h) 50 400 000

4 Write the following numbers in full:

(a) 10^3 (b) 10^5 (c) 10^6 (d) 10^7 (e) 9×10^6

(f) 5×10^2 (g) 8×10^5 (h) 6×10^1 (i) 4×10^8 (j) 2×10^4

5 Write the following numbers in full:

(a) $2·3 \times 10^3$ (b) $5·87 \times 10^6$ (c) $7·2 \times 10^5$

(d) $5·0 \times 10^4$ (e) $1·24 \times 10^7$ (f) $1·24 \times 10^1$

(g) $2·08 \times 10^2$ (h) $3·45 \times 10^9$ (i) $1·02 \times 10^4$

6 Write the following numbers in scientific notation:

(a) The age of the earth is about 6 000 000 000 years.

(b) The distance from the earth to the sun is approximately 150 000 000 kilometres.

(c) The closest star to the earth is Proxima Centauri at 24 800 000 000 000 miles.

(d) The total area of land on earth is approximately 131 100 000 square kilometres.

7 Write these numbers in full:

(a) The speed of light is about 3×10^8 metres per second.

(b) The circumference of the sun is about $4·37 \times 10^6$ kilometres.

(c) The mass of the earth is about 6×10^{24} kilograms.

1.12 Scientific notation – small numbers

$10^2 = 100$
$10^1 = 10$
$10^0 = 1$
$10^{-1} = 0.1$
$10^{-2} = 0.01$
$10^{-3} = 0.001$

To express numbers less than one in scientific notation, negative powers of 10 are used.

> **Scientific notation**
> $a \times 10^n$ where $1 \leqslant a < 10$ and $n \in Z$.

Example 1

Write the following numbers using scientific notation.

(a) 0·002

(b) 0·0000037

(c) 0·000125

(a) 0·002
$= 2 \times 0.001$
$= \mathbf{2 \times 10^{-3}}$

(b) 0·0000037
$= 3.7 \times 0.000001$
$= \mathbf{3.7 \times 10^{-6}}$

(c) 0·000125
$= 1.25 \times 0.0001$
$= \mathbf{1.25 \times 10^{-4}}$

Example 2

Write the following numbers in full.

(a) The wavelength of an X-ray is 5×10^{-10} metres

(b) The half life of plutonium is 1.5×10^{-4} seconds

(a) 5×10^{-10} metres
$= \mathbf{0.000\ 000\ 000\ 5\ metres}$

(b) 1.5×10^{-4} seconds
$= \mathbf{0.000\ 15\ seconds}$

Exercise 1.12

1 Express the following as powers of ten:

(a) 0·000 001

(b) 0·000 1

(c) 0·000 000 001

(d) 0·1

2 Write in scientific notation:

(a) 0·07

(b) 0·000 06

(c) 0·000 001

(d) 0·9

(e) 0·002

(f) 0·0034

(g) 0·000 000 059

(h) 0·000 032

(i) 0·124

(j) 0·000 138

(k) 0·005 06

(l) 0·000 000 667

3 Write these numbers in full:

(a) 2×10^{-3}

(b) 8×10^{-9}

(c) 5×10^{-12}

(d) 6.9×10^{-5}

(e) 1.1×10^{-7}

(f) 2.7×10^{-6}

(g) 3.61×10^{-4}

(h) 7.02×10^{-14}

(i) 7.11×10^{-10}

4 Write the following numbers in scientific notation:

(a) Light travels one metre in about 0·000 000 003 seconds.

(b) One second is equivalent to 0·000 000 03169 of a year.

(c) The mass of a dust particle is 0·000 000 000 753 kilogrammes.

5 Write these numbers in full:

(**a**) The mass of a proton is $1\cdot63 \times 10^{-27}$ kilogrammes.

(**b**) The charge of an electron is $1\cdot602 \times 10^{-19}$ coulombs.

(**c**) The Bohr radius of an atom is $5\cdot29 \times 10^{-11}$ metres.

1.13 Scientific notation – using a calculator

Calculators have an $\boxed{\text{EXP}}\boxed{\text{E}}$ or $\boxed{\text{EE}}$ button for calculations using scientific notation.

Different calculators have different displays. For example:

Type in $2\cdot4 \times 10^6$ $\boxed{2}\boxed{\cdot}\boxed{4}\boxed{\text{EXP}}\boxed{6}$. This may show $2\cdot4 \times 10^6$ on the calculator display. Check this on your calculator.

Example

Calculate $2\cdot3 \times 10^8 \times 754$

$2\cdot3 \times 10^8 \times 754$

$= \mathbf{1\cdot7342 \times 10^{11}}$

Using a calculator enter
$\boxed{2\cdot3}\boxed{\text{EXP}}\boxed{8}\boxed{\times}\boxed{754}\boxed{=}$

Exercise 1.13

1 Calculate, giving your answer in scientific notation:

(**a**) $4 \times 10^5 \times 2$ (**b**) $3 \times 10^7 \times 8$ (**c**) $5 \times 10^7 \times 5$

(**d**) $9 \times 10^{15} \times 3$ (**e**) $5\cdot2 \times 10^2 \times 16$ (**f**) $1\cdot3 \times 10^{20} \times 12$

(**g**) $3\cdot4 \times 10^{24} \times 23$ (**h**) $6\cdot6 \times 10^8 \times 1\cdot6$ (**i**) $3\cdot05 \times 10^6 \times 0\cdot5$

2 Calculate, giving your answer in full:

(**a**) $1 \times 10^8 \times 6$ (**b**) $7 \times 10^2 \times 8$ (**c**) $9 \times 10^7 \times 4$

(**d**) $6\cdot7 \times 10^7 \times 5$ (**e**) $1\cdot02 \times 10^5 \times 1\cdot7$ (**f**) $3\cdot7 \times 10^{10} \times 2\cdot3$

(**g**) $5\cdot6 \times 10^4 \times 23$ (**h**) $1\cdot7 \times 10^8 \times 0\cdot8$ (**i**) $5\cdot05 \times 10^1 \times 15$

3 The speed of light is 3×10^8 metres per second. Calculate how far light will travel in:

(**a**) 6 seconds   (**b**) 15 seconds.

Review exercise 1

1 Write:

(**a**) the whole numbers between 5 and 8 inclusive

(**b**) the integers between -4 and 2.

2 List the following values of x:

(**a**) $x \leqslant 2, x \in \mathbf{N}$ (**b**) $x \leqslant 5, x \in \mathbf{Z}$

3 Calculate:

(**a**) $16 + (-2)$ (**b**) $(-12) - (-30)$ (**c**) $-15 - 3 + (-4)$ (**d**) $21 - 5 - (-1)$

4 Calculate:

(**a**) $(-3) \times 15$ (**b**) $(-6) \times (-1 \cdot 2)$ (**c**) $(-3) \times (-7) \times 5$ (**d**) $(-3) \times (-9) \times (-6)$

5 Calculate:

(**a**) $\dfrac{48}{(-6)}$ (**b**) $\dfrac{(-35)}{(-7)}$ (**c**) $\dfrac{(-65)}{5}$ (**d**) $\dfrac{(-80)}{5}$ (**e**) $\dfrac{(-36)}{(-9)}$

6 Calculate:

(**a**) $\dfrac{3 \times (-8)}{6}$ (**b**) $\dfrac{(-6) \times (-8)}{2}$ (**c**) $\dfrac{(-5) \times (-9)}{15}$ (**d**) $\dfrac{7 \times 12}{(-3)}$

7 Calculate:

(**a**) $7 + (-34) \div 2$ (**b**) $16 - 3 \times (-5)$ (**c**) $(-12) \times 7 + 20$

(**d**) $(3 - 5) \times (6 - 4)$ (**e**) $(9 + 15) \div (13 - 19)$ (**f**) $(7 + 25) \div (-10 + 6)$

8 Use each formula to calculate the missing values.

(**a**) $K = 7T$ Find K when $T = -3$

(**b**) $F = 6c - 7$ Find F when $c = -12$

(**c**) $P = ab + c$ Find P when $a = 6, b = -6$ and $c = -15$

9 Evaluate:

(**a**) $\sqrt{25}$ (**b**) $\sqrt{100}$ (**c**) $\sqrt{9}$ (**d**) $\sqrt{900}$ (**e**) $\sqrt{144}$

10 Find to one decimal place:

(**a**) $\sqrt{8}$ (**b**) $\sqrt{17}$ (**c**) $\sqrt{135}$ (**d**) $\sqrt{29 \cdot 5}$ (**e**) $\sqrt{1000}$

11 Write as powers:

(**a**) $3 \times 3 \times 3$ (**b**) $(-6) \times (-6)$ (**c**) $7 \times 7 \times 7 \times 7 \times 7 \times 7$

12 Evaluate:

(**a**) 3^3 (**b**) 2^5 (**c**) 1^7 (**d**) 1^4 (**e**) 14^1 (**f**) 10^7

13 Which of the following numbers are prime?

16		57		9		43		81
	3		71		51		46	
1000		301		19		74		

14 Find the prime factors of:

(**a**) 18   (**b**) 26   (**c**) 54   (**d**) 135   (**e**) 182

15 Find the missing numbers if

(**a**) 23 ▢ 6 is divisible by 4   (**b**) 415 ▢ is divisible by 3

16 Write the following numbers using scientific notation:

(**a**) 300 000   (**b**) 270   (**c**) 28 000 000   (**d**) 624   (**e**) 18·2

(**f**) 0·000 000 04   (**g**) 0·0056   (**h**) 0·189   (**i**) 0·0348   (**j**) 0·708

17 Write the following numbers in full:

(**a**) 3×10^4 (**b**) $4·5 \times 10^3$ (**c**) $1·16 \times 10^2$ (**d**) $1·02 \times 10^1$

(**e**) 9×10^{-9} (**f**) $7·2 \times 10^{-6}$ (**g**) $4·6 \times 10^{-18}$ (**h**) $3·1 \times 10^{-12}$

18 Calculate, giving your answer in scientific notation:

(**a**) $5 \times 10^{16} \times 9$ (**b**) $5 \times 10^{28} \times 15$ (**c**) $1·7 \times 10^{24} \times 13·5$

Summary

Sets of numbers

Some sets of numbers are commonly used in mathematics

N = natural numbers $\{1, 2, 3, 4, \ldots\}$
W = whole numbers $\{0, 1, 2, 3, 4, \ldots\}$
Z = integers $\{\ldots, -3, -2, -1, 0, 1, 2, 3, \ldots\}$
Q = rational numbers – any number which can be written as a fraction $\{\ldots, -4, 1.5, 6\frac{1}{2}, \ldots\}$

Integers

- Adding a negative number is the same as subtracting the positive number.
- Subtracting a negative number is the same as adding the positive number.
- Multiplying a positive number by a negative number gives a negative number.
- Multiplying a negative number by a negative number gives a positive number.
- Dividing a positive number by a negative number gives a negative number.
- Dividing a negative number by a positive number gives a negative number.
- Dividing a negative number by a negative number gives a positive number.

Square roots

16 is a square number since $4^2 = 4 \times 4 = \mathbf{16}$.
The square root of 16 is 4. $\sqrt{16} = \mathbf{4}$.

Powers

$2^4 = 2 \times 2 \times 2 \times 2 = \mathbf{16}$ For 2^4 say 'two to the power of four.'

Prime factors

A **prime** number is a number which has exactly two factors.
The set of prime numbers = $\{2, 3, 5, 7, 11, 13, \ldots\}$.
To split a number into its **prime factors** use the following method

2	350
5	175
5	35
7	7
	1

$350 = 2 \times 5 \times 5 \times 7$
$\quad\;\; = \mathbf{2 \times 5^2 \times 7}$

Scientific notation

Numbers in scientific notation must be written in the form

$\quad a \times 10^n$ where $1 \leqslant a < 10$ and $n \in Z$

$3{\cdot}2 \times 10^4 = 32\,000$ $1{\cdot}5 \times 10^{-2} = 0.015$

2 Decimals and significant figures

In this chapter you will review and extend your understanding of decimal fractions, review mental calculations and learn about significant figures.

2.1 Rounding

Remember

46.8	is	47	rounded to the nearest whole number
513.24	is	513.2	rounded to 1 decimal place (1 d.p.)
15.685	is	15.69	rounded to 2 decimal places (2 d.p.)
91.862349	is	91.8623	rounded to 4 decimal places (4 d.p.)

The convention is to round up

Exercise 2.1

1 Round each figure to the nearest whole number.

(**a**) 5·6   (**b**) 16·39   (**c**) 102·247   (**d**) 0·55

(**e**) 6·099   (**f**) 1040·07   (**g**) 1000·49   (**h**) 32·81

2 Round each figure to 1 decimal place.

(**a**) 25·68   (**b**) 13·24   (**c**) 6·085   (**d**) 51·95

(**e**) 0·08   (**f**) 2·99   (**g**) 12·38   (**h**) 0·35

3 Round each figure to 2 decimal places.

(**a**) 3·456   (**b**) 21·073   (**c**) 0·906   (**d**) 120·6601

(**e**) 302·455   (**f**) 33·4329   (**g**) 45·009   (**h**) 0·034

4 Round each figure to the number of decimal places shown.

(**a**) 35·63 (1 d.p.)   (**b**) 15·068 (2 d.p.)   (**c**) 4·05 (1 d.p.)

(**d**) 0·234 (2 d.p.)   (**e**) 43·5555 (3 d.p.)   (**f**) 2·007 (2 d.p.)

(**g**) 32·109 (2 d.p.)   (**h**) 7·4055 (3 d.p.)   (**i**) 533·133 (2 d.p.)

5 Struan has to report percentage price rises to one decimal place.
List each rise to 1 decimal place.

Percentage price rises

House	Car	Holiday	Food	Petrol
15·56	3·06	6·98	2·333	8·02

2.2 Significant figures

The accuracy of a number may be measured in **significant figures**.
When zero is used as a place holder, it is not significant.
Otherwise all digits are always significant.

36 000 attend Hampden

155 000 viewers

25   has 2 significant figures (2 sig. figs.)
1025   has 4 sig. figs.
7·029   has 4 sig. figs.
0·0501   has 3 sig. figs.   The first two zeros are place holders

Example 1

16482 fans attended a Hearts football match.
This is   20000 to 1 sig. fig.
         16000 to 2 sig. figs.
         16500 to 3 sig. figs.
         16480 to 4 sig. figs.

Example 2

Round:

(**a**) 5632 to 2 sig. figs.   (**b**) 593 to 1 sig. fig.   (**c**) 0·0961 to 2 sig. figs.

(**a**) **5600**   (**b**) **600**   (**c**) **0·096**

Exercise 2.2

1 How many significant figures are there in each number?

(**a**) 546   (**b**) 23   (**c**) 1·578   (**d**) 309

(**e**) 0·09   (**f**) 7   (**g**) 30·6   (**h**) 50·00

(**i**) 3408   (**j**) 4·560   (**k**) 12·309   (**l**) 3·000

(**m**) 67·01   (**n**) 1654301   (**o**) 349   (**p**) 0·00036

2 The table shows the actual and rounded attendance figures at seven football grounds.

(**a**) How many significant figures are there in each rounded number?

(**b**) Which is the least accurate rounded attendance figure?

	Firhill	Hampden	Cappielow	Pittodrie	Rugby Park	Love Street
Actual	10345	38597	1478	21577	9873	8744
Rounded	10000	38600	1500	21580	9870	8700

3 A technician measures the thickness of six precision tools.
How many significant figures are there in each measurement?

Tool code number	75C	89A	36C	82C	55D
Thickness (mm)	0·002	0·010	0·0501	0·009	0·03

4   From the set of numbers, list those with
   (a)   1 significant figure
   (b)   2 significant figures
   (c)   3 significant figures
   (d)   4 significant figures

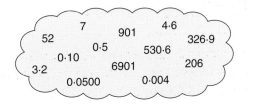

7   901   4·6
52   530·6   326·9
   0·5
0·10   206
3·2   6901
   0·0500   0·004

5   Round each number to 1 significant figure.
   (a) 58   (b) 3·6   (c) 0·066   (d) 521
   (e) 675   (f) 75   (g) 3890   (h) 7·9
   (i) 355   (j) 78 900   (k) 0·0078   (l) 780 000
   (m) 6·7   (n) 45 600   (o) 9·00   (p) 350

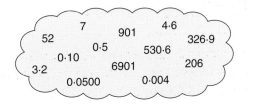

6   Round each number to 2 significant figures.
   (a) 356   (b) 7·29   (c) 1569   (d) 0·0981
   (e) 54600   (f) 1·23   (g) 45·09   (h) 2·09
   (i) 2300·5   (j) 45 600 000 (k) 1·6000   (l) 0·0908
   (m) 13·89   (n) 0·195   (o) 65·09   (p) 2·89

7   Round each number to 3 significant figures.
   (a) 2345   (b) 1·257   (c) 32 560   (d) 0·058 90
   (e) 3·000   (f) 305 400   (g) 12·09   (h) 34·5678
   (i) 0·011 11 (j) 123 000 000 (k) 23·23   (l) 45·009
   (m) 3010   (n) 40 506   (o) 3 567 000 (p) 7·008

8   Copy and complete the table:

Number	to 1 sig. fig.	to 2 sig. figs.	to 3 sig. figs.
5263	5000	5300	5260
4872			
3·201			
0·023 51			
54 657			
4·609			
4·5000			
3 349 000			
4 568 954			
0·005 409			
20·033			

9   Round each number to the given accuracy:
   (a)   560 (1 sig. fig.)   (b) 0·0046 (1 sig. fig.)   (c) 345·8 (2 sig. figs.)
   (d)   45·009 (3 sig. figs.)   (e) 14·007 (4 sig. figs.)   (f) 120 (1 sig. fig.)
   (g)   0·007 89 (2 sig. figs.) (h) 5 650 000 (2 sig. figs.) (i) 0·002 031 (2 sig. figs.)
   (j)   325 500 000 (3 sig. figs.) (k) 34·6666 (3 sig. figs.) (l) 50·099 (3 sig. figs.)

10 Complete each calculation.
Write your answers correct to two significant figures.

(**a**) $2 \cdot 31 \times 12 \cdot 4$ (**b**) $4 \cdot 097 \div 0 \cdot 43$ (**c**) $0 \cdot 6 \times 0 \cdot 003\,55$

(**d**) $1 \cdot 3 - 0 \cdot 999$ (**e**) $1 \cdot 3 + 2 \cdot 441 - 0 \cdot 8$ (**f**) $(3 \cdot 55 + 1 \cdot 231) \div 2 \cdot 1$

11 Calculate the mean height of these children.
Give your answer correct to
2 significant figures.

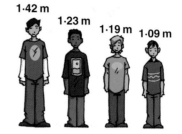

1·42 m 1·23 m 1·19 m 1·09 m

12 A punnet of strawberries weighs $0 \cdot 85$ kilogrammes.
To 1 significant figure calculate the weight of

(**a**) 5 punnets   (**b**) 9 punnets   (**c**) 11 punnets.

13 Calculate the profit on each house, to two significant figures.

House prices

Bought	£76 455	£89 534	£125 785	£209 544
Sold	£86 543	£97 678	£156 000	£245 676

14 For Alan's shelving unit he needs the following pieces of wood:
6 pieces $1 \cdot 85$ metres long and 4 pieces $2 \cdot 22$ metres long.
What total length of wood does he need, to 2 significant figures?

2.3 Mental calculations

Remember

$3 \cdot 1 \times 5$ ⟨$3 \times 5 = 15$ / $0 \cdot 1 \times 5 = 0 \cdot 5$⟩ $= 15 \cdot 5$

$-4 \cdot 8 \div 6$ ⟨$48 \div 6 = 8$⟩ $= -0 \cdot 8$

$-5 \cdot 9 \times 10$ ⟨Digits move left 1 place⟩ $= -59$

$0 \cdot 169 \times 100$ ⟨Digits move left 2 places⟩ $= 16 \cdot 9$

$28 \cdot 65 \times 1000$ ⟨Digits move left 3 places⟩ $= 28650$

$28 \div 10$ ⟨Digits move right 1 place⟩ $= 2 \cdot 8$

$-65 \cdot 2 \div 100$ ⟨Digits move right 2 places⟩ $= -0 \cdot 652$

$5 \cdot 29 \div 1000$ ⟨Digits move right 3 places⟩ $= 0 \cdot 00529$

Exercise 2.3

Calculate mentally:

1 4.1×6	**2** 2.3×3	**3** -3.3×4	**4** 10.2×5
5 6.5×7	**6** $5.4 \div 9$	**7** $16.4 \div 4$	**8** $0.18 \div 3$
9 $20.8 \div 4$	**10** $3.28 \div 8$	**11** 2.3×10	**12** 34.7×10
13 -0.2×10	**14** 0.1×10	**15** 4.45×10	**16** 3.4×100
17 0.9×100	**18** -6.2×100	**19** 1.03×100	**20** 0.2×1
21 -3.41×1000	**22** 0.089×1000	**23** 21.1×1000	**24** 0.003×1000
25 4.5×1000	**26** $-3.4 \div 10$	**27** $0.41 \div 10$	**28** $234 \div 10$
29 $1.23 \div 10$	**30** $-0.004 \div 10$	**31** $3.4 \div 100$	**32** $45 \div 100$
33 $0.78 \div 100$	**34** $0.08 \div 100$	**35** $876 \div 100$	**36** $56 \div 1000$
37 $34.8 \div 1000$	**38** $0.07 \div 1000$	**39** $-0.0057 \div 1000$	**40** $102 \div 1000$
41 $-13 + 9$	**42** $2 - (-12)$	**43** 7.2×8	**44** $-16.2 \div 2$
45 7.8×10	**46** 0.09×100	**47** 0.9×1000	**48** $6.7 \div 10$
49 $2.3 \div 100$	**50** $2 \div 1000$	**51** $3 - 16$	**52** $-12 - (-2)$
53 4.4×5	**54** $40.5 \div 5$	**55** 2.3×10	**56** 2.1×1
57 0.3×1000	**58** $0.09 \div 10$	**59** $1.2 \div 100$	

60 Find the total weight of ten boxes each weighing 0.76 kilogrammes.

61 One hundred lucky winners share £340. How much does each one get?

62 Sue needs 7 lengths of lace, each of 4.2 metres. What total length is this?

2.4 Decimal calculations without a calculator

Remember

$5.2 + 16.35$
$= \mathbf{21.55}$

$\begin{array}{r} 5.20 \\ + 16.35 \\ \hline 21.55 \end{array}$

$17.9 - 1.635$
$= \mathbf{16.265}$

$\begin{array}{r} 17.900 \\ - 1.635 \\ \hline 16.265 \end{array}$

52.86×9
$= \mathbf{475.74}$

$\begin{array}{r} 52.86 \\ \times 9 \\ \hline 475.74 \end{array}$

$3.509 \div 5$
$= \mathbf{0.7018}$

$\begin{array}{r} 0.7018 \\ 5\overline{)3.5090} \end{array}$

3.7×2.5
$= \mathbf{9.25}$

$\begin{array}{r} 3.7 \\ \times 2.5 \\ \hline 185 \\ 740 \\ \hline 9.25 \end{array}$

Answers have the same number of decimal places as in the calculation

3.8×20
$= 3.8 \times 2 \times 10$
$= 7.6 \times 10$
$= \mathbf{76}$

$9.6 \div 40$
$= 9.6 \div 4 \div 10$
$= 2.4 \div 10$
$= \mathbf{0.24}$

Exercise 2.4

Calculate:

1 $3\cdot45 + 12\cdot9$

2 $23\cdot5 + 0\cdot981$

3 $3\cdot4 + 1\cdot34 + 304$

4 $0\cdot98 + 4\cdot7 + 19\cdot21$

5 $0\cdot008 + 1\cdot1 + 11$

6 $12\cdot3 - 4\cdot7$

7 $3\cdot45 - 2\cdot8$

8 $0\cdot987 - 0\cdot08$

9 $2\cdot4 + 0\cdot98 - 1\cdot7$

10 $123 - 0\cdot99$

11 $3\cdot6 \times 5$

12 $16\cdot8 \div 80$

13 $0\cdot09 \times 9$

14 $2\cdot7 \times 40$

15 $46\cdot01 \times 6$

16 $14\cdot4 \div 30$

17 $234\cdot8 \div 4$

18 $0\cdot985 \div 5$

19 $4\cdot676 \div 7$

20 $46\cdot7 \div 5$

21 $3\cdot5 + 0\cdot89 - 1\cdot3$

22 $1\cdot11 - 0\cdot9$

23 $0\cdot76 \times 8\cdot2$

24 $1\cdot5 \times 3\cdot9$

25 $3\cdot46 \div 8$

26 $0\cdot045 \div 9$

27 $(2\cdot3 + 0\cdot75) \div 5$

28 $(12\cdot3 - 1\cdot64) \times 4$

29 $(2\cdot35 + 1\cdot007) \times 7$

30 $(0\cdot97 - 0\cdot89) \times 4$

31 $0\cdot23 \times 400$

32 $(2\cdot5 + 3\cdot6) \times 600$

33 $100 \div (5\cdot2 - 4\cdot8)$

2.5 Decimal calculations with a calculator

> **Example**
>
> Calculate: **(a)** $3\cdot09 + 0\cdot0543 - 1\cdot0265$ **(b)** $3\cdot42 \times 6\cdot7 \div 2\cdot6$
>
> **(a)** $\boxed{3\cdot09}\ \boxed{+}\ \boxed{0\cdot0543}\ \boxed{-}\ \boxed{1\cdot0265}$ **(b)** $\boxed{3\cdot42}\ \boxed{\times}\ \boxed{6\cdot7}\ \boxed{\div}\ \boxed{2\cdot6}$
>
> $\quad = \boxed{2\cdot1178}$ $\quad = \boxed{8\cdot8130769}$
>
> $\quad = \mathbf{2\cdot1178}$ $\quad = \mathbf{8\cdot81}$ to 3 sig. figs.

Exercise 2.5

Calculate:

1 $103\cdot1 + 34\cdot67 - 8\cdot99$

2 $4\cdot09 - 1\cdot233 + 10\cdot5$

3 $23\cdot1 \times 0\cdot092$

4 $4\cdot5 \times 67\cdot8 \times 0\cdot5$

5 $45 \div 3\cdot45$

6 $809\cdot7 \div 5\cdot6$

7 $5\cdot5 \times 3\cdot2 \div 2\cdot1$

8 $4\cdot15 \div 3 \times 0\cdot85$

9 $(55\cdot1 + 0\cdot99) \times 2\cdot3$

10 $(46\cdot1 - 5\cdot66) \div 0\cdot9$

2.6 Decimal applications

Example 1

£1 is worth €1.48 at August 2004 rates.
Calculate how much €18.50 is in pounds.

$\boxed{18.50}\ \boxed{\div}\ \boxed{1.48}\ \boxed{=}\ \boxed{12.5}$

Answer **£12.50**

Example 2

Merav wishes to cut 17·5 centimetre strips of ribbon from a 5 metre roll.
If she did this accurately   **(a)** how many strips could she cut?
                             (b) how much ribbon would be left?

(a) 5 m = 500 cm

$\boxed{500}\ \boxed{\div}\ \boxed{17.5}\ \boxed{=}\ \boxed{28.57}$ She can cut **28 strips.**

(b) $\boxed{28}\ \boxed{\times}\ \boxed{17.5}\ \boxed{=}\ \boxed{490}$

$\boxed{500}\ \boxed{-}\ \boxed{490}\ \boxed{=}\ \boxed{10}$ She has **10 cm** left.

Exercise 2.6

1 Using £1 = €1.48:

  (a) change to euros   **(i)** £52   **(ii)** £244   **(iii)** £450
  (b) change to pounds   **(i)** €64   **(ii)** €102   **(iii)** €346

2 At the exchange office, the rates are shown in a table.

  (a) Change £58.50 into

£1 =
€1.58, \$1.72, 1.8 Swiss francs

    (i) euros   **(ii)** Swiss francs   **(iii)** dollars.

  (b) Change into pounds

    (i) €72   **(ii)** \$182   **(iii)** 212 Swiss francs.

3 Carole is knitting a cardigan. The length of the back should be
18 centimetres. So far she has knitted 16·9 centimetres.
How much has she still to knit?

4 In Chicago, Ruth has bought five items at the outlet mall.

  (a) Calculate the total amount spent in \$.
  (b) How much is this in £, at the rate £1 = \$1.75?

5 In a 100 metre race the times below were recorded.

Name	Sam	Ian	John	Sean	Ben
Time (secs)	15·62	14·59	16·10	14·63	15·75

(a) Who won the race?

(b) How much faster was Sam than John?

(c) Calculate the mean time.

6 The 4 by 100 metres relay team members recorded the following times in seconds: 12·93, 13·51, 15·01 and 12·85.

(**a**) What was their total time?

(**b**) What was the time difference between the fastest and the slowest runners?

(**c**) How many of the team ran faster than the mean time?

7 In the Home Economics class, Mrs Macfarlane's sponge recipe requires the following ingredients per pupil:

flour	125 g
sugar	85 g
butter	75 g

(**a**) Express each weight in kilogrammes.

(**b**) For a class of 18 pupils, how much of each ingredient will she need?

8 John is fixing veneer edging to his table top. How much does he need?

0·75 m

0·95 m

9 The maximum weight limit for air luggage is 25 kilogrammes per person.

For each set of luggage   (**i**)   calculate the total weight

                                     (**ii**) does it meet the weight limit?

(**a**)   (**b**)   (**c**)

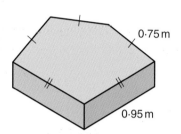

4·7 kg   16·8 kg   4·9 kg   5·2 kg   16·7 kg

19·6 kg   3·7 kg

10 (**a**) Calculate the mean weight of these children.

(**b**) If Sally loses 1·6 kg, what is the new mean weight?

39·4 kg   35·6 kg   32·1 kg   26·5 kg

11 Simon makes a small profit on each cake he sells.

(**a**) Calculate his total income from the sale of these cakes.

(**b**) Which cake generated the most profit?

Cake	Price (£)	Profit (£)	Sold
Eclair	0·85	0·15	16
Scone	0·35	0·07	56
Bun	0·41	0·10	48
Doughnut	0·62	0·12	46

Review exercise 2

1 Round each figure to 1 decimal place.

(**a**) 34·74   (**b**) 6·09   (**c**) 4·55   (**d**) 102·239   (**e**) 0·02

2 Round each figure to the number of decimal places indicated.

(**a**) 3·256 (2 d.p.)   (**b**) 13·07 (1 d.p.)   (**c**) 0·0456 (3 d.p.)

(**d**) 405·666 (2 d.p.)   (**e**) 0·503 (2 d.p.)   (**f**) 55·998 (2 d.p.)

3 How many significant figures are there in each number?

(**a**) 235   (**b**) 5067   (**c**) 23 001   (**d**) 0·89   (**e**) 0·00508

4 Round each number to 2 significant figures.

(**a**) 238   (**b**) 4650   (**c**) 0·0316   (**d**) 8·03   (**e**) 2 567 000

5 Round each number to the significant figures indicated.

(**a**) 23·7 (2 sig. figs.)   (**b**) 3·457 (3 sig. figs.)   (**c**) 0·055 (1 sig. fig.)

(**d**) 3·666 (2 sig. figs.)   (**e**) 15·09 (2 sig. figs.)   (**f**) 2347600 (4 sig. figs.)

6 Calculate mentally:

(**a**) $1·4 \times 4$ (**b**) $2·5 \times 5$ (**c**) $-16·5 \div 3$ (**d**) $24·68 \div 4$

(**e**) $0·9 \times 10$ (**f**) $3·02 \times 10$ (**g**) $-35·8 \div 10$ (**h**) $0·076 \div 10$

(**i**) $1·02 \times 100$ (**j**) $-0·87 \times 100$ (**k**) $23·45 \div 100$ (**l**) $0·051 \div 100$

(**m**) $6·75 \times 1000$ (**n**) $1·5 \times 1000$ (**o**) $23 \div 1000$ (**p**) $0·6 \div 1000$

7 Calculate without a calculator:

(**a**) $2·5 + 13 + 3·68$ (**b**) $56·7 - 9·88$ (**c**) $3·05 \times 8·9$

(**d**) $44·9 \times 5$ (**e**) $-4·842 \div 6$ (**f**) $(3·65 + 2·385) \times 7$

8 Calculate:

(**a**) $23·5 + 3·78 - 1·4$ (**b**) $3·09 - 1·54 + 47$ (**c**) $3·07 \times 1·1$

(**d**) $6·6 \times 1·25 \div 2·1$ (**e**) $(3·1 + 12·66) \times 4·5$ (**f**) $(14·3 - 3·88) \div 3·2$

9 Using the rate £1 = $1.75:

(**a**) change to dollars   (**i**) £54   (**ii**) £660   (**iii**) £125.50

(**b**) change to pounds   (**i**) $350   (**ii**) $460   (**iii**) $842

10 In a four lap cycle race, Nicole's lap times in minutes are:

32·5, 34·2, 33·1 and 32·1

(**a**) What was her total time?

(**b**) What was the difference in time between her fastest and slowest laps?

(**c**) What was her average lap time?

Summary

Decimal places

3·87   has 2 decimal places
125·0765   has 4 decimal places

Significant figures

1378   has 4 significant figures
36001   has 5 significant figures
0·0308   has 3 significant figures

Decimal calculations

$3·5 + 16·94$ 3·5
$= \mathbf{20·44}$ $+\underline{16·94}$
                      20·44   Align decimal points.

$7·46 \times 2·8$ 7·46
$= \mathbf{20·888}$ $\times \underline{\quad 2·8}$
                      5968
                      $\underline{14\,920}$
                      20·888   Answer has the same number of decimal places as the calculation.

3 Angles and scale drawing – review

In this chapter you will review your knowledge of related angles, the interior and exterior angles of polygons, and scale drawing.

3.1 Related angles

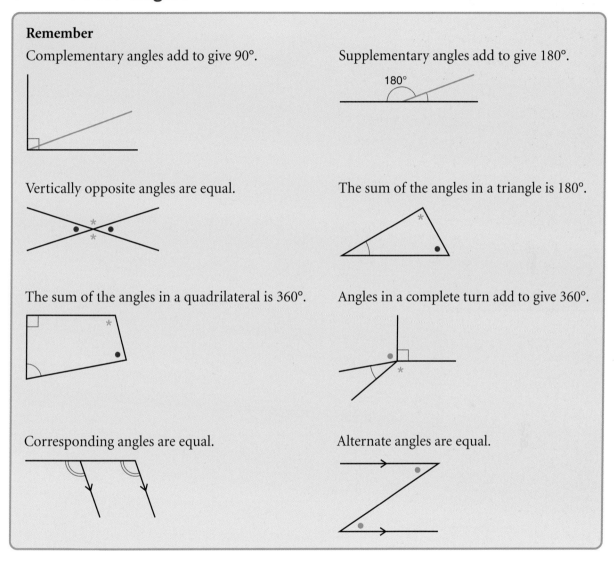

Remember

Complementary angles add to give 90°.

Supplementary angles add to give 180°.

180°

Vertically opposite angles are equal.

The sum of the angles in a triangle is 180°.

The sum of the angles in a quadrilateral is 360°.

Angles in a complete turn add to give 360°.

Corresponding angles are equal.

Alternate angles are equal.

Exercise 3.1

1 Calculate the size of each angle *a* to *e*.

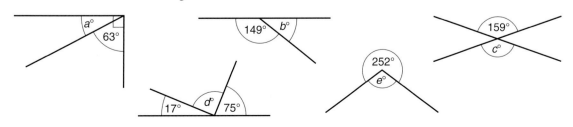

2 Calculate the value of *x* in each diagram.

(a)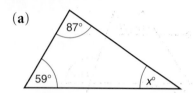

(b)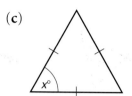

(c)

(d)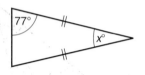

(e)

(f)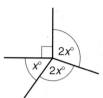

(g)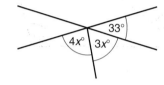

3 Copy each diagram and find the size of each angle marked *a* to *m*.

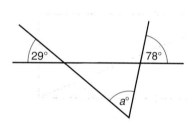

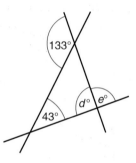

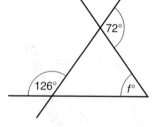

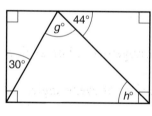

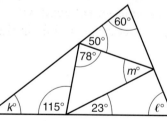

4 Without measuring, find the size of each angle marked *a* to *w*.

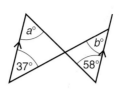 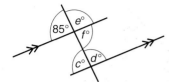 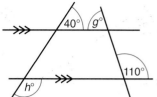

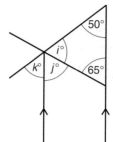 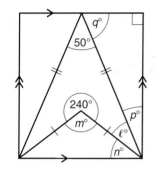 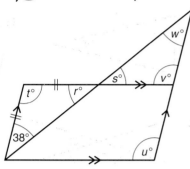

5 (**i**) Calculate the value of *x* in each diagram.
   (**ii**) Copy each diagram and fill in the size of every angle.

(**a**) 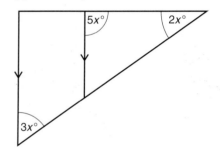   (**b**)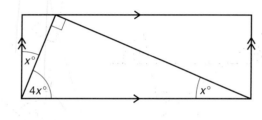

6 The diagram shows the hinge arrangement of parallelograms on John's replacement windows.
Copy the diagram and fill in the sizes of **every** angle.

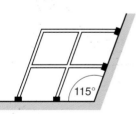

7 The diagram shows the side view of a symmetrical camping table.
Sketch the diagram and fill in the sizes of **every** angle.

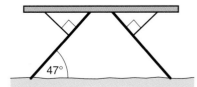

3.2 Angles of a polygon

Example

Find the interior and exterior angles of this octagon.

$x°$ is the interior angle.

$y°$ is the exterior angle.

Angle at centre $z° = \frac{360}{8}$

$z° = 45°$

$w° = \frac{1}{2}(180 - 45°)$

$w° = 67\frac{1}{2}°$

Hence $x° = 2 \times 67\frac{1}{2}°$

$x° = 135°$

And $y = 180° - 135°$

$y = 45$

The interior angle is **135°** and the exterior is **45°**.

Exercise 3.2

1 Find the interior and exterior angles of each regular polygon.

14 sides

(**a**)   (**b**)   (**c**)   (**d**)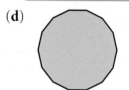

2 Find the interior and exterior angles of:

(**a**) a nonagon (9 sides)   (**b**) a decagon (10 sides)   (**c**) a dodecagon (12 sides)

3.3 Drawing regular polygons

Exercise 3.3

You need a protractor, compasses and ruler for this exercise.

1 Follow these steps to draw a regular hexagon.

Step 1
Draw a circle with a radius of 5 cm and mark its centre.

Step 2
Draw radii at intervals of 60°.

Step 3
Join the ends of the radii to form a regular hexagon.
Rub out the radii and circle.

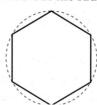

2 Use the method from question **1** to draw:

(**a**) an octagon (**b**) a pentagon (**c**) a square.

3 Draw a **hexagram** by carrying out
Steps 1 and 2 and joining alternate points.

4 Draw (**a**) a pentagram (**b**) an octagram.

3.4 Scale drawing – representative fractions

Example

The map shows five towns around Dommersee.
Ferries sail between the towns around the lake.
The scale of the map is 1 : 50000.

Calculate the true distance from Helligbrenge
to Engelhof.
Distance on map is 4·2 cm.

Map distance	True distance
1	50 000
4·2	210 000

×4·2 on Map distance; ×4·2 on True distance

True distance = 210 000 cm
= 2100 m
= **2·1 km**

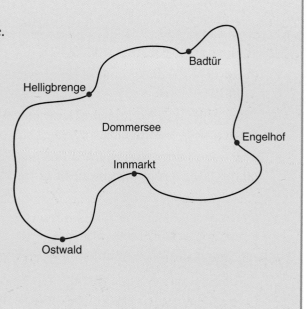

Exercise 3.4

1 Calculate the true distance between

(**a**) Innmarkt and Badtür

(**b**) Badtür and Engelhof

(**c**) Ostwald and Helligbrenge

(**d**) Ostwald and Badtür.

2 On an Ordnance Survey map, with a scale of 1 : 50 000, the distance
from Clydebank to Bowling is 12 centimetres.
How far is it from Clydebank to Bowling?

3 Rachel walked from the camp site to the Post Office. On her map, which has a scale of 1 : 25 000, it was a distance of 10·5 centimetres. How far did Rachel walk?

4 The distance on a map from the port at Roscoff to the camp site is 24 centimetres. The scale of the map is 1 : 200 000. Is the campsite within 50 kilometres of the port?

5 Alasdair's map has a scale of 1 : 130 000. The distance on the map from the airport to his holiday resort is 23 centimetres. The taxi driver said the distance was about 30 kilometres. Was he a truthful taxi driver?

6 Craig is making a scale drawing of his new bathroom which is 3 metres long and 2·5 metres wide.

(**a**) What will be the dimensions of his drawing if he uses a scale of
   (**i**) 1 : 10   (**ii**) 1 : 25   (**iii**) 1 : 50?

(**b**) Craig's paper is 29·5 centimetres long and 25 centimetres broad. Which scale is most suitable for Craig's size of paper? Explain.

(**c**) Craig wants to fit a bath which is 1·65 metres long. What length will this be on a plan with a scale of 1 : 15?

7 In Majorca, Ken took the bus from his resort into Palma, a distance of 15 kilometres. The scale on Ken's map is 1 : 100 000. What distance is it on the map for Ken's bus journey?

8 It is 30 kilometres from the airport on Ibiza to the northern tip of the island. What distance would this be on a map with a scale of 1 : 75 000?

3.5 Calculating the scale

The height of this photograph is 7 centimetres.
The original is 56 centimetres in height.

Find the scale and calculate the width of the original photo.

|← 5 cm →|

Scale

Photo	Original
÷7 ⟨ 7	56 ⟩ ÷7
1	8

7 cm

The scale is **1 : 8**

Using the scale

Width

Photo	Original
×5 ⟨ 1	8 ⟩ ×5
5	40

The true width is **40 cm**

Exercise 3.5

1 For each photograph, calculate the scale used and the missing
   dimension of the real picture.

(**a**)

True width 27 cm

(**b**)

True height 49·5 cm

(**c**)

True width 20·5 cm

2 A model locomotive, which is 26 centimetres long, is an exact scaled-
   down replica of a famous steam locomotive. The length of the real
   one is 19·5 metres.
   Find
   (**a**) the scale used to make the model
   (**b**) the true height if the model is 4 centimetres high.

3 Jill has a model of a World War Two bomber. She knows that the real
   plane was 23·65 metres long with a 16 metre wing span. On the model
   Jill found that it was 43 centimetres in length and had a wing span of
   32 centimetres. Is the model made to scale? Explain your answer.

3.6 Drawing scale diagrams

Example

The shadow of this building is 30 metres long. From the end of the shadow the angle of elevation of the sun is 40°. Make a scale drawing using a scale of 1 to 500 and find the height of the building.

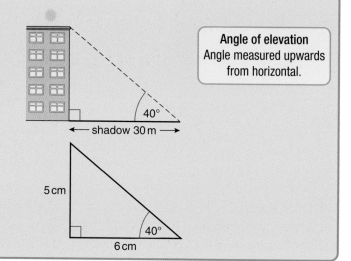

> **Angle of elevation**
> Angle measured upwards from horizontal.

Drawing height	True height
×5 ⟮ 1	500 ⟯ ×5
5	2500

$$\text{True height} = 2500\,\text{cm}$$
$$= 25\,\text{m}$$

The height of the building is **25 metres**.

Exercise 3.6

1 The angle of elevation of the sun is 45° and the shadow of the lighthouse is 20 metres long. Use a scale of 1 to 500 to make a scale drawing and find the height of the lighthouse.

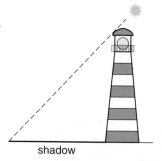

shadow

2 Using the scales given, make scale drawings to find the height of each building.

(a) Telecom Tower

Scale 1 : 2000

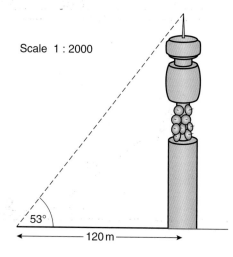

53°

120 m

(b) Eiffel Tower

Scale 1 : 5000

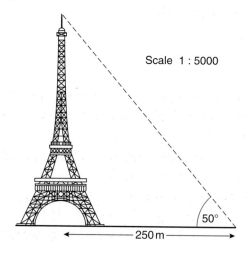

50°

250 m

3 From the top of a cliff the coastguard sees a ship out at sea. The angle of depression is 15° and the cliff is 60 metres high.

(**a**) Choose a suitable scale and make a scale drawing.

(**b**) How far is the ship from the foot of the cliff?

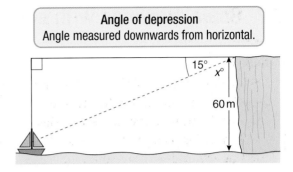

Angle of depression
Angle measured downwards from horizontal.

4 Steeplejack Fred is working at the top of the factory chimney.
He sees Linford on the ground with his lunchbox.
The chimney is 75 metres tall and the angle of depression is 55°.
Use a scale diagram to find how far Linford is from the base of the chimney.

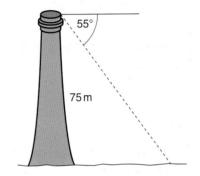

5 Sandyfield farm has an advertising balloon floating above their strawberry field.
The balloon is tied to a tractor on the ground by a long rope.
On a perfectly calm day, the angles of elevation from points 120 metres apart on either side of the tractor are 40° and 55°.
Use a scale diagram to find the height of the balloon above the ground.

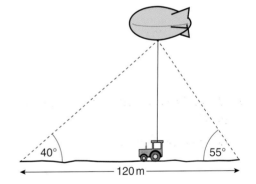

6 A paraglider is being towed at the end of a 20 metre rope by a speedboat. The angle of elevation of the rope is 37°.

(**a**) Use a scale diagram to find the height of the paraglider above sea-level.

(**b**) The paraglider loses height and the rope is now at an angle of elevation of 21°.
How much height has the paraglider lost?

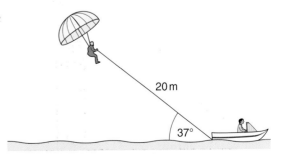

3.7 Scale drawings with bearings

Remember

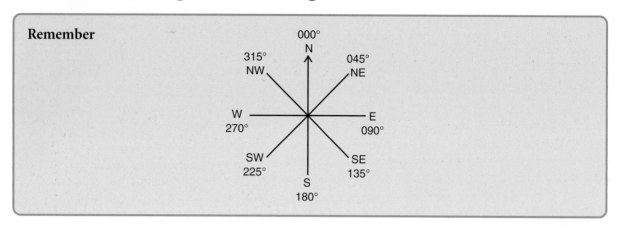

Exercise 3.7

1 The position of a buoy (B) is fixed by giving bearings from two points on the coast.

From A the buoy is on a bearing of 060°.

From C the buoy is on a bearing of 315°.

Point C is 18 km due East of point A.

Choose a suitable scale and draw a scale diagram to find how far the buoy is from A.

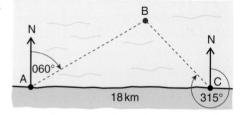

2 Morte Point is 10 miles due North of Westward Ho.

The bearing of a ship is 230° from Morte Point and 320° from Westward Ho.

(**a**) Make a scale drawing to show the position of the ship.

(**b**) How far is the ship from
   (**i**) Morte Point
   (**ii**) Westward Ho?

(**c**) From the ship what is the bearing of
   (**i**) Morte Point
   (**ii**) Westward Ho?

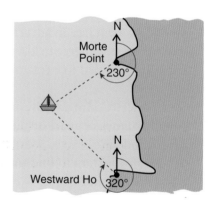

3 The air traffic control centre at Mainton is 60 kilometres due south of the direction beacon at Lowther.

A plane is on a bearing of 165° from Lowther and on a bearing of 110° from Mainton.

(**a**) Make a scale drawing to show the position of the plane.

(**b**) How far is the plane from
   (**i**) Lowther
   (**ii**) Mainton?

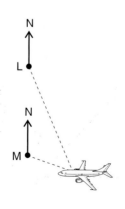

3.8 Angle problems involving bearings

Example

A ship at position A observes a lighthouse L on a bearing of 060°.
After sailing on a bearing of 135° to point B the lighthouse is observed
on a bearing of 340°. Calculate angles ∠ALB and ∠ABL.

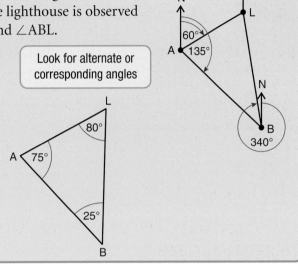

Draw a diagram and mark in equal angles.

∠LAB = 135 − 60 = 75°

∠ALB = 60 + 20 = **80°** (alternate angles)

∠ABL = 180 − (75 + 80) = **25°**

> Look for alternate or corresponding angles

Exercise 3.8

1 A ship at position A observes a lightship L on a bearing of 070°.
After sailing to B on a bearing of 110° the lightship is observed
on a bearing of 325°. Calculate angles ∠ALB and ∠ABL.

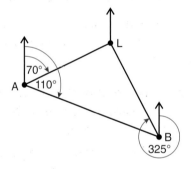

2 A ship at position P observes a rock R on a bearing of 330°.
After sailing on a bearing of 020° to position Q the rock is observed
on a bearing of 220°. Calculate angles ∠PQR and ∠PRQ.

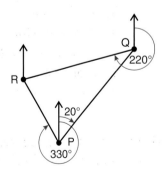

3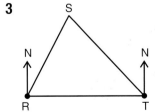

A steeple S bears 065° from R and 320° from T.
R lies due west of T.
Calculate angle ∠RST.

4 A, B and C are three harbours.
B lies on a bearing of 068° from A.
C lies on a bearing of 340° from A.
C lies on a bearing of 320° from B.
Calculate angle ∠ACB.

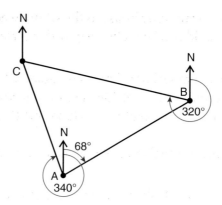

5 KLM is a triangular sailing course.
L lies on a bearing of 050° from K.
M lies on a bearing of 105° from K and 205° from L.

(**a**) Draw a clear diagram.

(**b**) Calculate angles ∠KLM and ∠KML.

Review exercise 3

1 Without measuring, find the size of each angle marked a to s.

(**a**)

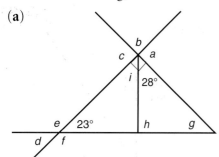

(**b**)

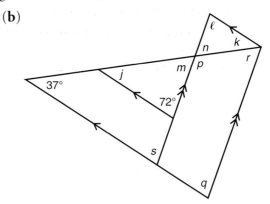

2 For each regular polygon find the sizes of the angles marked
(**i**) x (**ii**) y (**iii**) z.

(**a**)

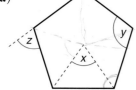

(**b**)

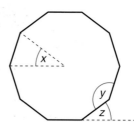

3 Gary's map has a scale of 1 : 75 000 and the distance on the map from
his holiday home to the main town is 16 centimetres.
Calculate the true distance.

4 It is 35 kilometres from Jim's house to the school where he works.
What distance would this be on the map with a scale of 1 : 200 000?

5 Winston's dad has a model of a famous battleship. The real ship was
94·5 metres long with a beam of 25·5 metres. Winston measured the
model and found it was 63 centimetres long and 17 centimetres across
the beam.
Was the model made exactly to scale? Explain your answer.

6 HMS Churchill (C) is 50 kilometres due East of HMS Eden (E).
Submarine Trafalgar (T) is on a bearing of 125° from Eden and
on a bearing of 210° from Churchill.

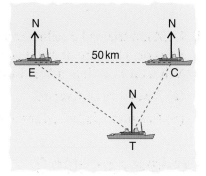

(**a**) Make a scale drawing to show the positions of the ships
and the submarine.

(**b**) How far is Trafalgar from
(**i**) HMS Eden
(**ii**) HMS Churchill?

7 The Cobbler hill is due south of Beinn Ime.
Ben Vane is on a bearing of 055° from Bienn Ime and on a bearing of
035° from The Cobbler.
Calculate the angle ∠IVC.

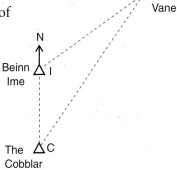

8 Jack is flying his kite. The length of the string is 25 metres and the angle
of elevation is 15°. As the wind increases the angle changes to 42°.
By how much did the kite rise?

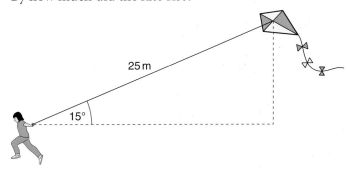

Summary

Angle facts

- Complementary angles add to give 90°

- Supplementary angles add to give 180°

- The sum of the angles of a triangle is 180°.

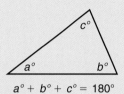

$$a° + b° + c° = 180°$$

- Vertically opposite angles are equal.

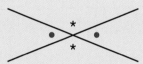

- Corresponding angles are equal.
  ∠ACG = ∠CDF

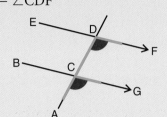

- Alternate angles are equal.
  ∠EDC = ∠DCG

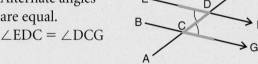

- Angles in a polygon

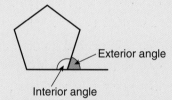

Using scales

A scale can be written as a representative fraction.
1 cm represents 25 000 cm is equivalent to 1 : 25 000.

Scale drawing (cm)	True length (cm)
1	6
4·8	6 × 4·8 = 28·8

Scale 1 cm to 6 cm.
The true wingspan of the bird is **28·8 centimetres**.

Calculating scales

The length of a tunnel is 240 metres.
On the engineer's plan the length is 6 centimetres.

Plan length	True length	
÷6 ⟨ 6 / 1	24 000 / 4000 ⟩ ÷6	The scale is **1 : 4000**

Bearings

Bearings are
- measured from north
- measured clockwise
- given as 3 figures.

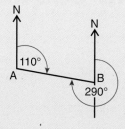

The bearing of B from A is 110°. The bearing of A from B is 290°.

Scale drawing

When constructing a scale drawing:
Step 1 Make a sketch.
Step 2 Calculate distances.
Step 3 Make a scale drawing.

Example

A ship at position A observes a lighthouse L on a bearing of 060°. After sailing on a bearing of 135° to point B the lighthouse is observed on a bearing of 340°. Calculate angles ∠ALB and ∠ABL.

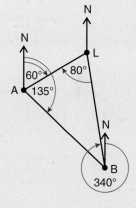

Draw a diagram and mark in equal angles.
∠LAB = 135 − 60 = 75°
∠ALB = 60 + 20 = **80°** (alternate angles)
∠ABL = 180 − (75 + 80) = **25°**

4 Formulae and sequences

4.1 Number machines

An internet site offers computer games for sale.
Each game costs £10 then £5 is added for postage.
This can be shown in a table.

Number of games	1	2	3	4
Cost	15	25	35	45

Each cost can be calculated using a number machine.

Notice the increase each time is 10.

For 2 games

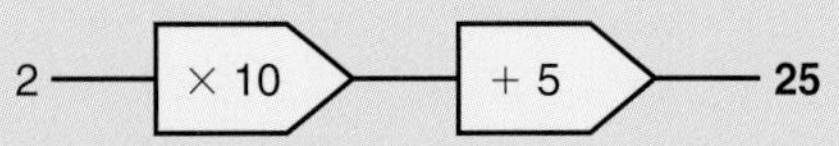

2 ——[× 10]——[+ 5]—— 25

For 4 games

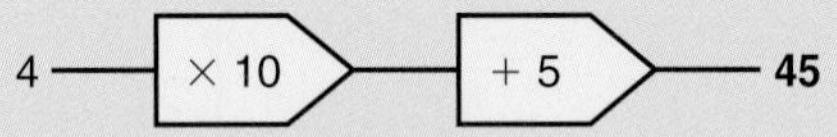

4 ——[× 10]——[+ 5]—— 45

For x games

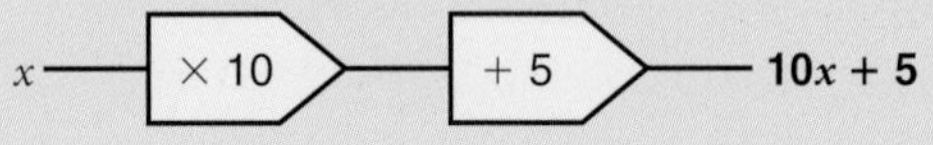

x ——[× 10]——[+ 5]—— $10x + 5$

A formula for the cost C, in £, of x games would be $C = 10x + 5$

Exercise 4.1

1 An internet company offers computer games for sale.
   Each game costs £12 then £3 is added for postage.
   (a) Draw number machines to find the cost of
       (i) 2 games   (ii) 3 games   (iii) x games
   (b) Write a formula for the cost C, in £, of x games.

2 City Taxis charge £2.50 per mile plus £3 for each journey.
   (a) Draw number machines to find the cost of travelling
       (i) 4 miles   (ii) 10 miles   (iii) x miles
   (b) Write a formula for the cost C, in £, of x miles.

3 An airport charges £1.20 per hour plus £5 to park a car.
   (a) Draw number machines to find the cost of parking a car for
       (i) 3 hours   (ii) 6 hours   (iii) x hours
   (b) Write a formula for the cost C, in £, of parking for x hours.

4 The following machines are used to calculate the cost C, in £, of hiring different sailing dinghies at Highport where x is the number of hours hired.
For each dinghy
(**a**) calculate the cost of a 4 hour hire
(**b**) write the formula for the cost of hiring each dinghy.

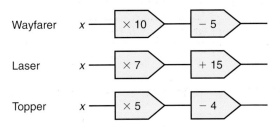

5 The cost of entry to the cinema is £5.20 per person. Greg has a voucher which allows £3 discount on the total for groups of 5 or more.
(**a**) Draw a number machine to illustrate this.
(**b**) Calculate the total cost of entry for
 (**i**) 6 people   (**ii**) 9 people   (**iii**) x people, where $x \geqslant 5$.
(**c**) Write a formula for the cost C, in £, of entry for x people, where $x \geqslant 5$.

6 In an experiment, a spring of length 15 centimetres increases in length by 2·5 centimetres for every kilogramme of weight added.
(**a**) Draw a number machine to illustrate this.
(**b**) Calculate the length of a spring with weights of
 (**i**) 8 kilogrammes   (**ii**) 20 kilogrammes   (**iii**) x kilogrammes.
(**c**) Write a formula for the length L, in centimetres, when x kilogrammes are added.

7 A tank of water containing 42 000 cubic centimetres fills at a rate of 80 cubic centimetres per second when the tap is turned on.
The following number machines can be used to calculate the volume of water in the tank x seconds after the tap is turned on.

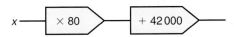

(**a**) Use the number machine to find the volume after
 (**i**) 10 seconds   (**ii**) 1 minute.
(**b**) Write the formula for the volume after x seconds.
(**c**) If the tank can hold 50 000 cubic centimetres, how long will it take for the tank to fill?

4.2 Reversing

Example

An internet site offers computer games for sale.
Each game costs £10 plus postage and packing at £5 per order.

How many games can be bought for £35?

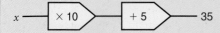

Work backwards, by reversing the number machine,

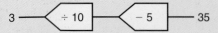

3 games could be bought.

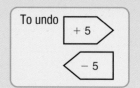

Exercise 4.2

1 Draw reverse number machines for each of the following number machines.
Find the value of *x*.

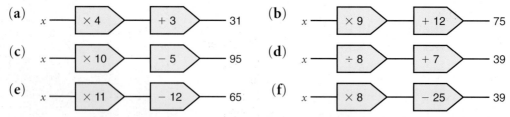

(a) x — × 4 — + 3 — 31

(b) x — × 9 — + 12 — 75

(c) x — × 10 — − 5 — 95

(d) x — ÷ 8 — + 7 — 39

(e) x — × 11 — − 12 — 65

(f) x — × 8 — − 25 — 39

(g) x — ÷ 20 — + 16 — 42

(h) x — ÷ 9 — − 25 — 72

2 An internet site offers CDs for sale at £12 each plus postage and packing at £7 per order.

(a) Draw a number machine to illustrate this.

(b) Draw a reverse number machine to find the number of CDs when the total cost is known.

(c) Find the number of CDs which can be bought for
  (i) £43   (ii) £91   (iii) £*c*.

3 Hightown Airport charges £2.50 per hour plus £4 to park a car.

(a) Draw a reverse number machine to find the number of hours a car can be parked if the total cost is known.

(b) Find the number of hours a car can be parked for
  (i) £11.50   (ii) £24   (iii) £*c*.

4.3 Evaluating formulae

Formulae are used to generalise situations. They are useful when the same calculations are likely to be repeated.

Example 1

The cost of a car service is calculated using the formula $C = 10h + 50$ where C is the total cost and h is the number of hours worked. Find the total cost for

(a) 3 hours   (b) $4\frac{1}{4}$ hours

(a) $C = 10h + 50$
   $C = 10 \times 3 + 50$ Substitute 3 instead of h
   $C = 30 + 50$
   $C = 80$

(b) $C = 10h + 50$
   $C = 10 \times 4{\cdot}25 + 50$ Substitute 4·25 instead of h
   $C = 42{\cdot}5 + 50$
   $C = 92.5$
   The total cost is **£92.50**

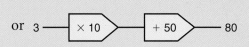

or 3 — ×10 — +50 — 80

The total cost is **£80**.

Example 2

This formula may be used to convert from degrees Fahrenheit to degrees Celsius:

$$C = \frac{5(F - 32)}{9}$$

Change 59 °F to Celsius.

$$C = \frac{5(F - 32)}{9}$$

$$C = \frac{5(59 - 32)}{9}$$

$$C = \frac{5 \times 27}{9}$$

$$C = 15$$

> **Remember:**
> **B**rackets
> **O**f
> **D**ivide
> **M**ultiply
> **A**dd
> **S**ubtract

59 °F is equivalent to **15 °C**.

Exercise 4.3

1 Evaluate each formula for the given value.

(a) $C = 8h + 16, h = 4$ (b) $C = 12h + 25, h = 9$

(c) $C = 1{\cdot}5h + 28, h = 6$ (d) $C = 5h + 5{\cdot}6, h = 1{\cdot}2$

(e) $C = 2{\cdot}5h + 1{\cdot}8, h = 5$ (f) $C = 2{\cdot}3h + 5{\cdot}4, h = 7$

(g) $C = 4h + 2{\cdot}4, h = 2{\cdot}5$ (h) $C = 4{\cdot}5h + 6{\cdot}7, h = 8$

2 A mail order firm uses the formula $C = 5w + 10$ to calculate the cost of shipping items, where C is the total cost in £ and w the weight in kilogrammes of the items.
Calculate the cost for

(**a**) 8 kg (**b**) 4·5 kg (**c**) $6\frac{3}{4}$ kg (**d**) 9·35 kg

3 The formula $F = \dfrac{9C}{5} + 32$ is used to change degrees Celsius into degrees Fahrenheit.

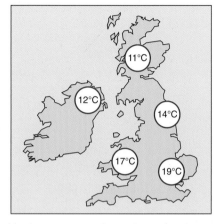

(**a**) Convert into degrees Fahrenheit:
   (**i**) 25 °C (**ii**) 50 °C (**iii**) 65 °C (**iv**) 42 °C

(**b**) Normal body temperature is 37 °C.
   What is the equivalent in degrees Fahrenheit?

(**c**) Convert each of the temperatures on the weather map into degrees Fahrenheit.

4 Evaluate each formula for the given value.

(**a**) $P = 2(b + 3·5), b = 2·7$

(**b**) $R = 4·5(c - 12·7), c = 32·7$

(**c**) $H = 9(8·7 - d), d = 3·9$

(**d**) $N = 8(k - 9), k = 5$

(**e**) $T = \dfrac{(26 + g)}{4}, g = 14$

(**f**) $W = \dfrac{3(h - 19)}{8}, h = 35$

(**g**) $Q = \dfrac{1·5(4·2 - p)}{5}, p = 2·2$

(**h**) $B = \dfrac{0·4(y + 2)}{y}, y = 5$

5 The formula $C = \dfrac{5(F - 32)}{9}$ is used to change degrees Fahrenheit, F, into degrees Celsius, C.

(**a**) Convert into degrees Celsius:
   (**i**) 50 °F (**ii**) 68 °F (**iii**) 122 °F (**iv**) 23 °F

(**b**) The boiling point of water is 212 °F.
   What is the equivalent in degrees Celsius?

(**c**) The freezing point of water is 32 °F.
   What is the equivalent in degrees Celsius?

4.4 Further formulae

Some formulae may require substitution for more than one variable.

Example 1

Which of these lawns has the greater area?
Find the area of each of these triangular lawns.

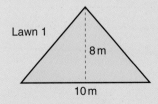

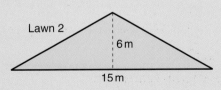

$A = \dfrac{1}{2}bh$

$A = \dfrac{1}{2} \times 10 \times 8$

$A = 40 \text{ m}^2$

$A = \dfrac{1}{2}bh$

$A = \dfrac{15 \times 6}{2}$

$A = 45 \text{ m}^2$

Lawn 2 is 5 square metres greater than Lawn 1.

Example 2

Use the formula $d = 5t^2$ to find d
when $t = 8$.

$d = 5t^2$
$d = 5 \times 8^2$
$d = 5 \times 64$
$d = 320$

When $t = 8$, $d = \mathbf{320}$

Example 3

The distance, s, a particle travels is given by

$s = ut + \dfrac{1}{2}at^2$.

Calculate s when $u = 5$, $t = 10$ and $a = 3$

$s = ut + \dfrac{1}{2}at^2$

$s = 5 \times 10 + \dfrac{1}{2} \times 3 \times 10^2$

$s = 50 + \dfrac{1}{2} \times 300$

$s = \mathbf{200}$

Exercise 4.4

1 Use the formula, $A = \dfrac{1}{2}bh$ to calculate the area of each triangle.

(a)

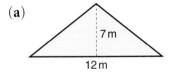

(b)

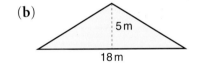

(c)

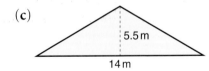

2 Evaluate each formula for the given values.

(a) $V = Ah$ when   (i) $A = 29$ and $h = 5$ (ii) $A = 1·2$ and $h = 8$

(b) $F = ma$ when   (i) $m = 23$ and $a = 10$ (ii) $m = 6·7$ and $a = 20$

(c) $s = ut$ when   (i) $u = 68$ and $t = 9$ (ii) $u = 8·9$ and $t = 11$

(d) $V = IR$ when   (i) $I = 25$ and $R = 40$ (ii) $I = 5·2$ and $R = 40$

(e) $a = bc + 5$ when   (i) $b = 87$ and $c = 8$ (ii) $b = 5·4$ and $c = 8$

(f) $B = cd + r$ when   (i) $c = 12, d = 8$ and $r = 26$ (ii) $c = 5·3, d = 8$ and $r = 8·95$

(g) $f = th + rt$ when   (i) $h = 64, r = 47$ and $t = 9$ (ii) $h = 7·2, r = 3·2$ and $t = 7$

3 The time taken to climb a mountain can be calculated using Naismith's Rule. This can be stated as $t = 12d + 0·1h$ where t is the time in minutes, d is the distance in kilometres walked and h is the height climbed in metres.

(a) Calculate the time taken for a walk of 10 kilometres, climbing 600 metres.

(b) Eirean is planning a trip which involves walking on 3 separate days. She wants to walk for the longest time on the first day, and the shortest time on the last day. On which of her three days should she plan these walks?

Walk A   8 kilometres, 2000 metres climbed

Walk B   10 kilometres, 1000 metres climbed

Walk C   5 kilometres, 1500 metres climbed.

4 The distance travelled by a coin dropped down a well can be calculated using the formula $d = 5t^2$ where d is the distance in metres and t is the time in seconds. Find the distance travelled after

(a) 3 seconds   (b) 10 seconds   (c) 6 seconds   (d) 1·5 seconds.

5 Evaluate each formula for the given values.

(a) $A = 2d^2$ when $d = 3$ (b) $A = (2d)^2$ when $d = 3$

(c) $G = x^2 + 5$ when $x = 7$ (d) $G = (x + 5)^2$ when $x = 7$

(e) $s = \frac{1}{2}gt^2$ when $g = 9·8$ and $t = 10$ (f) $t = a^2 - bc$ when $a = 9, b = 4·2$ and $c = 9$

(g) $T = (x + y)^2$ when $x = 6·5$ and $y = 4·5$ (h) $K = (st - 9g)^2$ when $s = 25, t = 5$ and $g = 12$

6 Body Mass Index, B, can be used to plan the training of athletes.

The formula for this is $B = \dfrac{w}{h^2}$ where w is a person's weight in

kilograms and h is a person's height in metres.

The table gives the heights and weights of three athletes.

Athlete	Weight	Height
Lee	62	1·77
Shirley	90	1·75
Liz	56	1·74

(a) Calculate the Body Mass Index for each athlete.

(b) One of the athletes is a sprinter, one is a hammer thrower and one is a marathon runner. Which athlete do you think competes in each event? Explain your answer.

(c) You are classified as overweight if your Body Mass Index is more than 25. Which athlete could be classified as overweight?

4.5 Finding the missing variable

A formula can be used to find the value of an unknown variable if all other values in the formula are known.

Example

The cost of hiring a bike is given by $C = 10h + 50$ where C is the cost in pounds and h is the number of hours. Find the number of hours if the cost of hire was £90.

$$
\begin{array}{rl}
C & = 10h + 50 \\
90 & = 10h + 50 \\
-50 & \qquad -50 \\
\\
40 & = 10h \\
\div 10 & \quad \div 10 \\
\\
4 & = h
\end{array}
$$

Substitute the values.

Solve the equation.

Notice this is the same as reversing the number machine.

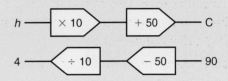

The bike was hired for **4 hours**.

Exercise 4.5

1 For each formula, substitute the values to form an equation and solve to find the missing value.

(**a**) $C = 8h + 25$ find h when $C = 65$

(**b**) $C = 12h + 18$ find h when $C = 78$

(**c**) $V = IR$ find R when $V = 240$ and $I = 5$

(**d**) $F = ma$ find a when $F = 100$ and $m = 2{\cdot}5$

(**e**) $s = ut$ find u when $s = 72$ and $t = 6$

(**f**) $T = 2p + 3q$ find q when $T = 540$ and $p = 120$

(**g**) $t = 12k + 0{\cdot}1h$ find h when $t = 42$ and $k = 2$

(**h**) $P = 2l + 2b$ find b when $P = 60$ and $l = 16$

2 The sum, S, in right angles, of the angles in a polygon is calculated from the formula $S = 2n - 4$ where n is the number of sides.
How many sides has

(**a**) an enneagon if its angle sum is 14 right angles

(**b**) a hendecagon if its angle sum is 18 right angles?

3 Two different hire companies, Better Bikes and Boneshakers, use the formulae shown to calculate the cost of hiring bikes, where C is the cost in pounds and t is the time in hours.

Better Bikes	Boneshakers
$C = 6t + 25$	$C = 5t + 30$

(**a**) Calculate the length of time for which a bike could be hired from Better Bikes for

  (**i**) £37   (**ii**) £85   (**iii**) £145.

(**b**) Calculate the length of time for which a bike could be hired from Boneshakers for

  (**i**) £45   (**ii**) £75   (**iii**) £100.

(**c**) Which of the companies gives better value if Jenni can spend (**i**) £50   (**ii**) £60?

(**d**) If £55 is available to hire a bike, which company gives better value? Explain your answer clearly.

4 The perimeter of a rectangle can be calculated from the formula
$P = 2(l + b)$ where l is its length and b its breadth.

(**a**) A rectangle has a perimeter of 50 cm and a breadth of 17 cm. What is its length?

(**b**) A rectangle has a perimeter of 74 cm and a length of 23 cm. What is its breadth?

5 The total surface area of a cuboid can be calculated using the formula
$A = 2(lb + bh + hl)$.
Find

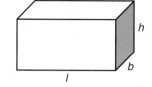

(**a**) the height of a cuboid with surface area 72 cm², length 6 cm
and breadth 2 cm

(**b**) the breadth of a cuboid with a surface area 142 cm², length 7 cm and height 3 cm

(**c**) the length of a cuboid with surface area 180 cm², height 6 cm and breadth 6 cm.

Review exercise 4

1 Tom can complete a canoe course in 120 seconds. For each gate he
hits, 10 seconds is added to his time.

(**a**) Draw number machines to find his total time if he hits
　　(**i**) 5 gates　　(**ii**) x gates

(**b**) Write a formula for the total time t, in seconds, of hitting x gates.

2 Evaluate each formula for the given values.

(**a**) $V = Ah$ when $A = 45$ and $h = 9$

(**b**) $m = pn + 8$ when $p = 4·2$ and $n = 7$

(**c**) $F = \dfrac{9C}{5} + 32$ when $C = 75$

(**d**) $x = yz + w$ when $y = 1·6$, $z = 6$ and $w = 8·7$

(**e**) $s = \frac{1}{2}at^2$ when $a = 3·5$ and $t = 12$

(**f**) $C = \dfrac{5(F - 32)}{9}$ when $F = 95$

3 A garden centre sells bags of compost at £3.50 each. In addition they
have a home delivery service which costs £5 per order.

(**a**) Draw a number machine to illustrate this.

(**b**) Draw a reverse number machine to find the number of bags of compost when the total cost is
known.

(**c**) Find the number of bags which can be bought for　(**i**) £40　　(**ii**) £75.

4 The formulae shown are used to calculate the cost C, in pounds, of
hiring two different types of dinghy, for h hours.

Otter
$C = 8h + 20$

Lazer
$C = 6h + 30$

(**a**) For how long could you hire an Otter dinghy if the total cost was £52?

(**b**) For how long could you hire a Lazer dinghy if the total cost was £54?

(**c**) For how long could you hire each dinghy if the total cost was £40?

(**d**) Find the number of hours for which the hire cost would be the same for both dinghies.

Summary

Number machines

Number machines can be used to illustrate formulae.

An internet site offers computer games for sale.
Each game costs £10 then £5 is added for postage.
This can be shown in a table.

Number of games	1	2	3	4
Cost	15	25	35	45

Each cost can be calculated using a number machine.
For 2 games:

$$2 \longrightarrow \boxed{\times\ 10} \longrightarrow \boxed{+\ 5} \longrightarrow \mathbf{25}$$

Reversing number machines

An internet site offers computer games for sale.
Each game costs £10 plus postage and packing at £5 per order.

How many games can be bought for £35?

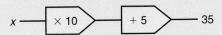

$$x \longrightarrow \boxed{\times\ 10} \longrightarrow \boxed{+\ 5} \longrightarrow 35$$

Work backwards, by reversing the number machine:

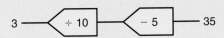

$$3 \longleftarrow \boxed{\div\ 10} \longleftarrow \boxed{-\ 5} \longleftarrow 35$$

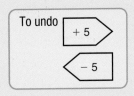

To undo

$\boxed{+\ 5}$

$\boxed{-\ 5}$

3 games could be bought.

Evaluating formulae

Formulae can be evaluated by substituting values for variables.
Calculate C when $h = 3$

$C = 10h + 50$
$C = 10 \times 3 + 50$ $\boxed{\text{Substitute 3 instead of } h}$
$C = \mathbf{80}$

or $3 \longrightarrow \boxed{\times\ 10} \longrightarrow \boxed{+\ 50} \longrightarrow \mathbf{80}$

The distance, s, a particle travels is given by
$s = ut + \frac{1}{2}at^2$.
Calculate s when $u = 5$, $t = 10$ and $a = 3$
$s = ut + \frac{1}{2}at^2$
$s = 5 \times 10 + \frac{1}{2} \times 3 \times 10^2$
$s = 50 + \frac{1}{2} \times 300$
$s = \mathbf{200}$

Finding the missing variable

A formula can be used to find the value of an unknown variable if all other values are known.

The cost of hiring a bike is given by $C = 10h + 50$ where C is the cost in pounds and h is the number of hours.
Find the number of hours if the cost of hire was £90.

$$C = 10h + 50$$
$$90 = 10h + 50$$ Substitute the values.
$$-50 \qquad -50$$

$$40 = 10h$$ Solve the equation.
$$\div 10 \qquad \div 10$$

$$4 = h$$

The bike was hired for **4 hours**.

Notice this is the same as reversing the number machine.

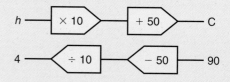

The bike was hired for **4 hours**.

5 Fractions and percentages

In this chapter you will review and extend your knowledge of fractions, decimals and percentages.

5.1 Fractions, decimals and percentages

> **Remember**
>
> $57\% = \frac{57}{100} = 0\cdot57$ $57\%, \frac{57}{100}$ and $0\cdot57$ are equivalent.
>
> $56\% = \frac{56}{100} = \frac{14}{25}$ in **simplest form**.
>
> **Example**
>
> Calculate **(a)** 20% of £240   **(b)** $66\frac{2}{3}\%$ of 63 kilogrammes
>
>   **(a)** 20% of £240   **(b)** $66\frac{2}{3}\%$ of 63 kilogrammes
>
> $= \frac{1}{5} \times £240$ $= \frac{2}{3}$ of 63 kg
>
> $= \textbf{£48}$ $\frac{1}{3} \times 63 = 21$
>
>   So, $\frac{2}{3}$ of 63 kg $= 2 \times 21$ kg $= \textbf{42 kg}$

Exercise 5.1

1 Write each as a fraction in simplest form:

   (a) 35%   **(b)** 60%   **(c)** 66%   **(d)** 24%   **(e)** $37\frac{1}{2}\%$

   (f) $\frac{12}{30}$ **(g)** $\frac{16}{56}$ **(h)** $\frac{21}{77}$ **(i)** $\frac{123}{666}$ **(j)** $\frac{34}{102}$

   (k) $0\cdot55$ **(l)** $0\cdot81$ **(m)** $0\cdot38$ **(n)** $0\cdot05$ **(o)** $0\cdot005$

2 Calculate:

   (a) 20% of £36   **(b)** 60% of 50 kg   **(c)** 75% of 60 cm

   (d) $33\frac{1}{3}\%$ of 930 litres   **(e)** $66\frac{2}{3}\%$ of 36p   **(f)** 70% of $50

3 A sweet company sells 40% of their warehouse stock. How many tonnes of sweets are now in the warehouse if they started with 20 tonnes?

4 You have won a prize in a maths competition.

      Prize A is 5% of £250.   **Prize B** is $2\frac{1}{2}\%$ of £600.

Which prize should you choose?

5.2 Using one percent and ten percent

Example

Calculate (a) $3\frac{1}{2}$% of 250 kg   (b) 17·5% of £150

(a) 1% of 250   = 2·5   (b) 10% of £150 = £15

$\frac{1}{2}$%   = 1·25   5%   = £ 7.50

3%   = 7·5 $2\frac{1}{2}$%   = £ 3.75

So, $3\frac{1}{2}$% of 250 kg = **8·75** kg   So, 17·5%   = **£26.25**

Exercise 5.2

1 Calculate:

(a) 3% of £75   (b) 9% of 500 g   (c) 7% of 350 cm

(d) 4% of 80 mm   (e) 8% of 200 ml   (f) 6% of £35

2 Calculate:

(a) $\frac{1}{2}$% of £400   (b) $1\frac{1}{2}$% of €800   (c) $3\frac{1}{2}$% of £150

3 Calculate:

(a) 30% of 550 kg   (b) 40% of 240 m   (c) 70% of £30

(d) 20% of 60p   (e) 90% of £120   (f) 30% of 225 litres

4 Calculate:

(a) 5% of £240   (b) 15% of 90 kg   (c) 5% of $6   (d) 35% of £8

5 Calculate:

(a) $2\frac{1}{2}$% of $880   (b) $17\frac{1}{2}$% of £350   (c) 17·5% of £80

6 Calculate the VAT ($17\frac{1}{2}$%) on:

(a) £300   (b) £42

(c) £15   (d) £120

£300

7 Calculate:

(a) 11% of €3000   (b) 13% of 600 kg   (c) 18% of £50

(d) 31% of $450   (e) 63% of 8000 mm   (f) 99% of £7

5.3 Percentages using a calculator

Example 1

Calculate 16% of £350

16% of £350

= 0·16 × £350

= **£56**

Example 2

A shop adds 12% to a £40 item. How much does the item cost now?

112% of 40

= 1·12 × £40

= 44·80

The item costs **£44.80**

Example 3

Sue has an 8% employee's discount. Calculate what she pays for an £87 dress.

0·92 × 87 = 80·04

She pays **£80.04**

Exercise 5.3

1 Calculate:
   (**a**) 18% of £360
   (**b**) 37% of €250
   (**c**) 54% of £18
   (**d**) 3% of £9
   (**e**) 8·8% of $250
   (**f**) 5·5% of £1000

2 A shop raises prices by 16%.
   Calculate each new selling price.

   (**a**)
   Shirt
   £25

   (**b**)
   Train set
   £40

   (**c**)
   CD player
   £260

3 A £40 clock has its price reduced by 35%. How much will it now cost?

4 Billy makes 8 litres of fruit punch for his party.
   He uses 56% lemonade, 22% orange juice,
   14% pineapple juice and 8% grapefruit juice.
   Calculate the volume of each ingredient in the punch.

5 A shop gives a 33% discount on some items.
   Calculate the new price of each of these items:

   (**a**)

   £65

   (**b**)

   £140

   (**c**)

   £79

6 Add VAT at 17·5% to each bill:

(a) TOTAL: £45

(b) TOTAL: £126

(c) TOTAL: £3760

7 A bank pays 3·5% interest per annum on their Gold Savers accounts.
Bob puts £450 into a Gold Savers account.
How much will he have in his account after a year?

> Per annum means each year.

8 Jill has £8200 to deposit in an account for one year.

(a) Which account should she choose?
Why this account?

(b) Calculate how much interest she would
have received in each account.

(c) What is the difference in interest paid
between the best and worst accounts?

Account	Interest Rate
CityBank	2%
P.O. Account	3·25%
Hullifax	1·75%
B.S.T	3·5%

9 A shop increases prices by $12\frac{1}{2}$%.
Find the new cost of a shirt which had cost £30.

10 Add V.A.T. at 17·5% to find the total cost of each item:

(a) T.V. £850   (b) Car £8600   (c) Conservatory £12 800

5.4 Percentage of a total

Example

A basket of fruit has 12 apples, 6 oranges, 4 pears and 5 bananas.
What percentage of the fruit are pears?
Total = 12 + 6 + 4 + 5 = 27
Pears: 4 out of 27 = $\frac{4}{27}$ = 0·148
To the nearest whole percent, **15% are pears**.

Exercise 5.4

1 Change each fraction to a percentage:

(a) $\frac{17}{25}$ (b) $\frac{34}{40}$ (c) $\frac{45}{60}$ (d) $\frac{37}{45}$

2 Zak scores $\frac{35}{45}$ in his Maths test, $\frac{68}{80}$ in his English test and $\frac{17}{22}$ in his French test.

    (**a**) What percentage did he score for each subject?

    (**b**) List his subjects from best to worst.

3 Eddie drives 30 kilometres of an 80 kilometre journey.
What percentage of the journey has he still to drive?

4 Helen scored 24 out of 30 in her assessment.
What percentage of marks did she **lose**?

5 A box of sweets has 20 milk chocolates, 16 plain chocolates and 4 jellied sweets. What percentage of the box are:

    (**a**) plain chocolates   (**b**) jellied sweets?

6 A bag of marbles has 20 orange, 30 red, 15 green, 24 blue and 1 black marble.
What percentage, to the nearest whole percent, of the marbles are

    (**a**) orange   (**b**) green   (**c**) black   (**d**) blue   (**e**) red?

5.5 Percentage increase and percentage decrease

Percentage increase	Percentage decrease
Example	**Example**
Jay's weight increases from 32 kg to 34 kg. Calculate the percentage increase in weight.	A car worth £11 000 in 2005 was only worth £7000 in 2006. Calculate the percentage decrease in value.
Increase is 2 kg.	Decrease is £4000.

$$\text{Fractional increase} = \frac{\text{increase}}{\text{original amount}}$$

$$= \frac{2}{30}$$

$$= 0.0625$$

$$= \textbf{6.25\% increase}$$

$$\text{Fractional decrease} = \frac{\text{decrease}}{\text{original amount}}$$

$$= \frac{4000}{11\,000}$$

$$= 0.364, \text{ to 3 sig. figs.}$$

$$= \textbf{36.4\% decrease}$$

Exercise 5.5

1 Alfie weighed 76 kilograms last year. This year he weighs 84 kilograms.
Calculate his percentage weight increase to one decimal place.

2 In the first week of training for a half marathon Baz ran 20 kilometres.
In the second week he ran 26 kilometres.
Calculate the percentage increase to two significant figures.

3 (**a**) For each plant in the table calculate the percentage height increase to two decimal places.

(**b**) Which plant showed the greatest percentage increase in height?

	Month 1	Month 2
Plant 1	12 cm	15 cm
Plant 2	15 cm	25 cm
Plant 3	16 cm	17 cm

4 The value of a car over three years is shown in the table. Calculate the percentage decrease from:

(**a**) 2004 to 2005   (**b**) 2005 to 2006

(**c**) 2004 to 2006

Year	Value
2004	£8500
2005	£6500
2006	£5000

5.6 Finding the original amount

Example

A car servicing bill is £470, including VAT at 17·5%.
Calculate the cost **excluding** VAT.

Cost + VAT = 117·5% = 1·175
1·175 × Cost = 470

Hence, Cost = $\dfrac{470}{1·175}$ = **£400**

Check: 117·5% of 400 = 1·175 × 400
= 470

Exercise 5.6

1 For each bill, including VAT, calculate the original cost, **excluding** VAT.

(a) £70.50   (b) £293.75   (c) £211.50   (d) £14 100

2 Schools do not pay VAT. Find what a school would pay for furniture at the following prices, which include VAT.

(a) £58.75   (b) £352.50   (c) £258.50   (d) £752

3 For each employee calculate the salary before the 5% pay rise.

(a) Manager £31 500   (b) Foreman £16 800   (c) Tradesman £22 050

4 For each item calculate the price **before** the 15% discount.

(a)
Jacket
discount price
£200

(b)
Briefcase
dicounted
£128

(c)
Shoes
discounted
£75

5 Macy has £650 000 left from her £1.2 million lottery win.
What is the percentage decrease in amount?

6 In a sale a coat was reduced from £260 to £199 and an £18 scarf was reduced by £5.
Which had the greater percentage price reduction?

7 A square piece of fabric of side 20 centimetres is trimmed by 1 centimetre on all sides.
Calculate the percentage decrease in area.

5.7 Compound interest

When money is invested in a bank or building society, each year's interest is calculated on the amount at the start of each year.
The annual interest is added to the account.
The next year, interest is calculated on the new amount.
This is called **compound interest**.

Example

Ben deposited £200 in a bank.
The bank gave an interest rate of 6% per annum. Calculate his interest after 3 years.

Year 1:   Amount = 106% of £200
                 = 1·06 × £200
                 = £212

Year 2:   Amount = 106% of £212
                 = 1·06 × £212
                 = £224·72

Year 3:   Amount = 106% of £224.72
                 = 1·06 × £224·72
                 = £238·20

After 3 years Ben has a total amount of **£238·20**.
His total interest is £238·20 − £200 = **£38·20**.

Exercise 5.7

1 Sally deposited £400 in a bank.
The bank gave an interest rate of 4% per annum.
Calculate:

(**a**) the total amount in her account after 3 years

(**b**) the compound interest after 3 years.

2 Calculate the total amount in each account:

(**a**) £250 for 2 years at 7% p.a.   (**b**) £625 for 3 years at 5% p.a.

(**c**) £7000 for 4 years at 6% p.a.   (**d**) £850 for 5 years at 4·5% p.a.

3 Gary deposits £2000 in the Bank of Motherton at 3·5% per annum.
Lindsay deposits £1500 in Town Building Society at 6% per annum.
Who will receive the most compound interest after 2 years?

4 Jeri borrows £3000 from the Shark Investment company.
Jeri agrees to repay the loan and interest in one payment after 3 years.
The company charges an interest rate of 26% per annum.

(**a**) Calculate the total interest on the loan.

(**b**) How much will Jeri have to pay back after 3 years?

Review exercise 5

1 Write as a fraction, percentage and decimal:

(**a**) 57%   (**b**) $\frac{1}{4}$ (**c**) 0·69   (**d**) $\frac{3}{100}$ (**e**) 0·1

2 Calculate:

(**a**) 20% of £250   (**b**) $33\frac{1}{3}$% of 660 kg   (**c**) 40% of $280   (**d**) 15% of 60 cm

3 Find:

(**a**) 23% of €750   (**b**) 79% of $600   (**c**) 4% of £3460   (**d**) 9·5% of £160

4 Add VAT at 17·5% to find the total cost of:

(**a**) a pair of shoes at £140   (**b**) a garage bill of £1242.

5 Jackie decides to put £2600 in a bank account.

(**a**) Which bank will give her the most interest after one year?

(**b**) How much more interest (in £) will this bank give?

| High St. Bank | 4% per annum |
| Local Bank | 4·5% p.a. |

6 A shop increases its prices by 15%.
Find the new costs of these items:

(**a**) jumper, original price £33   (**b**) blouse, original price £12·50.

7 Change each score to a percentage:

(**a**) Jon – 24 out of 30   (**b**) Ben – 33 out of 60   (**c**) Beth – 34 out of 45.

8 A car worth £4500 in 2001 was only worth £1250 in 2003.
Calculate the percentage decrease in value.

9 For each bill, calculate the cost before VAT is added.

(**a**) £56·40 including VAT   (**b**) £7990 including VAT.

10 Barry deposited £3500 in a bank for 3 years at a rate of 4% per annum.
Calculate the total amount in his account after 3 years.

Summary

Equivalent fractions and simplest form

57%, $\frac{57}{100}$ and 0·57 are **equivalent**.

56% $= \frac{56}{100} = \frac{14}{25}$ in **simplest form**.

Percentages of quantities

Without a calculator:
Calculate $3\frac{1}{2}$% of 250 kg

1% of 250	$= 2\cdot5$
$\frac{1}{2}$%	$= 1\cdot25$
3%	$= \underline{7\cdot5}$

So, $3\frac{1}{2}$% of 250 kg $= \mathbf{8\cdot75}$ kg

With a calculator:
56% of 130 kg
$= 0\cdot56 \times 130$ kg
$= \mathbf{72.8\ kg}$

A shop adds 12% to a £40 item
How much does the item cost now?
112% of 40
$= 1\cdot12 \times 40$
$= 44\cdot80$
The item costs **£44.80**

Percentage increase and percentage decrease

Percentage increase
Jay's weight increases from
32 kg to 34 kg.
Calculate the percentage increase in weight.
Increase is 2 kg.

$$\text{Fractional increase} = \frac{\text{increase}}{\text{original amount}}$$
$$= \frac{2}{32}$$
$$= 0\cdot0625 = \mathbf{6\cdot25\%\ increase}$$

Percentage decrease
A car worth £11 000 in 2005 was only
worth £7000 in 2006.
Calculate the percentage decrease.
Decrease is £4000.

$$\text{Fractional decrease} = \frac{\text{decrease}}{\text{original amount}}$$
$$= \frac{4000}{11\ 000}$$
$$= \mathbf{36\cdot4\%\ decrease}$$

Finding original amount

Example

A car servicing bill is £470, including VAT at 17·5%.
Calculate the cost **excluding** VAT.
Cost + VAT = 117·5% = 1·175

Hence, cost $= \dfrac{£470}{1\cdot175} = \mathbf{£400}$

Check: 117·5% of 400 $= 1\cdot175 \times 400$
$\qquad\qquad\qquad\quad = 470$

Compound interest

Example

Ben deposited £200 in a bank.

The bank gave an interest rate of 6% per annum. Calculate his interest after 3 years.

Year 1:   Amount = 106% of £200
            = 1·06 × £200
            = £212

Year 2:   Amount = 106% of £212
            = 1·06 × £212
            = £224·72

Year 3:   Amount = 106% of £224.72
            = 1·06 × £224·72
            = £238·20

After 3 years Ben has a total amount of **£238·20**.

His total interest is £238·20 − £200 = **£38·20**.

6 Proportion

In this chapter you will learn how to solve problems using proportion.

6.1 Direct proportion

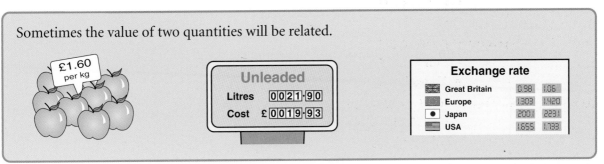

Sometimes the value of two quantities will be related.

Exercise 6.1

You need 2 mm graph paper for questions **4** and **5**.

1 Michael can type 50 words per minute.

(**a**) Copy and complete the table.

Number of minutes	1	2	3	4	5	6	7	8
Number of words								

(**b**) What happens to the number of words when the number of minutes is

(**i**) doubled　　(**ii**) trebled　　(**iii**) quadrupled?

2 Alfred works in The Excelsior hotel.

(**a**) Copy and complete the table.

Number of hours worked	1	2	3	4	5	6	7	8
Wage (£)								48

(**b**) What happens to Alfred's wages when the number of hours worked is

(**i**) doubled　　(**ii**) halved　　(**iii**) quartered?

3 Sue works in a petrol station which sells petrol at 80 pence per litre.

(**a**) Copy and complete the table.

Petrol (litres)	1	2	3	4	5	6	7	8
Cost (£)								£6·40

(**b**) What happens to the cost when the amount of petrol is

(**i**) doubled　　(**ii**) halved　　(**iii**) multiplied by 3?

> If an increase in one quantity causes a proportional increase in the other or a decrease in one quantity means a decrease in the other, this is called **direct proportion**.

4 Sam sells pic 'n' mix sweets for 99 pence per 100 grams.

(**a**) Copy and complete the table.

Sweets (g)	100	200	300	400	500	600	700
Cost (£)	0.99						

(**b**) Use the information in the table to copy and complete the graph.

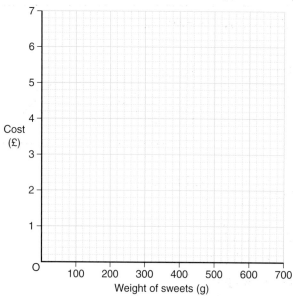

5 A phone call on Jan's phone costs 5 pence per minute.

(**a**) Copy and complete the table.

Length of call (min)	1	2	3	4	5	6
Cost (p)						

(**b**) Use the information in the table to copy and complete the graph.

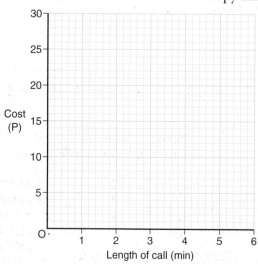

6 What do you notice about the graphs in questions **4** and **5**?

7 The graph shows the cost of B & B at the Bella Rosa guest house.

(**a**) Describe the graph

(**b**) Copy and complete:

   The cost and the number of nights are in _____

(**c**) What happens to the cost when the number of nights

   (**i**)   halves   (**ii**)   trebles

 (**iii**) quarters   (**iv**) multiplies by 5?

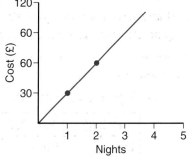

> When two quantities are in direct proportion the graph is a straight line through the origin.

8 (**a**) Which of these graphs shows quantities in direct proportion?

(**b**) Explain why the other graphs do not.

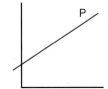   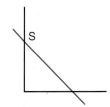

9 Go Fast taxis charge £0.20 per half kilometre and £0.50 hire charge.

(**a**) Copy and complete the table.

Distance (km)	1	2	3	4	5	6	7
Cost (£)							

(**b**) Use the information in the table to draw a graph.

(**c**) Are the distance and cost in direct proportion? Explain your answer.

10 The table below shows the area of squares.

Length (cm)	1	2	3	4	5	6	7
Area (cm²)	1	4					

(**a**) Copy and complete the table.

(**b**) Are the length and area in direct proportion? Explain your answer.

6.2 Using proportion

Proportion tables may be used to solve problems involving two quantities which are in proportion.

Example 1

(**a**) Four nights at the Tulip Hotel costs £208. Find the cost of 5 nights.

Nights	Cost (£)
4	208
1	52
5	260

÷4 and ×5

The cost for 5 nights is **£260**.

(**b**) Three nights at the Bluebell Hotel costs £165. How many nights could you stay for £385?

Cost (£)	Nights
165	3
55	1
385	7

÷3 and ×7

This is called the **unitary method** because one unit of the quantity is found first.

You could stay for **7 nights**.

Example 2

(**a**) Ronan earns £36.40 for 7 hours. How much does he earn for working 40 hours?

	Hours	Wage (£)	
÷7	7	£36.40	÷7
×40	1	£5.20	×40
	40	£208	

Ronan earns **£208.**

(**b**) Cathy earns £210 for working a 35 hour week. How many hours did she work if she earned £108?

	Wage (£)	Hours	
÷35	210	35	÷35
×18	6	1	×18
	108	18	

Cathy worked **18 hours.**

Exercise 6.2

1 Ariel works part time and earns £32.10 for working 6 hours. How much will he earn if he works 5 hours instead?

2 Maia earns £57.60 for working 8 hours. How much will she earn for working 15 hours?

3 The cost for 7 nights at the Gold Hotel is £539. Find the cost for
(**a**) 14 nights　　　(**b**) 3 nights　　　(**c**) 10 nights.

4 18 packets of cat food feed a cat for 6 days.
(**a**) How many would be needed for
　(**i**) 2 days　　　(**ii**) 15 days　　　(**iii**) 3 weeks?
(**b**) How many days could the cat be fed with
　(**i**) 27 packets　　　(**ii**) 42 packets　　　(**iii**) 5 dozen packets?

5 Jeffrey wants to make muffins for 10 people. Calculate how much of each ingredient he will need.

> Makes 6　**Fruity muffins**
> 180g　dried fruit
> 600 ml boiling water
> 450g　self raising flour
> 210g　caster sugar
> 120g　butter
> 3　　　eggs

6 Richard uses 4 gallons of petrol to travel 128 miles.
(**a**) How far could he travel with 3 gallons?
(**b**) How many gallons would he need to travel 288 miles?

7 A video with eight episodes of Maths Fun has a total running time of 1 hour 36 minutes. If Miss Marple wants to show the class three episodes, how long will this take?

8 Andrew changes £25 into euros and receives €35. How much would Salma receive if she exchanged £48?

9 A 4 litre tin of paint covers 15 square metres of wall. How many litres would be needed to cover 36 square metres?

10 A 200 gram box of grass seed covers 6 square metres. How much grass seed will be needed to cover 50 square metres?

POUNDS
EURO
U$S 1.79
.... 1.32
U$ CANADIAN 1.01
YEN 1.00
PESO 1.65
.... 0.20

11 Mr Feldman saw on his phone bill that one hour and twenty minutes of internet time cost him 56 pence. How much would half an hour cost him?

12 £50 is changed into 500 Hong Kong dollars. How many dollars would be received when changing:

(**a**) £20   (**b**) £3   (**c**) £4.50?

13 £200 is changed into €290. How many euros would be received when changing:

(**a**) £60   (**b**) £145   (**c**) £180?

14 A 250 g packet of broccoli costs 59 pence. A 150 g piece of loose broccoli costs 29 pence.

(**a**) Find the cost of 50 g of each kind of broccoli.

(**b**) Which is better value for money?

15 When on holiday in America, Janet buys a handbag costing $120. If the exchange rate was £1 = $1.78, how much did the handbag cost in pounds sterling? Give your answer to the nearest penny.

16 A packet of biscuits, which has 50% extra free, weighs 300 g. What was the weight of the original pack?

Find 100%

17 The cost of hiring a bicycle for the day, including 15% deposit, is £34.50. What is the cost without the deposit?

18 The cost of a DVD recorder including VAT at 17.5% is £282. Calculate the cost without VAT.

19 The cost of a car including VAT at 17.5% is £6995. Calculate the cost without VAT.

6.3 Inverse proportion
Exercise 6.3

1 A new drainage pipe is to be laid along 120 metres of motorway. The pipe is available in sections of different lengths.

(**a**) Copy and complete the table.

Length of each section (metres)	Number of sections needed
1	
2	
4	30
6	
12	

(**b**) When the length of each section is doubled, what happens to the number of sections needed?

2 A crash barrier is to be fitted along a 200 metre stretch of motorway.

  (**a**) How many sections of barrier will be needed when the length of each section is

    (**i**) 2 metres   (**ii**) 4 metres   (**iii**) 8 metres?

  (**b**) When the length of each section is doubled, what happens to the number of sections needed?

3 480 minutes of programmes can be recorded on a video tape.

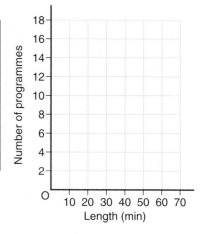

  (**a**) Copy and complete the table below.

Length of programmes (minutes)	Number of programmes
10	
20	
30	
40	
60	
120	
240	

  (**b**) Copy and complete the graph using the information in the table above.

  (**c**) Explain how the graph differs from a graph showing direct proportion.

4 A car can travel 30 miles in one hour. What happens to the time taken if its speed is:

  (**a**) halved   (**b**) doubled   (**c**) trebled?

5 How long will it take **one** pump to empty each of these pools when

(**a**)	(**b**)	(**c**)
2 pumps take 6 days	2 pumps take 3 days	3 pumps take 6 days

6.4 Using inverse proportion

Example

At 40 kilometres per hour a journey takes 6 hours.

How long would the journey take at a speed of 30 kilometres per hour?

Speed (km/h)	Time (h)
40	6
1	240
30	8

÷40, ×30 (left); ×40, ÷30 (right)

The journey would take **8 hours**.

> If an increase in one quantity causes a proportional decrease in the other or a decrease in one quantity means an increase in the other, this is called **inverse proportion**.

Exercise 6.4

1 It takes 12 hours for 3 bricklayers to build a wall.
How long will it take 2 bricklayers?

2 White lines have to be painted along a stretch of road using a line painting machine. If the machine has a speed of 2 miles per hour it takes 24 minutes to paint the road. A faster machine is bought which has a speed of 3 miles per hour. How long will it take to complete the same job?

3 At 30 kilometres per hour a train takes 6 hours for its journey from Edinburgh to Kyle of Lochalsh. How long would the same journey take at:

(**a**) 60 km/h   (**b**) 36 km/h   (**c**) 45 km/h?

4 An engineer calculates that two pumps will take 30 hours to clear the water from a mine shaft. How long would it take to clear the water with

(**a**) 4 pumps   (**b**) 5 pumps   (**c**) 6 pumps   (**d**) 8 pumps?

5 A construction company needs to hire 25 joiners to complete a job in 32 days. If they can only afford to hire 20 joiners how long will the job take them?

6 A harvest of apples are packed in 7 boxes each holding 200 apples. How many apples would be in each box if

(**a**) 5 boxes   (**b**) 8 boxes were used?

7 Miss Brodie has enough money to buy 30 calculators at £4 each. If she decides to buy the more expensive calculators at £5, how many could she buy?

8 At 30 kilometres per hour a train takes 6 hours for its journey.
How long would it take at:

(**a**) 40 km/h   (**b**) 90 km/h   (**c**) 50 km/h?

9 A shelf can hold exactly 18 encyclopedias, each 4 centimetres thick. If the encyclopedias are to be replaced by CD Roms with a thickness of 8 millimetres, how many will fit onto the shelf?

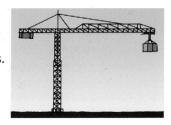

10 A crane can lift a maximum of 50 blocks each weighing 27 kilograms. How many 25 kilogram blocks could it lift?

11 It takes Jessie 3 hours to type her essay on 4 pages with 45 lines per page. If the pages had 30 lines, how many pages would she have used?

6.5 Mixed proportion questions

Decide whether a question is
- direct proportion
- inverse proportion
- not in proportion

Check that your answer is sensible.

Exercise 6.5

1 A car can travel 240 miles in 4 hours. How far will it travel in 7 hours?

2 On a plan 5 centimetres represents 3 metres. What length is represented by 12 centimetres?

3 Stephanie can fit forty-two, 10 centimetre, square tiles along her bathroom wall. How many will fit if she decides to use 12 centimetre, square tiles?

4 Tony measures that he takes 30 steps in 12 metres. How many steps would he take in 200 metres?

5 Mr Benn takes 40 minutes, at a steady speed of 45 kilometres per hour, to travel to work. If, on another day, the journey takes him 1 hour, how fast was he travelling?

6 If one man can see for 15 kilometres from the top of a hill, how far will three men see?

7 A car travelling at a speed of 35 miles per hour can complete a journey in 3 hours. How long will it take at a speed of 25 miles per hour?

8 If 2 eggs take 8 minutes to boil, how long will 5 take?

9 At a speed of 50 kilometres per hour a car can travel a distance of 325 kilometres in a certain length of time. If its speed is reduced to 30 kilometres per hour how far will it travel in the same time?

10 If it takes 50 minutes to play Beethoven's second symphony, how long will it take to play his fifth symphony?

11 A firm with 40 staff has a monthly wage bill of £52 000. At the same average wage what would be the wage bill if another 5 staff were taken on?

12 Sally exchanged £120 for 360 Singapore dollars. Her brother changed his money for 520 Singapore dollars. If he spent 380 dollars how much would he receive when he changed it back into pounds sterling?

13 Fourteen lottery winners are to share the jackpot equally. Each person will receive £450 000. If another four people claim a share of the jackpot, how much will each person receive now?

Review exercise 6

1 Mr Lister saw on his phone bill that fifty minutes of internet time cost him 70 pence. How much would one hour and ten minutes cost him?

2 Shareen wants to make coffee cakes for 14 people. Calculate how much of each ingredient she will need.

Makes 8	**Coffee cakes**
180g	butter
400ml	milk
480g	self raising flour
210g	caster sugar
20g	instant coffee
4	eggs

3 A 750 gramme packet of rice in Saveways costs 83 pence.
A 630 gramme bag of rice in Scoop-A-Mix costs 74 pence.

(**a**) Find the cost of 100 grammes of rice in each shop.

(**b**) Which is better value for money?

4 At 40 kilometres per hour a train takes 6 hours for its journey.
How long would it take at:

(**a**) 30 km/h   (**b**) 20 km/h   (**c**) 100 km/h   (**c**) 36 km/h?

5 A company needs to hire 18 plumbers to complete a job in 21 days.
If they can only afford to hire 12 plumbers how long will the job take them?

6 A harvest of peaches is packed in 9 boxes each holding 150 peaches.
How many peaches would be in each box if

(**a**) 5 boxes   (**b**) 15 boxes were used?

Summary

Direct proportion

If an increase in one quantity causes a proportional increase in the other or a decrease in one quantity means a decrease in the other, this is called **direct proportion**.

When two quantities are in direct proportion the graph connecting them is a straight line through the origin.

Four nights at the Tulip Hotel costs £208. Find the cost of 5 nights.

The cost for 5 nights is **£260**.

Nights	Cost (£)
4	208
1	52
5	260

÷4   ×5   ÷4   ×5

This is called the **unitary method** because one unit of the quantity is found first.

The cost for 5 nights is **£260**.

Inverse proportion

If an increase in one quantity causes a proportional decrease in the other or a decrease in one quantity means an increase in the other, this is called **inverse proportion**.

At 40 kilometres per hour a journey takes 6 hours. How long would the journey take at a speed of 30 kilometres per hour?

Speed (km/h)	Time (h)
40	6
1	240
30	8

÷40   ×30   ×40   ÷30

The journey would take **8** hours.

Decide whether a question is
- direct proportion
- inverse proportion
- not in proportion

Check that your answer is sensible.

7 Area

In this chapter you will revise the area of a triangle and find the area of common quadrilaterals and composite shapes.

7.1 Area of a triangle

Remember
Area of a triangle $= \frac{1}{2} \times$ base $\times$ height

$$A = \frac{1}{2}bh$$

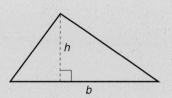

Example
Calculate the area of the triangle.

$$A = \frac{1}{2}bh$$
$$= \frac{1}{2} \times 8 \times 6$$
$$= 24 \text{ cm}^2$$

The area of the triangle is **24 cm²**

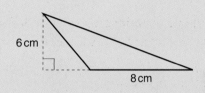

Exercise 7.1

1 Calculate the area of each triangle.

(a)
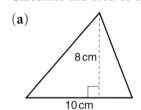

(b) 8 cm, 9 cm

(c) 7 mm, 12 mm

(d)
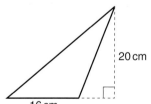

(e)
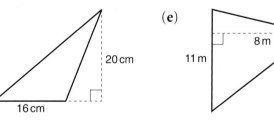
11 m, 8 m

(f) 12 cm, 12 cm

(g)
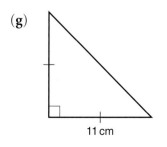
11 cm

(h)
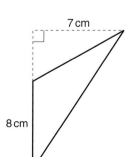
7 cm, 8 cm

(i)
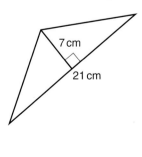
7 cm, 21 cm

Units must match.

(j)

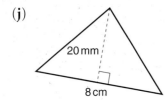

20 mm

8 cm

(k)

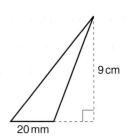

8 cm

30 mm

(l)

9 cm

20 mm

2 (**a**) Draw coordinate axes from -10 to 10.

 (**b**) Plot each set of points and join them to form a triangle.
  Calculate its area in square units.
   (**i**) $(-8, -3)$, $(-3, -3)$, $(-4, 3)$
   (**ii**) $(-7, 6)$, $(2, 6)$, $(-1, 10)$
   (**iii**) $(2, -5)$, $(1, 1)$, $(8, -5)$
   (**iv**) $(7, 1)$, $(7, 10)$, $(6, 3)$

3 Ian is ordering bark for his flower beds. Find the total area he has to cover.

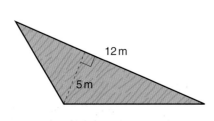

12 m

5 m

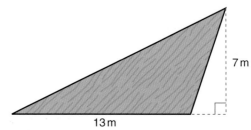

7 m

13 m

4 Alan has two areas of ground to turf. What will be the total area of grass?

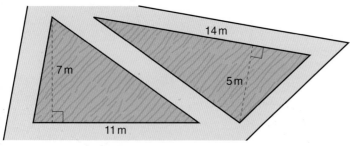

14 m

7 m

5 m

11 m

5 Carole uses patches of silk to construct bedcovers.
 The area of each patch is shown.
 (**a**) Find the length of the base. (**b**) Find the height.

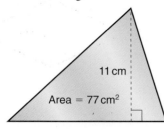

11 cm

Area = 77 cm²

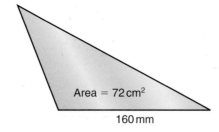

Area = 72 cm²

160 mm

7.2 Area of a rhombus

The area of a rhombus is half the area of the surrounding rectangle.

Area of rhombus $= \frac{1}{2} \times$ breadth $\times$ length

$\qquad = \frac{1}{2} \times$ diagonal$_1$ $\times$ diagonal$_2$

$\qquad \mathbf{A = \frac{1}{2} d_1 d_2}$

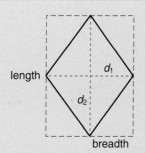

Example

Calculate the area of the rhombus.

$A = \frac{1}{2} d_1 d_2$

$\quad = \frac{1}{2} \times 20 \times 16$

$\quad = 160 \text{ mm}^2$

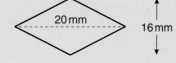

The area of the rhombus is **160 mm²**.

Exercise 7.2

1 Calculate the area of each rhombus.

(a)

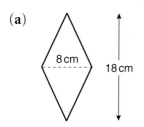

(b)

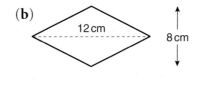

(c)

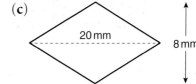

(d)

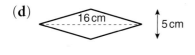

(e)

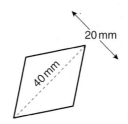

(f)

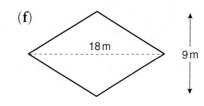

(g)

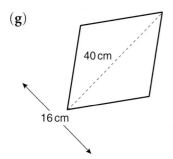

(h)

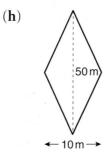

(i)

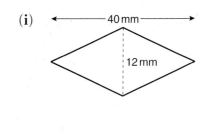

(j)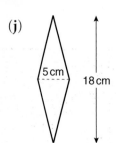

(k)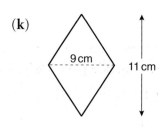

(l)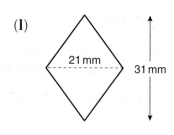

2 (**a**) Draw coordinate axes from -10 to 10.

   (**b**) Plot each set of points and join them to form a rhombus.
   Calculate its area in square units.
   (**i**) $(-7, 1)$, $(-9, 5)$, $(-7, 9)$ $(-5, 5)$
   (**ii**) $(-5, -3)$, $(-10, -5)$, $(-5, -7)$, $(0, -5)$
   (**iii**) $(8, -1)$, $(7, -5)$, $(8, -9)$, $(9, -5)$
   (**iv**) $(4, 0)$, $(-2, 5)$, $(4, 10)$, $(10, 5)$

3 Colin uses leather patches to upholster furniture. Calculate the area of each patch.

(**a**)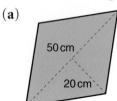

(**b**)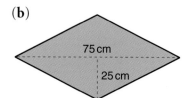

4 Dermid uses concrete rhombuses to create patios. Calculate the area of each patio.

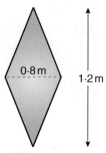

(**a**)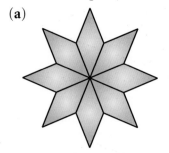

(**b**)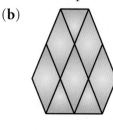

5 For each rhombus calculate the missing dimension.

(**a**)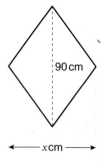

Area 2700 cm²

(**b**)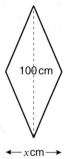

Area 1500 cm²

(**c**)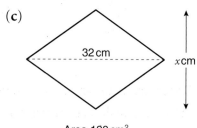

Area 128 cm²

7.3 Area of a kite

The area of a kite is half the area of the surrounding rectangle.

Area of kite $= \frac{1}{2} \times$ breadth $\times$ length

Area $= \frac{1}{2} \times$ diagonal$_1 \times$ diagonal$_2$

$\mathbf{A} = \frac{1}{2}\mathbf{d_1 d_2}$

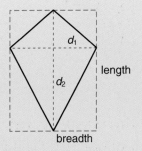

Example

Calculate the area of the kite.

$$A = \frac{1}{2}d_1 d_2$$
$$= \frac{1}{2} \times 12 \times 8$$
$$= 48$$

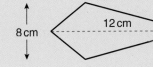

The area of the kite is **48 cm²**

Exercise 7.3

1 Calculate the area of each kite.

(**a**) 8 cm, 14 cm

(**b**) 8 cm, 20 cm

(**c**) 20 mm, 48 mm

(**d**) 12 m, 12 m

(**e**) 9 cm, 16 cm

(**f**) 2 mm, 48 mm

2 Sketch this V-kite and surrounding rectangle.

(**a**) Calculate the area of the rectangle.

(**b**) Calculate the total area shaded blue.

(**c**) What is the area of the V-kite?.

(**d**) Does the formula $A = \frac{1}{2}d_1 d_2$ hold for a V-kite?

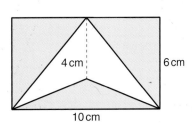

3 Calculate the area of each kite.

(**a**)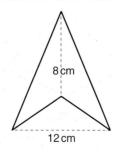

8 cm

12 cm

(**b**)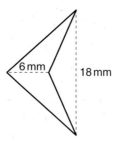

6 mm   18 mm

(**c**)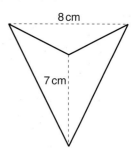

8 cm

7 cm

4 (**a**) Draw coordinate axes from −10 to 10.

(**b**) Plot each set of points and join them to form a kite.
Calculate its area in square units.
- (**i**) $(-6, 1)$, $(-9, 7)$, $(-6, 9)$, $(-3, 7)$
- (**ii**) $(-1, 6)$, $(2, 9)$, $(10, 6)$, $(2, 3)$
- (**iii**) $(-6, -2)$, $(-9, -10)$, $(-6, -8)$, $(-3, -10)$
- (**iv**) $(5, -1)$, $(9, -6)$, $(5, -9)$, $(1, -6)$

5 Alistair is making model kites using wood and tissue paper.
Calculate the area of tissue paper used for each kite.

(**a**)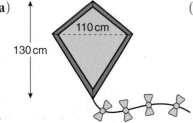

110 cm

130 cm

(**b**)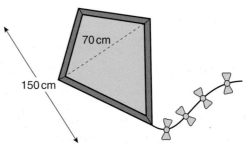

70 cm

150 cm

6 Morag makes beaded kite decorations. Calculate the area of each.

(**a**)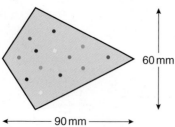

60 mm

90 mm

(**b**)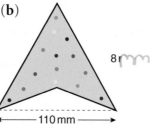

8 mm

110 mm

7 (**a**) Find the area of each decorative concrete slab.

(**b**) List them in order from smallest to largest.

(**i**)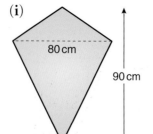

80 cm

90 cm

(**ii**)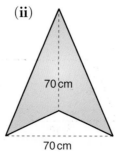

70 cm

70 cm

(**iii**)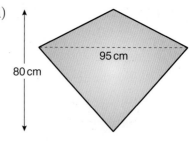

95 cm

80 cm

8 For each kite find the missing dimension.

(a)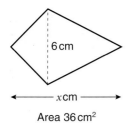

Area 36 cm²

(b)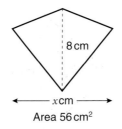

Area 56 cm²

(c)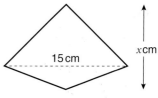

Area 75 cm²

(d)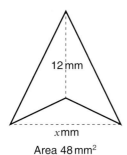

Area 48 mm²

(e)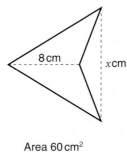

Area 60 cm²

(f)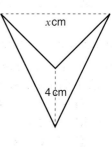

Area 23 cm²

7.4 Area of a parallelogram

A parallelogram may be converted to a rectangle.

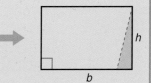

Area of rectangle = base × height
Hence, area of parallelogram = base × height
$A = bh$, where h is the perpendicular height.

Example

Find the area of the parallelogram.

$A = bh$
$= 12 \times 5$
$= 60$

The area of the parallelogram is **60 cm²**.

Exercise 7.4

1 Calculate the area of each parallelogram.

(a)

6 cm

5 cm

(b)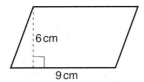

6 cm

9 cm

(c)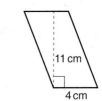

11 cm

4 cm

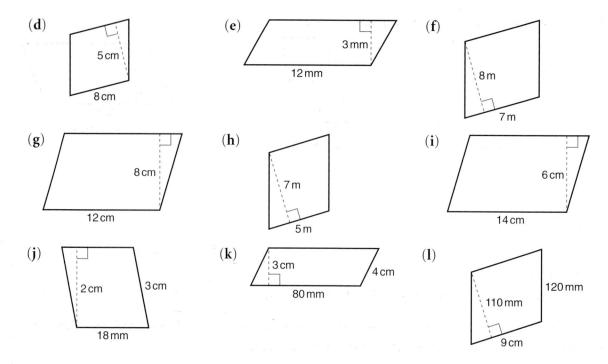

(d) 5 cm, 8 cm

(e) 3 mm, 12 mm

(f) 8 m, 7 m

(g) 8 cm, 12 cm

(h) 7 m, 5 m

(i) 6 cm, 14 cm

(j) 2 cm, 3 cm, 18 mm

(k) 3 cm, 4 cm, 80 mm

(l) 120 mm, 110 mm, 9 cm

2 (a) Draw coordinate axes from −10 to 10.

(b) Plot each set of points and join them to form a parallelogram.
Calculate its area in square units.
- (i) $(−10, 1)$, $(−8, 5)$, $(−2, 5)$, $(−4, 1)$
- (ii) $(−10, −2)$, $(−4, −2)$, $(−3, −8)$, $(−9, −8)$
- (iii) $(1, 2)$, $(3, 10)$, $(7, 10)$, $(5, 2)$
- (iv) $(1, −2)$, $(2, −10)$, $(10, −10)$, $(9, −2)$

3 Monty's demonstration garden has parallelogram shaped plots for each vegetable.
Calculate the area of each.

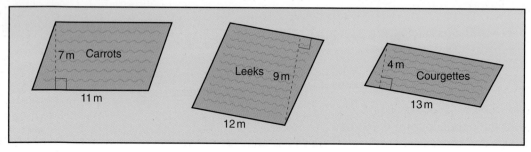

4 Carolyn is creating a collage using suede patches.

(a) Find the area of each patch.

(b) List the patches in order of size, from smallest to largest.

(i)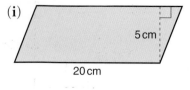
5 cm, 20 cm

(ii)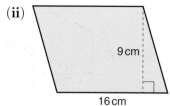
9 cm, 16 cm

(iii)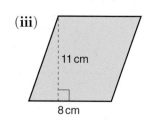
11 cm, 8 cm

5 Find the missing dimension of each parallelogram.

(**a**)

9 cm

x cm

Area 108 cm²

(**b**)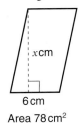

x cm

6 cm

Area 78 cm²

(**c**)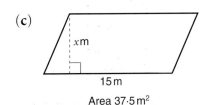

x m

15 m

Area 37·5 m²

7.5 Area of a trapezium

Remember
A trapezium is a **quadrilateral** with two parallel sides.

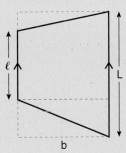

The area of a trapezium is the average of the area of the outer rectangle and the inner rectangle. This means calculating the breadth times the average length.

Outer rectangle $A = bL$ **Inner rectangle** $A = b\ell$

Trapezium $A = \dfrac{(bL + b\ell)}{2}$ or $A = \dfrac{b(L + \ell)}{2}$

Example
Calculate the area of the trapezium.

$$A = \frac{b(L + \ell)}{2}$$

$$= 7 \times \frac{(12 + 8)}{2}$$

$$= 7 \times 10$$

$$= 70$$

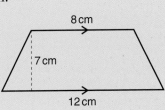

8 cm

7 cm

12 cm

The area of the trapezium is **70 cm²**.

Exercise 7.5

1 Calculate the area of each trapezium.

(**a**)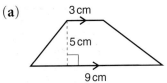

3 cm

5 cm

9 cm

(**b**)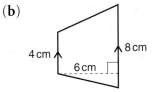

4 cm

6 cm

8 cm

(**c**)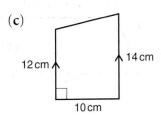

12 cm

14 cm

10 cm

(d)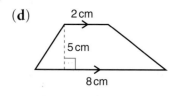

(e)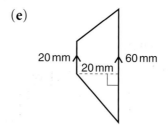

(f)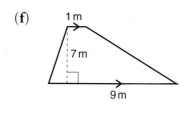

(g)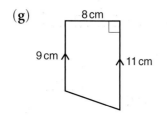

(h)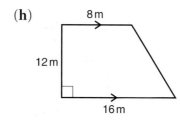

(i)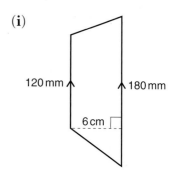

2 (a) Draw coordinate axes from -10 to 10.

(b) Plot each set of points and join them to form a trapezium.
Calculate its area in square units.

   (i) $(3, 1)$, $(8, 1)$, $(8, 9)$, $(3, 5)$

   (ii) $(-6, 4)$, $(-10, 4)$, $(-10, 10)$, $(-4, 10)$

   (iii) $(-2, -2)$, $(-2, -5)$, $(-9, -9)$, $(-9, -2)$

   (iv) $(3, -2)$, $(2, -7)$, $(10, -7)$, $(9, -2)$

7.6 Area of composite shapes

Many 2D shapes are composed of simpler shapes. These are called **composite** shapes.

Example

Find the area of each shape.

(a)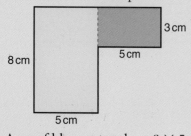

(b)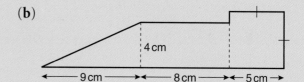

(a) Area of blue rectangle = $8 \times 5 = 40$ cm²
Area of red rectangle = 5×3 = $\underline{15 \text{ cm}^2}$
Total area   = 55 cm²

Area of the shape is **55 cm²**

(b) Area of triangle = $\frac{1}{2} \times 9 \times 4 = 18$ cm²
Area of rectangle = 8×4 = 32 cm²
Area of square = 5×5 = $\underline{25 \text{ cm}^2}$
Total area   = 75 cm²
Area of the shape is **75 cm²**

Exercise 7.6

1 Calculate the area of each composite shape.

(a)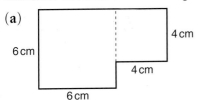

(b)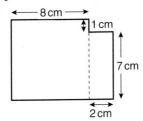

(c)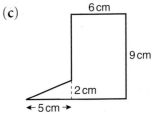

(d)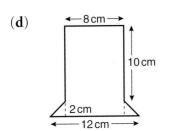

(e)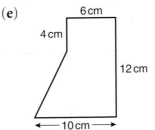

(f)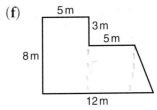

(g)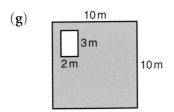

(h)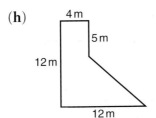

(i)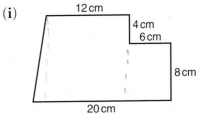

(j)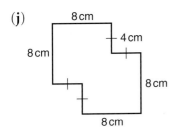

(k)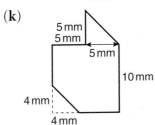

(l)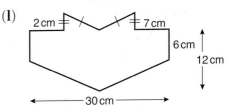

2 (a) Draw coordinate axes from -10 to 10.

(b) Plot each set of points and join them to form a 2D shape.
Calculate its area in square units.

    (i)　$(2, 2)$,　$(9, 2)$,　$(9, 4)$,　$(5, 6)$,　$(5, 10)$,　$(2, 10)$

    (ii)　$(-2, 4)$,　$(-2, 10)$,　$(-4, 10)$,　$(-9, 7)$,　$(-9, 4)$

    (iii)　$(-9, -2)$,　$(-9, -10)$,　$(-6, -9)$,　$(-6, -7)$,　$(-2, -7)$,　$(-2, -3)$

    (iv)　$(2, -2)$,　$(2, -9)$,　$(5, -7)$,　$(8, -7)$,　$(10, -10)$,　$(10, -1)$,　$(8, -1)$,　$(6, -3)$

3 For each 2D shape calculate the missing dimension.

(a)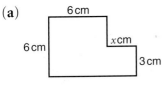

Total area 48 cm²

(b)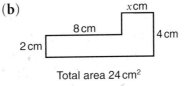

Total area 24 cm²

(c)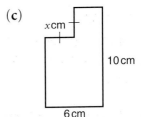

Total area 51 cm²

Review exercise 7

1 Calculate the area of each triangle.

(a)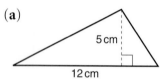

(b)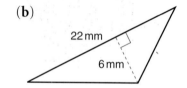

(c)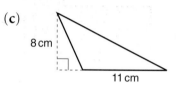

2 Calculate the area of each rhombus.

(a)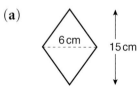

(b)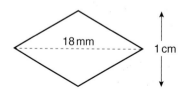

3 Calculate the area of each kite.

(a)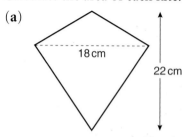

(b)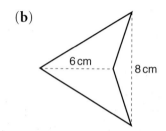

4 Calculate the area of each parallelogram.

(a)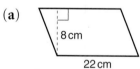

(b)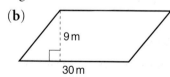

(c)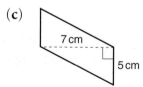

5 For each 2D shape calculate the missing dimension.

(a)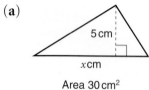

(b)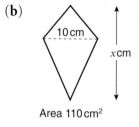

(c)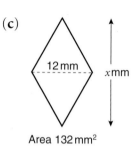

6 Calculate the area of each trapezium.

(a)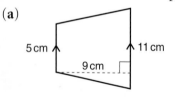

(b)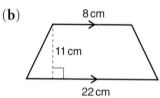

7 Calculate the area of each composite shape.

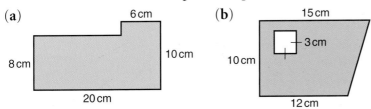

(a)

6 cm

10 cm

8 cm

20 cm

(b)

15 cm

3 cm

10 cm

12 cm

8 (a) Draw coordinate axes from -10 to 10.

(b) Plot the points and join them to form a 2D shape.
Calculate its area in square units.

(i) $(1, 1,)$, $(5, 4)$, $(1, 5)$

(ii) $(8, 2)$, $(10, 6)$, $(8, 10)$, $(6, 6)$

(iii) $(-2, 6)$, $(-3, 9)$, $(-9, 6)$, $(-3, 3)$

(iv) $(-7, 4)$, $(-10, 0)$, $(-7, 1)$, $(-4, 0)$

(v) $(-4, -2)$, $(-2, -5)$, $(-7, -5)$, $(-9, -2)$

(vi) $(2, -2)$, $(2, -5)$, $(6, -7)$, $(6, -2)$

(vii) $(-7, -7)$, $(-7, -10)$, $(8, -10)$, $(5, -9)$, $(2, -9)$, $(2, -7)$

9 The design of garden plots is shown below.

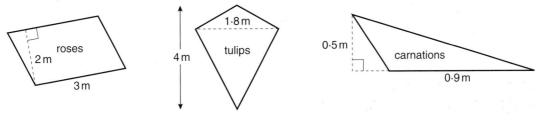

roses

2 m

3 m

1·8 m

tulips

4 m

0·5 m

carnations

0·9 m

(a) Calculate the area of each flower bed.

(b) List the flower beds in order of size, from smallest to largest.

Area of a triangle

$$A = \tfrac{1}{2}bh$$
$$= \tfrac{1}{2} \times 8 \times 6$$
$$\mathbf{A = 24\ cm^2}$$

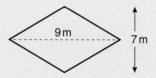

Area of a rhombus.

$$A = \tfrac{1}{2}d_1d_2$$
$$= \tfrac{1}{2} \times 9 \times 7$$
$$\mathbf{A = 31{\cdot}5\ m^2}$$

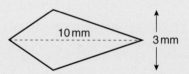

Area of a kite

$$A = \tfrac{1}{2}d_1d_2$$
$$= \tfrac{1}{2} \times 10 \times 3$$
$$\mathbf{A = 15\ mm^2}$$

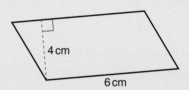

Area of a parallelogram

$$A = bh$$
$$= 6 \times 4$$
$$\mathbf{A = 24\ cm^2}$$

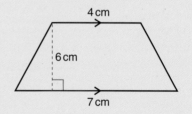

Area of a trapezium

$$A = \frac{b(L + \ell)}{2}$$
$$= 6 \times \frac{(7 + 4)}{2}$$
$$= 6 \times 5{\cdot}5$$
$$\mathbf{A = 33\ cm^2}$$

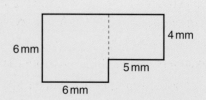

Area of composite shapes

Total area = sum of areas
$$A = 36 + 20$$
$$\mathbf{A = 56\ mm^2}$$

8 Information handling

In this chapter you will learn further techniques and methods to handle data.

8.1 Types of data

Biologists, psychologists, physicists and statisticians are some of the people who analyse data. Data is collected to answer a question about a real situation. You will gain greater insight if you can collect and analyse your own data.

Data can be either categorical or numerical

Categorical	Numerical	
	Discrete	Continuous
Data collected in categories e.g. colours	Data restricted to a number of values e.g. shoe sizes Count	Data unrestricted within a range e.g. people's heights Measure

Exercise 8.1

1 (**a**) Copy this table.

Categorical	Numerical	
	Discrete	Continuous
	Children in a family	

(**b**) Put each statement in the correct column in your table.

Children in a family	TVs in a household	Time watching TV
Length of words	Rainfall	T-shirt size
Life expectancy	Favourite style of music	Time taken to eat a cream cracker
A round of golf	Audience viewing figures	Fat content of different foods
Favourite TV channel	Number of leaves on a plant	Height of trees in a forest

(**c**) Which statements could go in more than one column?

(**d**) Think of some statements of your own. Put them in the correct column in your table.

8.2 Organising data

The following steps are useful when investigating data.

- Ask a question
- Collect data – survey or experiment
- Organise data
- Display data
- Draw a conclusion to answer the original question

Example

In 2002 a biologist asked the question "How healthy is the blue tit population in Ross Wood near Loch Lomond?" She counted the number of fledglings from each nest.

```
5   4   4    6   6
4   4   5   10   7
3   7   4    6   3
5   6   4
```

> The minimum value is 3 and the maximum value is 10

Organise the data into a frequency table.

Number of fledglings	Tally	Frequency
3	||	2
4	|||| |	6
5	|||	3
6	||||	4
7	||	2
8		0
9		0
10	|	1

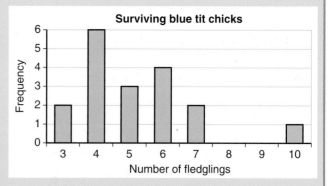

From this information a bar graph can be drawn.

The graph indicates that there is some variation in the number of surviving chicks. Shelter and availability of food play a part in causing this. The population is healthy.

The value of 10 fledglings looks out of place. Any piece of data like this is called an **outlier**. In this case, the nest could have been in a particularly sheltered location near a very plentiful source of food.

Exercise 8.2

1 The biologist revisited Ross Wood in 2003 to determine whether the blue tit population was more or less healthy than in 2002. She counted the number of fledglings from each nest.

6 6 4 2 8 5 7 5
5 4 5 4 7 6 3 7

For this data:

(**a**) construct a frequency table

(**b**) draw a bar graph

(**c**) describe the health of the blue tit population.

2 Bryony played 2 rounds of golf at Millarcraig Golf Club. She recorded the number of shots she took at each hole. She wanted to know if she was improving.

Round 1	Round 2
5 6 6 5 7	5 4 4 5 4
4 4 4 8 5	4 3 6 9 4
3 7 2 7 3	4 7 4 10 3
6 7 4	4 5 5

(**a**) For Round 1:
  (**i**) construct a frequency table
  (**ii**) draw a bar graph.

(**b**) Repeat part (**a**) for Round 2.

(**c**) Do you think Bryony has improved from Round 1 to Round 2? Explain.

3 A national survey asked pupils to record the number of canned drinks they had consumed in the last two days. They were also asked to say if they attended an urban or a rural school. The results were as follows:

Rural										Urban									
3	1	0	2	0	0	0	2	4	10	11	2	3	3	5	1	5	0	4	6
1	12	0	1	0	7	0	0	0	2	0	0	12	1	1	4	2	0	2	4
0	0	2	5	0	4	0	3	0	1	3	0	2	0	1	2	1	1	2	0
0	2	0	0	0	1	0	0	1	12	7	0	3	5	2	2	0	2	0	8
3	0	1	0	0	0	2	0	1	0	0	10	0	3	1	2	1	4	3	0

Adapted from: The *CensusAtSchool* Project

(**a**) For the rural data:
  (**i**) construct a frequency table
  (**ii**) draw a bar graph.

(**b**) Repeat part (**a**) for the urban data.

(**c**) Compare and then comment on your two graphs.

(**d**) Collect the data from your own class and compare the results with those from the national survey.

8.3　Stem and leaf diagrams

A **stem and leaf diagram** may be used to display data.

Example

It is suggested that many European football leagues can only be won by a small number of sides in each league. To decide if this is true, the points totals in the Scottish Premier League in season 2003/04 were collected.

98　81　68　53　49　34
46　46　44　43　42　26

Min	26	Max	98

Draw a **stem and leaf diagram** to decide.

For this data, use the tens digits for the stem and the units digits for the leaves.

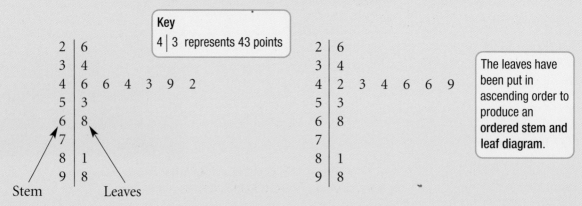

```
2 | 6          Key                      2 | 6
3 | 4          4 | 3 represents 43 points 3 | 4
4 | 6  6  4  3  9  2                     4 | 2  3  4  6  6  9
5 | 3                                    5 | 3
6 | 8                                    6 | 8
7 |                                      7 |
8 | 1                                    8 | 1
9 | 8                                    9 | 8
Stem      Leaves
```

Key
4 | 3 represents 43 points

The leaves have been put in ascending order to produce an ordered stem and leaf diagram.

This diagram shows clearly that two teams were much better than the rest of those in the league. The diagram also shows that most teams scored between 40 and 50 points.

Exercise 8.3

1 The points totals for the Scottish First Division for the 1979/80 season are shown.

(a) Find the maximum and minimum points totals.

(b) Decide upon the values in your stem.

(c) Draw an ordered stem and leaf diagram.

(d) Looking at your stem and leaf diagram, do you think that in this league more teams had a chance of winning than in season 2003/4?

Scotland 79/80	Pts
Aberdeen	48
Celtic	47
Dundee	26
Dundee United	37
Hibernian	18
Kilmarnock	33
Morton	36
Partick Thistle	36
Rangers	37
St. Mirren	42

2 The points totals for the French First Division for the 2003/4 season are shown.

France 2003/04	Pts		Pts
Ajaccio	40	Metz	42
Auxerre	65	Monaco	75
Bastia	39	Montpellier	31
Bordeaux	50	Nantes	60
Guingamp	38	Nice	50
Le Mans	38	Paris S.G.	76
Lens	53	Rennes	52
Lille	51	Sochaux	63
Lyon	79	Strasbourg	43
Marseille	57	Toulouse	39

(a) Find the maximum and minimum points totals.

(b) Draw an ordered stem and leaf diagram.

(c) Looking at your stem and leaf diagram, how many teams do you think had a realistic chance of winning the league?

3 In a recent national survey pupils were asked how many minutes in a typical day they spent watching TV. Some of the results are shown below.

    101   118   150   147   203   124   135   164   105   134
    184   157   132   104   177   156   148   122   139   108

> Use 10, 11, 12 … as stems.

(a) Find the maximum and minimum times.

(b) Draw an ordered stem and leaf diagram.

(c) Looking at your stem and leaf diagram, do you think there is anything to worry about?

(d) Collect the same data from your own class and compare your results with those from the national survey.

4 In an angling competition on Loch Maree, the total weight (in kg) of fish caught in one day by each competitor was recorded.

    0·6   5·4   2·3   1·7   1·1   4·3   2·5   1·6   1·2
    0·8   2·6   6·7   5·1   2·8   2·3   1·5   3·2   3·1

(a) Find the maximum and minimum weights.

(b) Draw an ordered stem and leaf diagram.

(c) The average weight of a single fish in Loch Maree is 1 kilogramme. Looking at your stem and leaf diagram, do you think the anglers did well?

8.4 Back to back stem and leaf diagrams

A **back-to-back** stem and leaf diagram can be useful when comparing two sets of data.

Example

To compare the question of male and female life expectancy (LE), the following data (in years) was collected from some countries in the European Union.

Country	Male LE	Female LE	Country	Male LE	Female LE
Austria	74·7	81·2	Italy	76	82·5
Belgium	74·6	81·5	Luxembourg	74	80·8
Cyprus	74·6	79·3	Malta	75·6	80·8
Czech Republic	71·2	78·4	Netherlands	75·6	81·4
Denmark	74·1	79·5	Portugal	72·4	79·7
Finland	73·9	81·4	Slovenia	71·2	79·2
France	75	83	Spain	75·5	82·6
Germany	74·5	80·9	Sweden	77·1	82·5
Greece	76	81·3	United Kingdom	75·1	80·7
Ireland	74·2	79·9			

The minimum value is 71·2 and the maximum value is 83

Draw a back-to-back stem and leaf diagram to illustrate the data and reach a conclusion.

```
        Male life expectancy           Female life expectancy

                    2   2 | 71 |
                        4 | 72 |
                        9 | 73 |
        7  6  6  5  2  1  0 | 74 |
              6  6  5  1  0 | 75 |
                    0  0 | 76 |
                        1 | 77 |
                          | 78 | 4
                          | 79 | 2  3  5  7  9
                          | 80 | 7  8  9
                          | 81 | 2  3  4  4  5
                          | 82 | 5  5  6
                          | 83 | 0
```

Key   Key
9 | 73 represents 73·9 years   80 | 7 represents 80·7 years

The diagram shows that the life expectancy of women in the European Union is clearly greater than that of the men. The difference appears to be around five years.

Exercise 8.4

1 The World Health Organisation wants to know if the difference between male and female life expectancy in Africa is similar to Europe's. To investigate this question they collected the life expectancy (LE) data, in years, in some African countries.

Country (Africa)	Male LE	Female LE	Country (Africa)	Male LE	Female LE
Angola	37·4	39·9	Mozambique	37·3	35·6
Botswana	36·8	37·5	Namibia	42·5	38·7
Burkina Faso	45·9	47	Niger	41·7	41·4
Burundi	45·2	47	Rwanda	38·4	39·7
Central African Republic	42·2	45·5	Sierra Leone	42·7	48·6
Congo, Republic of the	44·4	50·9	Somalia	45	48·3
Cote d'Ivoire	43·6	46·3	South Africa	47·6	48·6
Ethiopia	43·9	45·5	Swaziland	37·9	39·4
Kenya	46·6	48·4	Uganda	42·6	44·2
Lesotho	48	49·7	Zambia	37·1	37·5
Malawi	36·6	37·6	Zimbabwe	38·5	35·7
Mali	45·8	48·2			

(**a**) Find the maximum and minimum life expectancies for all the countries.

(**b**) Draw an ordered, back-to-back stem and leaf diagram.

(**c**) Looking at your stem and leaf diagram, and the example in the panel, how similar are the results?

2 "Does the weight of a rugby player determine whether he plays in the forwards or the backs?" The weights (in pounds) of the Welsh national rugby squad in 2004 were collected.

Backs	224	207	210	196	208
	220	210	190	218	186
	194	181	201	190	172
	178				

Forwards	265	254	249	245	248
	245	238	262	243	224
	242	241	256	245	254
	217	269	242	234	238
	210	214			

(**a**) Find the maximum and minimum weights for the whole squad.

(**b**) Draw a back-to-back stem and leaf diagram.

(**c**) Answer the original question.

3 A Manchester City fan asked, "Was English football more competitive 20 years ago than it is now?" To investigate this question, the points were collected from the 1983/4 season and the 2003/4 season.

(a) Find the maximum and minimum points totals for both leagues.

(b) Draw an ordered, back-to-back stem and leaf diagram.

(c) Looking at your stem and leaf diagram, answer the original question.

England 1983/4	Pts
Arsenal	63
Aston Villa	60
Birmingham	48
Coventry	50
Everton	62
Ipswich	53
Leicester	51
Liverpool	80
Luton	51
Manchester Utd.	74
Norwich	51
Nottingham Forest	74
Notts County	41
QPR	73
Southampton	77
Stoke City	50
Sunderland	52
Tottenham	61
Watford	57
West Bromwich Albion	51
West Ham United	60
Wolves	29

England 2003/4	Pts
Arsenal	90
Aston Villa	56
Birmingham	50
Blackburn	44
Bolton	53
Charlton	53
Chelsea	79
Everton	39
Fulham	52
Leeds	33
Leicester	33
Liverpool	60
Manchester City	41
Manchester Utd.	75
Middlesborough	48
Newcastle	56
Portsmouth	45
Southampton	47
Tottenham	45
Wolves	33

4 Class activity

You need a die for this question.

The aim of the game is to get the highest number of points.

At the start of the game all players stand up. The die is rolled **twice**. Every player writes down the total of the two rolls.

From now on, before each roll of the die, a player has two choices.

    A   Sit down and record their total points, or

    B   Remain standing.

For those players still standing the die is rolled once. If the number is a five, all players still standing lose all of their points. They sit and record a score of 0. If the number is not a five, the number is added to their total score. Repeat the second step until all players are seated. This completes a round. Play five rounds. Each player adds the scores for their five rounds to get their final total.

(a) Record all the final totals of the players in your class.

(b) Play the game a second time, trying to improve your strategy from the first game.

(c) Record all the final totals for the second game.

(d) Draw a back-to-back stem and leaf diagram to illustrate the totals from the two games.

(e) Describe any changes in performance between the two games.

8.5 Grouping continuous data

It may be useful to group data before it is displayed.

Example
"Who eats more quickly – boys or girls?" The times taken (in seconds) for 30 pupils to eat one cream cracker were recorded.

Girls   42   85   92   112   124
        63   75   72   80   103
        74   78   93   118   95

Boys   95   50   64   87   66
       49   72   81   98   77
       66   68   72   61   88

Use a frequency table and **histogram** to investigate.

Time is continuous data.

The class intervals must include all data with no gaps.

> There are usually 6 to 10 intervals in a frequency table.

Time, t (secs)	Tally		Frequency	
	Girls	Boys	Girls	Boys
$40 \leqslant t < 50$					1	1
$50 \leqslant t < 60$				0	1
$60 \leqslant t < 70$				1	5
$70 \leqslant t < 80$	||||	|||	4	3
$80 \leqslant t < 90$	||	|||	2	3
$90 \leqslant t < 100$	|||	||	3	2
$100 \leqslant t < 110$				1	0
$110 \leqslant t < 120$	||		2	0
$120 \leqslant t < 130$				1	0

Since the data is continuous, the horizontal axis must be labelled as a continuous scale. A graph like this is called a **histogram**.

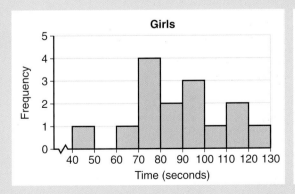

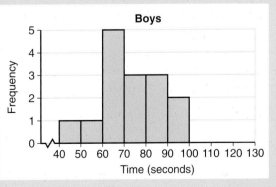

The graphs indicate that generally the boys ate more quickly than the girls.

Exercise 8.5

1 In season 2002/3, a football fan argued that Hearts was a more
determined team than Hibs, and that they continued to attack and
defend for the full 90 minutes. The fan collected the times (in
minutes) of all goals scored and conceded by both teams that season.

Hearts scored

33	18	40	65	90	78	53	57	30	34	63	74	76	25	56
37	79	46	89	60	86	90	53	48	51	5	70	90	26	41
51	4	66	42	80	30	62	90	90	90	45	49	90	50	53
79	30	72	8	69	78	79	73	90	57	78				

Hearts conceded

65	51	72	44	41	78	12	27	27	78	41	3	9	36	41
26	27	36	65	76	90	52	81	79	90	15	19	26	36	66
90	63	22	44	68	73	57	11	17	89	90	41	53	61	40
73	59	29	29	65	73									

Hibs scored

31	51	35	88	9	14	71	41	8	11	45	28	51	43	81
89	70	36	45	12	49	59	64	90	55	83	89	70	85	11
17	89	90	71	67	37	60	3	15	18	83	44	53	58	90
42	62	72	66	38	69	8	34							

Hibs conceded

63	90	18	40	65	90	6	45	64	86	78	90	10	23	57
31	31	75	86	90	11	35	90	47	76	90	63	88	78	30
62	90	90	58	85	31	41	20	39	55	9	86	90	1	23
90	69	24	42	11	47	62	90	87	89	32	88	87	29	52
86														

(a) (i) Copy and complete the following table for the 'Hearts
scored' goal times.

Time of goal (minutes)	Tally	Frequency
$0 \leqslant t < 15$		
$15 \leqslant t < 30$		
$30 \leqslant t <$		
$\quad \leqslant t <$		
$\quad \leqslant t <$		
$\quad \leqslant t \leqslant 90$		

(ii) Draw a histogram to illustrate the 'Hearts scored' goal times.

(b) Repeat for 'Hearts conceded' goal times.

(c) Repeat for 'Hibs scored' goal times.

(d) Repeat for 'Hibs conceded' goal times.

(e) By comparing the four histograms, explain whether you think the
fan was correct.

2 Question: "Are breakfast cereals a healthy option?"
A dietician collected data about salt and sugar content for
some breakfast cereals.

For 11–14 year olds, the recommended daily allowance for
salt is 6 grammes and for sugar it is 75 grammes. The figures
in the table are for an average portion of 40 grammes.

Cereal	Salt(g)	Sugar(g)
Frosties	0·60	15·2
Rice Krispies	0·60	4
Golden Nuggets	0·50	16
Cheerios	0·70	8·6
All Bran	1·68	6·2
Corn Flakes	1·16	3·0
Alpen	0·17	8·8
Shredded Wheat	0·01	0·2
Special K	0·88	3·8
Sugar Puffs	0·01	22·6
Weetabix	0·36	2·4

Cereal	Salt(g)	Sugar(g)
Lion Cereal	0·30	14·4
Frosties Turbos	0·60	16
Cookie Crisp	0·60	16·5
Golden Grahams	1·00	12·8
Frosties Chocolate	0·65	16·4
Hunny B's	0·50	14·8
Cinnamon Grahams	0·70	13·7
Bart Simpson's Eat My Shorts	0·55	14·4
Choco Corn Flakes	0·65	16
Coco Pops	0·45	15·6

(a) (i) Copy and complete the following table for the salt content.

Salt (s) in grammes	Tally	Frequency
$0 \leqslant s < 0.2$		
$0.2 \leqslant s < 0.4$		
$0.4 \leqslant s <$		
$\leqslant s <$		
$\leqslant s <$		
$\leqslant s <$		
$\leqslant s <$		
$\leqslant s <$		
$\leqslant s < 1.8$		

(ii) Draw a histogram to illustrate this data.

(iii) How would you answer the question?

(b) Choose suitable class intervals for the sugar content and
then repeat part (a) for this data.

3 This question is designed for working in groups.

A biologist was investigating how Scots Pine trees adapt to different climates and asked the question "Is the rainfall in the west of Scotland higher than in the east?" She collected data from the River Inver and the River Almond areas.

Rainfall data in millimetres:

River Inver

Year	Mar	May	Aug	Nov
2001	74	96	99	299
2000	266	84	123	274
1999	219	144	62	304
1998	239	92	161	223
1997	255	160	89	113
1996	80	87	97	379
1995	213	109	61	229
1994	328	34	122	180
1993	171	92	113	64
1992	261	109	284	305
1991	146	124	108	367
1990	507	78	244	186
1989	274	80	237	107
1988	244	58	208	134
1987	206	112	121	193
1986	223	183	118	330
1985	132	58	250	230
1984	140	26	85	198
1983	359	37	123	120
1982	192	153	259	370
1981	197	70	121	527
1980	98	25	179	291
1979	283	127	143	414
1978	202	47	113	373
1977	102	118	92	445

River Almond

Year	Mar	May	Aug	Nov
2001	59	36	100	71
2000	59	38	100	143
1999	60	67	53	134
1998	70	81	88	116
1997	63	111	43	75
1996	26	60	47	119
1995	80	55	25	83
1994	170	16	66	107
1993	49	134	55	54
1992	142	37	152	129
1991	75	17	32	87
1990	93	41	70	51
1989	110	35	125	23
1988	82	58	97	61
1987	82	43	106	51
1986	82	110	100	111
1985	82	52	134	72
1984	91	40	34	181
1983	89	95	34	19
1982	80	63	86	149
1981	116	56	19	104
1980	94	16	112	135
1979	127	65	90	138
1978	89	25	90	107
1977	80	44	103	114

(**a**) Decide upon the comparisons you wish to make.

(**b**) Decide upon your class intervals.

(**c**) Construct and complete frequency tables.

(**d**) Draw histograms to illustrate your chosen data.

(**e**) Explain how you would answer the biologist's question.

8.6 Scatter diagrams

A **scatter diagram** is used to display the relationship between two variables.

In 1948 a physics professor, George W. Pierce, asked the question "Is the rate at which crickets chirp related to the temperature?" He collected the following data and plotted it on a set of axes to create a scatter diagram.

Temperature (°F)	88·6	71·6	93·3	84·3	80·6	75·2	69·7	82	69·4	83·3	79·6	82·6	80·6	83·5	76·3
Chirps per second	20	16	19·8	18·4	17·1	15·5	14·7	17·1	15·4	16·2	15	17·2	16	17	14·4

The plotted points show a general trend, but not an exact relationship. As the temperature increases, the number of chirps per second increases.

This is called a **positive correlation** between the temperature and the number of chirps per second.

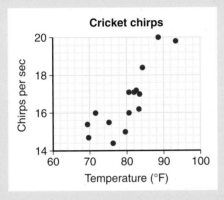
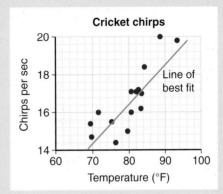

A **line of best fit** can be added to the graph. This line can be used to make predictions.

If the temperature was 78°F, the number of chirps per second would be around 16.

Exercise 8.6

1 Town planners wanted to investigate the relationship between road traffic and pollution. They collected the data shown below.

Traffic in hundreds per day	79	109	90	124	111	114	127	102	121	119	131	135	75	92	81	98
Lead in parts per million	34	58	43	60	53	48	74	38	50	55	67	68	30	39	33	48

(**a**) Draw axes as shown and plot this data to give a scatter diagram.

(**b**) Describe the correlation and add your line of best fit.

(**c**) Use your line of best fit to
  (**i**) estimate the amount of lead you might expect when 8500 vehicles use a road in one day
  (**ii**) estimate the number of vehicles when the amount of lead was 52 parts per million.

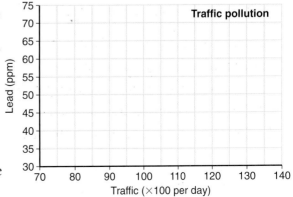

2 Biologists need to know the weight of a bear to assess its health. Research was undertaken to see if there was a connection between the chest girth of a bear and its weight. The following data was collected.

Chest in inches	23	25	26	28	29	30	31	32	33	34	34	35
Weight in pounds	46	60	65	90	114	114	140	125	166	152	146	172
Chest in inches	35	37	39	40	41	42	48	49	50	53	54	55
Weight in pounds	184	160	180	224	262	220	356	360	400	416	514	478

(**a**) Draw a scatter diagram of this data.

(**b**) Describe the correlation and add your line of best fit.

(**c**) Use your line of best fit to estimate
   (**i**) the weight of a bear with a chest measurement of 45 inches
   (**ii**) the chest measurement if the weight was 350 pounds.

3 A salmon population was investigated to determine the relationship between the length of a female salmon and the mass of eggs it produced. The following data was collected.

Length in mm	566	459	519	451	457	474	472	560	470	518	484
Egg mass in mg	297	199	182	215	237	196	188	207	207	207	171

(**a**) Draw a scatter diagram of this data.

(**b**) Describe the correlation and consider whether it is appropriate to add your line of best fit.

4 An ornithologist wants to know the relationship between the amount of energy a blue tit uses and the air temperature. He collects the following data.

Temperature °C	1	3	5	7	9	11	13
Energy kJ/day	52·6	47·2	47·5	41·1	43·8	41·6	36·5

(**a**) Draw a scatter diagram of this data.

(**b**) Describe the correlation and add your line of best fit.

(**c**) Use your line of best fit to estimate
   (**i**) the air temperature when a blue tit has used 43 kJ per day
   (**ii**) the amount of energy used when the temperature is 10°C.

5 In 2004 scientists from Oxford University wondered if women would ever be able to run faster than men. They collected the following data of the winning times in the men's and women's 100 metres finals at all the recent Olympic games.

Year	1928	1932	1936	1948	1952	1956	1960	1964	1968
Men's time (s)	10·8	10·3	10·3	10·3	10·4	10·5	10·2	10	9·95
Women's time (s)	12·2	11·9	11·5	11·9	11·5	11·5	11	11·4	11·08
Year	1972	1976	1980	1984	1988	1992	1996	2000	2004
Men's time (s)	10·14	10·06	10·25	9·99	9·92	9·96	9·84	9·87	9·85
Women's time (s)	11·07	11·08	11·06	10·97	10·54	10·82	10·94	10·75	10·93

(a) Draw a scatter diagram of men's times against the year.

(b) Draw the line of best fit.

(c) Predict the men's winning time in the year 2020.

(d) Repeat parts (a) to (c) for the women's times.

(e) Answer the scientists' question.

8.7 Measures of central tendency

To convey information about a data set, three measures of central tendency may be used: **mean**, **median** and **mode**.

Mean
The mean is found by adding all the data and dividing by the number of pieces of data.

Median
The median is the middle value when all the data is written in numerical order.

These may also be called averages.

Mode
The mode is the value that occurs most often.

Example
The number of broad beans in a sample of pods was found to be:

3, 8, 2, 6, 7, 4, 3, 9

For this data, calculate (a) the mean   (b) the median   (c) the mode

(a) Mean $= \dfrac{3+8+2+6+7+4+3+9}{8} = \dfrac{42}{8} = \mathbf{5.25}$ broad beans per pod

(b) | 2, 3, 3, 4 | | 6, 7, 8, 9 | Median = **5** broad beans   Halfway between 4 and 6.

(c) Mode = **3** broad beans   Occurs twice.

Exercise 8.7

1 Find the mean of each set of data:

(a) 2, 4, 6, 8, 10

(b) 2, 4, 6, 8, 10, 12, 14, 16, 18

(c) 24, 36, 44, 67, 48

(d) 33, 43, 46, 67, 72, 88, 89, 95

(e) 12, 16, 18, 21, 24, 28, 33, 37, 45, 46

2 Find the mean of each set of numbers:

(a) 5·6, 3·75, 7·8, 9, 6·27, 9·34, 8·24, 7·6

(b) 12, −15, 62, −47, 38, 55, −35, −30, −22, 37

(c) 47, 36, 28, 99, 73, 94, 45, 38, 62

(d) 147, 136, 128, 199, 173, 194, 145, 138, 162

(e) Using your answers to parts (c) and (d), state the value of the mean of
2847, 2836, 2828, 2899, 2873, 2894, 2845, 2838, 2862

3 Find the number that is halfway between

(a) 12 and 16   (b) 14 and 24   (c) x and y

4 The number halfway between 7 and x is 15. Find x.

5 Find the median of each set of numbers

(a) 46, 67, 123, 24, 86, 44, 39, 77, 101, 92, 52

(b) 44, 68, 75, 39, 12, 88, 64, 73

(c) 2·3, 4, 2·1, 3·04, 3, 4·6, 2·09, 3·8

(d) 7·2, 8·09, 6·4, 7, 6·13, 7·75, 6·06, 7·08, 8, 7·9

(e) 754, 800, 1064, 999, 852, 791, 1102, 861, 901, 738, 834, 950

(f) 13·6, 13·8, 14·3, 15·9, 17·2, 17·8, 18·3

(g) 5·6, 13·8, 14·3, 15·9, 17·2, 17·8, 78·3

(h) £27.60, £28.46, £29.30, £29.32, £31.56, £33.33, £34.72, £35.00

(i) £17.60, £18.46, £19.30, £29.32, £31.56, £63.33, £64.72, £65.00

6 What does the median tell you about the range of the data?

7 The weights of a pod of 10 bottlenose dolphins in the Moray Firth
are found. The mean weight is 372 kg.
A new dolphin, weighing 427 kg, joins the pod. What is the new
mean weight of the pod?

8 In an African forest, a researcher identifies two different families of
chimpanzees, which she labels family A and family B.

Family A has 10 members and a mean weight of 46 kg.
Family B has 15 members and a mean weight of 32 kg.

Calculate the mean weight of the two families combined.

9 List 5 whole numbers that are all different and have:

(a)   (i) a mean of 10

(ii) a mean of 10, a range of 10 and contain the value 10

(iii) a mean of 10, a range of 10 and do NOT contain the value 10

(b) Find all possible sets of 5 numbers that are all different, have a
mean of 12, a range of 10, a minimum of 6 and do NOT contain
the value 12.

10 The salaries (in £) of the employees in a small firm are:

90 000	30 000	20 000	20 000	11 400	10 000	10 000
10 000	7400	7400	7400	7400	6000	4000
4000	4000	4000	4000	4000	4000	4000
4000	4000	4000	4000			

(a) Find the mean, median and modal wage.

(b) Which average would you quote if

(i) you were a trade union representative arguing for more
money on behalf of the workforce

(ii) you were trying to attract someone to a new management position?

11 A shoe shop manager records the sizes of all women's shoes sold in one week.

> 3, 4, 4, 10, 11, 12, 6, 9, 10, 8, 7, 3, 6, 5,
> 10, 7, 9, 8, 6, 3, 2, 4, 4, 7, 6, 5, 4, 5, 9

(**a**) Find the modal shoe size.

(**b**) Construct a frequency table for the shoe sales and use it to calculate the mean of the shoe sizes.

(**c**) Why do you think the mode is a more useful average than the mean in this case?

12 In a concert orchestra, different people are paid very different amounts, depending on what they do. For a performance in London, the amount they earn for *one* concert is given in the table.

(**a**) Find the mean, median and modal wage.

(**b**) How would you feel if you were a string player or a principal?

(**c**) What would happen to the three different averages if the soloist was less well known and charged only £5,000?

Role	Number	Earnings
Soloist	1	£10 000
Conductor	1	£3000
Leader	1	£1000
Associate leader	2	£750
Principals	19	£250
Brass	5	£120
Percussion	1	£120
Woodwind	3	£120
Strings	51	£90

Review exercise 8

1 For each data set decide if the data is categorical or numerical. If it is numerical, decide if it is discrete or continuous.

(**a**) Fruit eaten per day

(**b**) Cars owned per household

(**c**) Car colour

(**d**) Notes played on a flute

(**e**) Time spent travelling to school

(**f**) Height

2 There is concern that Scotland's population is falling. To find out whether or not this is true, some families were asked "How many children are in your family?" The results were:

> 4 0 0 3 2 1 1 0 3 5 2 2 0 0 1
> 1 3 1 1 2 0 0 1 4 2 2 3 3 1 0

> The TFR (total fertility rate) in Scotland in 2002 was 1·48.

(**a**) For this data
  (**i**) construct a frequency table
  (**ii**) draw a bar graph
  (**iii**) calculate the mean number of children per family.
  (**iv**) Do you think this data shows that Scotland's population is rising or falling? Explain.

(**b**) Collect the same data from your class and then
  (**i**) construct a frequency table
  (**ii**) draw a bar graph
  (**iii**) calculate the mean number of children per family.
  (**iv**) Do you think this data shows that Scotland's population is rising or falling? Explain.

3 Media Studies students have asked the question, "Which is more popular, BBC1 or ITV?" The viewing figures (in millions of people) of the top 30 programmes on each channel for one week are shown below.

BBC1	18	17·8	17·8	16·8	9·8	9·3	9·1	8·9	8·8	8·8	8·7	8·6	8·4	8·2	8·1
	7·9	7·9	7·8	7·5	7·1	7	6·9	6·8	6·8	6·7	6·6	6·5	6·4	6·3	6·3
ITV	16·8	15·6	15·6	13·7	13·4	12·3	12·2	11·7	11·4	10·8	10·4	10·1	9·6	9·5	9·3
	8·9	8·5	8·4	8·2	8·1	7·8	7·8	7·3	7·3	7	7	6·9	6·8	6·6	6·3

(**a**) Find the maximum and minimum number of viewers.

(**b**) Draw a back to back stem and leaf diagram.

(**c**) Answer the students' question.

4 In a recent national lifestyle survey, 8–15 year olds were asked how many minutes in a typical day they spent playing computer games. The results are shown below.

Boys
35	5	16	24	65
24	74	120	53	36
53	38	79	20	8
44	32	17	0	88

Girls
43	22	7	0	12
28	8	5	3	15
42	12	6	7	0
15	0	2	3	11

(**a**) Draw a histogram for the boys' data by constructing and completing a frequency table.

(**b**) Repeat part (**a**) for the girls' data.

(**c**) How do the results compare?

5 The total oil consumption and oil production (in thousands of barrels per day), and population (in millions) of various countries in 2000 is shown below.

(**a**) Find the mean consumption and production.

(**b**) Find the median consumption and production.

(**c**) Compare and comment upon the consumption and population for USA, United Kingdom, Japan and India.

Country	Consumption	Production	Population	Country	Consumption	Production	Population
USA	18745	7745	290·3	Saudi Arabia	1335	9145	24·3
Canada	1775	2710	32·2	Egypt	545	795	74·7
Brazil	1825	1255	234·9	Australia	870	815	19·7
Argentina	430	820	38·7	Japan	5525	0	127·2
Germany	2760	0	82·4	India	2070	785	1049·7
Sweden	320	0	8·9	China	4840	3245	1287·0
United Kingdom	1675	2660	60·1	Pakistan	385	0	150·7
Russian Federation	2475	6535	144·5	New Zealand	135	0	4
Ukraine	210	0	48·1	South Africa	475	0	32·8
Iran	1170	3770	68·3				

6 Scientists wanted to see if they could predict how far a discus could be thrown in future. They collected the gold medal winning throws (in metres) from the modern Olympic Games.

Year	1896	1900	1904	1908	1912	1920	1924	1928	1932	1936	1948
Distance	29·1	36·0	39·3	40·9	45·2	44·7	46·2	47·3	49·5	50·5	52·8
Year	1952	1956	1960	1964	1968	1972	1976	1980	1984	1988	1992
Distance	55·0	56·3	59·2	61·0	64·8	64·4	67·5	66·6	66·6	68·8	65·1

(a) Draw appropriate axes, with the horizontal axis up to 2004, and plot this data to make a scatter diagram.

(b) Describe the correlation and add your line of best fit.

(c) Use your line of best fit to estimate the distance thrown in 1996, 2000 and 2004.

(c) Do you think the trend you have seen could carry on forever?

Summary

Types of data

Data can be either categorical or numerical.

Categorical	Numerical	
	Discrete	Continuous
Data collected in categories	Data restricted to a number of values	Data unrestricted within a range

Organising data

The following steps are useful when investigating data.

- Ask a question
- Collect data – survey or experiment
- Organise data
- Display data
- Draw a conclusion to answer the original question

Stem and leaf diagram

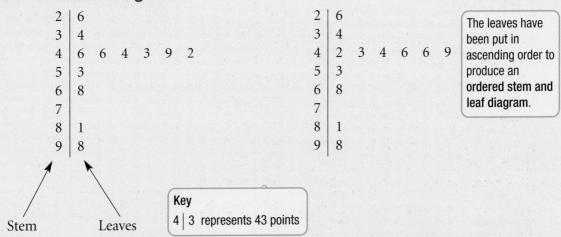

2	6
3	4
4	6 6 4 3 9 2
5	3
6	8
7	
8	1
9	8

2	6
3	4
4	2 3 4 6 6 9
5	3
6	8
7	
8	1
9	8

The leaves have been put in ascending order to produce an ordered stem and leaf diagram.

Stem   Leaves

Key
4 | 3 represents 43 points

Back to back stem and leaf diagram

Male life expectancy | | Female life expectancy

Male		Female
2 2	71	
4	72	
9	73	
7 6 6 5 2 1 0	74	
6 6 5 1 0	75	
0 0	76	
1	77	
	78	4
	79	2 3 5 7 9
	80	7 8 9
	81	2 3 4 4 5
	82	5 5 6
	83	0

Key
9 | 73 represents 73·9 years

Key
80 | 7 represents 80·7 years

Grouped continuous data

Time, t (secs)	Tally		Frequency	
	Girls	Boys	Girls	Boys
$40 \leqslant t < 50$	|	|	1	1
$50 \leqslant t < 60$		|	0	1
$60 \leqslant t < 70$	|	||||	1	5
$70 \leqslant t < 80$	||||	|||	4	3
$80 \leqslant t < 90$	||	|||	2	3
$90 \leqslant t < 100$	|||	||	3	2
$100 \leqslant t < 110$	|		1	0
$110 \leqslant t < 120$	||		2	0
$120 \leqslant t < 130$	|		1	0

Histogram

Boys

Frequency vs Time (seconds)

Scatter diagram

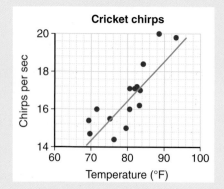

Cricket chirps

Chirps per sec vs Temperature (°F)

Measures of central tendency

Mean
The mean is found by adding all the data and dividing by the number of pieces of data.

Median
The median is the middle value when all the data is written in numerical order.

Mode
The mode is the value that occurs most often.

9 Algebra

In this chapter you will extend your knowledge of algebraic expressions and learn how to solve more complex equations.

9.1 Review – simplifying expressions

Example

Simplify: (**a**) $5c + 3d - c$ (**b**) $4x + 3y - 2x - 7y$ (**c**) $8 - 5p - 3q + 4p - 2q$

$$\begin{aligned}(\mathbf{a})\quad & 5c + 3d - c \\ = \ & 5c - c + 3d \\ = \ & \mathbf{4c + 3d}\end{aligned}$$
$$\begin{aligned}(\mathbf{b})\quad & 4x + 3y - 2x - 7y \\ = \ & 4x - 2x + 3y - 7y \\ = \ & \mathbf{2x - 4y}\end{aligned}$$
$$\begin{aligned}(\mathbf{c})\quad & 8 - 5p - 3q + 4p - 2q \\ = \ & 8 - 5p + 4p - 3q - 2q \\ = \ & \mathbf{8 - p - 5q}\end{aligned}$$

Exercise 9.1

1 Simplify each expression:

(**a**) $3p + 4p$

(**b**) $7c - 2c$

(**c**) $14q + 6q - q$

(**d**) $11z - 2z + 3z$

(**e**) $4e + 9f + 7e$

(**f**) $2y + 3y + 7g - 3g$

(**g**) $13x - 16y + 2x$

(**h**) $20p + q - p + 6q$

(**i**) $11f + 9f + 4g + 3f$

(**j**) $3a + 2b + 5a + b$

(**k**) $2s + 2c + 4s + 3c$

(**l**) $8s + 5 + 7s + 4$

(**m**) $5p + 3 - 2p - 2$

(**n**) $6 + 3p - 2 - p$

(**o**) $4p + 3q - 3p - q$

2 Simplify each expression:

(**a**) $5p + 8 + 2p + 3$

(**b**) $4t + 9 - 3t + 5$

(**c**) $7x + 3 - 2x - 2$

(**d**) $6 + 8y + 9 + 3y$

(**e**) $5a + 4b - 2a + 9b$

(**f**) $7q + 7 - 3q - 3$

(**g**) $4k + 8l - 3k - 6l$

(**h**) $4b - 3a + 7b + 8a$

(**i**) $3 - x + 7 + 5x - 6$

(**j**) $5 + 30y + 20 - 15y$

(**k**) $20z - 25w + 30z + 12w$

(**l**) $5p + 4p - 2q + 2p - 15q$

3 Simplify each expression:

(**a**) $9a - 2b + 6a - 4b$

(**b**) $17n - m + 16m - 4m$

(**c**) $6r + 7s - 20r + 2r + s$

(**d**) $t - s - 16t + 6s$

(**e**) $11f + g - f - 11g$

(**f**) $3x + 2y - 14x - y + 12x$

(**g**) $8x - 4y + 16y - 10x$

(**h**) $19a - 13b + 13a + 5b$

(**i**) $-2x + 3y - 4z + x - z$

(**j**) $22m - 3p + 7m - 16p$

(**k**) $4j - 7k - 8j - k$

(**l**) $4f - 5g + f - 4h - 2h$

9.2 Review – solving equations

Example

Solve: **(a)** $9x + 5 = 59$ **(b)** $3y - 8 = 5y$ **(c)** $35 - 5p = 25$

(a) $9x + 5 = 59$
$-5 \qquad -5$
$9x = 54$
$\div 9 \qquad \div 9$
$x = 6$

(b) $3y - 8 = 5y$
$-3y \qquad -3y$
$-8 = 2y$
$\div 2 \qquad \div 2$
$-4 = y$
$y = -4$

(c) $35 - 5p = 25$
$35 - 5p = 25$
$+5p \qquad +5p$
$35 = 25 + 5p$
$-25 \qquad -25$
$10 = 5p$
$\div 5 \qquad \div 5$
$2 = p$
$p = 2$

Exercise 9.2

1 Solve each equation:
- **(a)** $x + 4 = 11$
- **(b)** $2 + p = 22$
- **(c)** $2 = 9 - b$
- **(d)** $17 - r = 7$
- **(e)** $14 = g + 13$
- **(f)** $t + 7 = -3$
- **(g)** $3 - a = 1$
- **(h)** $w - 14 = -5$
- **(i)** $-4 = 3 - g$

2 Solve each equation:
- **(a)** $2x + 10 = 30$
- **(b)** $3p + 15 = 45$
- **(c)** $4 + 7t = 32$
- **(d)** $16 = 3y + 7$
- **(e)** $31 = 6 + 5s$
- **(f)** $1 + 2y = 9$
- **(g)** $4p + 9 = 1$
- **(h)** $2 = 5s + 7$
- **(i)** $3t - 1 = -7$
- **(j)** $-17 = 2w - 3$
- **(k)** $5x + 1 = -9$
- **(l)** $-3 = 4y + 5$

3 Solve each equation:
- **(a)** $5x = 2x + 15$
- **(b)** $7p = 18 + p$
- **(c)** $4r + 10 = 9r$
- **(d)** $24 + 2m = 8m$
- **(e)** $8s = 15 + 3s$
- **(f)** $6x = 2x + 20$
- **(g)** $5x = 3x - 6$
- **(h)** $4y - 10 = 9y$
- **(i)** $8t = 7t - 5$

4 Solve each equation:
- **(a)** $17 - 2p = 7$
- **(b)** $12 - 3x = 6$
- **(c)** $10 = 15 - 5x$
- **(d)** $20 - 4t = 8$
- **(e)** $8 = 16 - 4y$
- **(f)** $35 = 5 - 6m$
- **(g)** $5 - 2p = 13$
- **(h)** $11 = 4 - 7v$
- **(i)** $1 - 4q = 9$

5 Solve each equation:
- **(a)** $5x - 3 = 17$
- **(b)** $22 = 3y + 4$
- **(c)** $5a = 2a + 12$
- **(d)** $12 + b = 5b$
- **(e)** $3t + 9 = 0$
- **(f)** $1 = 4p + 9$
- **(g)** $17 - 3s = 2$
- **(h)** $1 = 5 - 4x$
- **(i)** $2x - 1 = 0$
- **(j)** $5x = 3x - 7$
- **(k)** $4 - 3y = 5$
- **(l)** $3m + 9 = 7$

9.3 More complex equations

Example

Solve: (a) $5x + 3 = 3x + 13$ (b) $10 - 2x = 3x + 25$

(a)
$$5x + 3 = 3x + 13$$
$$-3x \qquad -3x$$
$$2x + 3 = 13$$
$$-3 \qquad -3$$
$$2x = 10$$
$$\div 2 \qquad \div 2$$
$$x = 5$$

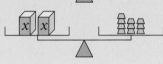

(b)
$$10 - 2x = 3x + 25$$
$$+2x \qquad +2x$$
$$10 = 5x + 25$$
$$-25 \qquad -25$$
$$-15 = 5x$$
$$\div 5 \qquad \div 5$$
$$-3 = x$$
$$x = -3$$

Exercise 9.3

1 Solve each equation:

(a) $4x + 2 = 2x + 8$ (b) $3y + 10 = y + 18$ (c) $5z + 2 = 3z + 6$

(d) $4x + 3 = 2x + 15$ (e) $7m - 3 = 3m + 17$ (f) $8v + 10 = 7v + 5$

(g) $5w - 1 = 4w + 5$ (h) $9y - 8 = 2y + 20$ (i) $4r + 7 = 8r - 13$

(j) $4x - 8 = 6x - 20$ (k) $9y + 8 = 3y - 4$ (l) $f - 31 = 5f - 3$

(m) $4q - 8 = 6q + 12$ (n) $9t + 5 = 15t - 1$ (o) $5y - 4 = 3y + 10$

(p) $6t + 1 = 3t - 2$ (q) $5s - 2 = 7s + 12$ (r) $4t - 3 = 7t - 9$

2 Solve:

(a) $4r + 12 = 48 - 2r$ (b) $13 - 4y = 2y - 11$ (c) $5k + 4 = 44 - 3k$

(d) $7b + 3 = 93 - 2b$ (e) $9 - 3s = 4s + 30$ (f) $14 - 6b = 4b + 34$

(g) $4 - 5x = 9x + 18$ (h) $7 - a = 4a - 18$ (i) $50 - 3z = 2z + 15$

(j) $3 - x = 9 - 3x$ (k) $4 - 3x = 12 - 5x$ (l) $10 - 7x = 1 - 4x$

(m) $7 - 2x = 4 - 5x$ (n) $3 - 6x = 18 - x$ (o) $7 - 2x = 7 - 9x$

3 Solve:

(a) $15 - 2x = 9$ (b) $7p - 6 = 4p$ (c) $10 - 2p = 3p$

(d) $9t + 8 = 5t$ (e) $12 = 2 - 5x$ (f) $20 - 3p = 7p$

(g) $6y - 2 = 2y - 8$ (h) $2m + 9 = 5m + 7$ (i) $5x - 3 = 3x + 4$

(j) $p - 7 = 4 - p$ (k) $3x + 1 = 3 - x$ (l) $10 - 5x = 8 - 2x$

(m) $5 - 4x = 6 - 2x$ (n) $30 - 8t = 2 + 10t$ (o) $10x + 1 = 15 - 5x$

9.4 The distributive law

$3(y + 4)$ is an algebraic expression.

This notation means every term **inside** the brackets is to be multiplied by the term **outside** the brackets.

So $\quad 3(y + 4)$
$\quad\quad = 3y + 12$

$3 \times y = 3y$
$3 \times 4 = 12$

$\begin{array}{r} y + 4 \\ y + 4 \\ y + 4 \\ \hline 3y + 12 \end{array}$

This is known as the distributive law.

This is called **expanding** or **multiplying out**.

Example Expand each expression (a) $4(y - 3)$ (b) $-3(4m + 2n - 6)$ (c) $6(3p - q) - 2p$

(a) $\quad 4(y - 3)$
$\quad = 4y - 12$

(b) $-3(4m + 2n - 6)$
$\quad = -12m - 6n + 18$

$-3 \times -6 = 18$

(c) $\quad 6(3p - q) - 2p$
$\quad = 18p - 6q - 2p$
$\quad = 18p - 2p - 6q$
$\quad = 16p - 6q$

$-2p$ is not in the brackets.

Collect like terms.

Exercise 9.4

1 Multiply out these brackets:
- (a) $3(x + 2)$
- (b) $6(7 + 4f)$
- (c) $3(3r + 6p + 2)$
- (d) $2(3z - 4)$
- (e) $8(9y - 2)$
- (f) $5(7q - 2w + 1)$
- (g) $9(6e - 2)$
- (h) $4(x + 6)$
- (i) $8(2r + 10s - 5)$
- (j) $3(y - 4)$
- (k) $7(3r - 4s)$
- (l) $11(5 - 2d + 6e)$
- (m) $10(5y - 8)$
- (n) $8(3 - 5y)$
- (o) $2(6x - y - 3)$

2 Expand and simplify:
- (a) $2(x + 3) + 5$
- (b) $3(y + 4) + 2y$
- (c) $5(3x + 4y - z) - 2x$
- (d) $2(8m - 3) - 4m$
- (e) $9(1 - 2p) + 3$
- (f) $11(2a + 3b + c) + 3c$
- (g) $12(4f - 2g) - 40f$
- (h) $10(3x + 4y) + 2x$
- (i) $4(3p + 2q - 7) - 6q$
- (j) $3(5x - 2y) - 6x$
- (k) $4(3f + 11) - 20$
- (l) $3(2 + 4e - f) - e$
- (m) $2(x + 3) + 4x$
- (n) $5(3y + 6) - 7y$
- (o) $5(3y + 6 - x) - 20$

3 Write without brackets:
- (a) $-4(q + 3)$
- (b) $-3(2p + 7)$
- (c) $-2(p + 3q + 5)$
- (d) $-3(y - 7)$
- (e) $-1(3w - 2z)$
- (f) $-7(4j - 5k + 2)$
- (g) $-5(2y + 5)$
- (h) $-3(4x + 5)$
- (i) $-4(3n - 7m - 5)$
- (j) $-6(2m - 2)$
- (k) $-8(8d - 6f)$
- (l) $-8(3m - 2n - 1)$

4 Expand and simplify:
- (a) $-3(2y + 7) + 2y$
- (b) $-4(8n + 1) + 7$
- (c) $2(4x + 5y - 3z) - 2y$
- (d) $-10(3x + 4y) + 2x$
- (e) $-3(5x - 2y) + 5y$
- (f) $4(3a + 6b - 2c) - 6c$
- (g) $-4(3f - 11) + 20$
- (h) $-5(4m - 2n) + 3m$
- (i) $12(3d - c - 5) + 70$
- (j) $-20(4s - 6) - 90$
- (k) $-9(3w - 3v) - 3v$
- (l) $10(-x - y - z) - x$
- (m) $15(6g - f) - f$
- (n) $7(4e - f) - f$
- (o) $-x + 2y - 3(x - y)$
- (p) $5 - 2(a + 2)$
- (q) $7b - 3(2b - 1)$
- (r) $p - q - 2(q - p)$

9.5 Simplifying using the distributive law

Example

Expand and simplify:

(a) $2(3x + 4y) + 3(x + y)$ **(b)** $2(x - 5) - 3(2x + 1)$ **(c)** $-3(2 + 4p) - (p - 8)$

(a) $2(3x + 4y) + 3(x + y)$	**(b)** $2(x - 5) - 3(2x + 1)$	**(c)** $-3(2 + 4p) - (p - 8)$
$= 6x + 8y + 3x + 3y$	$= 2x - 10 - 6x - 3$	$= -6 - 12p - p + 8$
$= 6x + 3x + 8y + 3y$	$= 2x - 6x - 10 - 3$	$= -6 + 8 - 12p - p$
$= 9x + 11y$	$= -4x - 13$	$= 2 - 13p$

$-(p - 8)$
$= -1(p - 8)$

Exercise 9.5

1 Multiply out the brackets and then simplify:

(a) $2(x + 3) + 3(2x + 5)$

(b) $5(2 + p) + 2(7 + 3p)$

(c) $3(2y + 7) + 2(5 - y)$

(d) $4(3m + 1) + 2(2m + 3)$

(e) $4(3x + y) + 3(x + 4y)$

(f) $4(6t + s) + 3(2s + t)$

(g) $7(1 + 2e) + e - 1$

(h) $6(2h - 3) + 2(15 - 4h)$

(i) $5(2x + 4y + 3z) + 4(x + 6y + 5z)$

(j) $p + 2(p + q) - q$

(k) $3(x + y) + 3(y - x)$

(l) $4(a + b + c) + 2(c - b - a)$

2 Expand and simplify each expression:

(a) $4(7r - 5) + 5(6r + 10)$

(b) $3(9x + 6) + 10(2x - 3)$

(c) $4(b + 3c - 2d) + 6(2b + 6c + 2d)$

(d) $8(b - 7c) + 9(2b - c)$

(e) $2(a + 5b) - (a + 3b)$

(f) $8(4r - 5s - t) + 3(r + 3s + 4t)$

(g) $5(p + 2q) - (p - 3q)$

(h) $4(r + 6) - (4 - r)$

(i) $10(5x - 2y + 6z) + 2(x - 5y - z)$

(j) $3(a + 1) - 2(a + 2)$

(k) $4(3b + 1) - 5(2b - 1)$

(l) $4(3g + 5h) - (2g + 5h) - g$

(m) $5(2 - 3c) - (c - 2)$

(n) $9(2d - 6) - (10 + 3d)$

(o) $2(p - q - r) - 3(r + q - p)$

(p) $2(x - y) - 2(y - x)$

3 Expand and simplify:

(a) $-9(2 + 4x) + 2(3 + x)$

(b) $-7(3 - 2m) + 6 - m$

(c) $-2(4 - 4z) + 2(z - 1)$

(d) $-2(7 + 6p) - 3(3 + 2p)$

(e) $6(2r - 3) - 3(r - 8)$

(f) $-10(2x - 3y) - 3(x - y)$

(g) $-6(3b - 6c) - (3b - 2c)$

(h) $-5(10d + 1) - (d - 5)$

(i) $-5(4x + y) - (x + y)$

(j) $-10(3y - 2) - (2y - 3)$

(k) $-20(4m - n) - (m - 2n)$

(l) $-4(5 - 2x) - 3(x - 1)$

(m) $-5(2p - 3q) - 7(p - 8q)$

(n) $-10(r - s) - 8(2r - 3s)$

(o) $3(2y + 4) + 5(3y - 2x - 3) + 6x$

(p) $-2(1 - x) - 2(x - 1)$

(q) $2(p - 3q - 1) - 3(1 - p - q)$

(r) $5(y - 8) + 8y - 4(2x - y - 7)$

9.6 Solving equations using the distributive law

Example

Solve the equations   (**a**) $3(2x - 4) = 6$ (**b**) $34 = 8 - 2(3y - 1)$

(**a**) $3(2x - 4) = 6$

$6x - 12 = 6$

$\quad +12 \qquad +12$

$6x = 18$

$\quad \div 6 \qquad \div 6$

$x = 3$

(**b**) $34 = 8 - 2(3y - 1)$

$34 = 8 - 6y + 2$ **Multiply bracket.**

$34 = 10 - 6y$ **Collect like terms.**

$\quad +6y \qquad +6y$

$6y + 34 = 10$

$\quad -34 \qquad -34$

$6y = -24$

$\quad \div 6 \qquad \div 6$

$y = -4$

Exercise 9.6

1 Solve the equations:

(**a**) $2(2x + 3) = 14$

(**b**) $3(3p + 2) = 60$

(**c**) $5(x + 1) = 25$

(**d**) $3(x - 1) = 18$

(**e**) $20 = 5(x - 4)$

(**f**) $100 = 10(x - 5)$

(**g**) $2(y + 13) = 32$

(**h**) $5(y - 7) = 10$

(**i**) $2(5x - 10) = 30$

(**j**) $21 = 3(3x - 2)$

(**k**) $2(z + 3) = 36$

(**l**) $100 = 5(1 + x)$

(**m**) $2 = 2(x + 7)$

(**n**) $3(2x + 10) = 30$

(**o**) $2(c + 1) = -4$

2 Solve:

(**a**) $2(x + 3) - 1 = 7$

(**b**) $5(3y - 2) + 15 = 35$

(**c**) $5(x - 1) + 2 = 12$

(**d**) $3(3x + 5) + 6 = 3$

(**e**) $5(2x - 3) - 4 = 21$

(**f**) $6(4a + 3) - 1 = 17$

(**g**) $2(x + 3) - 4 = 6$

(**h**) $3(1 + 2y) + 2 = 23$

(**i**) $15 = 5(3a - 1) + 5$

(**j**) $6(p - 1) + 11 = 17$

(**k**) $20 = 10 + 2(3x - 1)$

(**l**) $16 = 8 - 2(5 - x)$

3 Solve:

(**a**) $2(18 - x) = 18$

(**b**) $5(5 - x) = 5$

(**c**) $3(40 - 2s) = 42$

(**d**) $7(12 - 5x) = 14$

(**e**) $2(100 - x) = 300$

(**f**) $7(3 - 2y) = 49$

(**g**) $-2(2x + 4) = -16$

(**h**) $-2(g - 3) = -12$

(**i**) $-4(3x + 5) = -32$

(**j**) $-9(20 - y) = -9$

(**k**) $-30 = -6(8 + 3x)$

(**l**) $-5(3 - p) = -25$

4 Solve:

(**a**) $10 - (3y + 2) = 2$

(**b**) $11 + 2(6 - 2x) = 7$

(**c**) $28 = 1 - (2g - 1)$

(**d**) $20 - 7(2y - 3) = -1$

(**e**) $4(5 - 2z) - 5 = 39$

(**f**) $43 = 3 - 5(3m - 2)$

(**g**) $15 - 3(x - 1) = 6$

(**h**) $30 = 4 - 2(3a - 1)$

(**i**) $28 = 3 - 5(3s - 2)$

5 Solve:

(a) $3(2x + 7) = 24$

(b) $2(c + 1) = -7$

(c) $5(6a - 1) = 5$

(d) $2(3t + 17) = 38$

(e) $3(8 - 8x) = 18$

(f) $6(9 - 8x) = 38$

(g) $2(6 - 4x) = 24$

(h) $5(9 + 10x) = 35$

(i) $-2(4 - 3x) = 44$

(j) $6(4a + 3) - 1 = -7$

(k) $10(5x - 3) + 20 = 180$

(l) $10 - 3(x + 2) = 23$

9.7 Complex equations using the distributive law

Example

Solve   (a) $4(2x + 3) = 2(5x + 4)$ (b) $3(9 - x) = 15 - 2(2x - 3)$

(a)
$$4(2x + 3) = 2(5x + 4)$$
$$8x + 12 = 10x + 8$$

$-8x$ $\qquad$ $-8x$

Expand.

$$12 = 2x + 8$$

-8 $\qquad$ -8

Simplify.

$$4 = 2x$$

$\div 2$ $\qquad$ $\div 2$

Solve.

$$2 = x$$

$$x = 2$$

(b)
$$3(9 - x) = 15 - 2(2x - 3)$$
$$27 - 3x = 15 - 4x + 6$$
$$27 - 3x = 21 - 4x$$

$+4x$ $\qquad$ $+4x$

$$27 + x = 21$$

-27 $\qquad$ -27

$$x = -6$$

Exercise 9.7

1 Solve the equations:

(a) $3(x + 2) = 2(x + 5)$

(b) $4(y + 7) = 6(y + 2)$

(c) $5(2n + 1) = 7(n + 2)$

(d) $2(5s - 1) = 3(2s + 2)$

(e) $10(2m + 3) = 5(m + 3)$

(f) $2(3x + 3) = 3(x + 5)$

(g) $6(4x - 3) = 10(4x - 5)$

(h) $2(y - 3) = 3(8 - y)$

(i) $3(2y + 10) = 2(5 - 2y)$

(j) $3(2t + 4) = 4(8 - t)$

(k) $7(2z + 6) = 4(3z + 12)$

(l) $5(3r + 2) = 4(6r - 2)$

2 Solve:

(a) $2(3c - 8) = -2(4c - 6)$

(b) $5(2x + 1) - 2(x + 1) = 11$

(c) $6(x + 2) + 6 = 3(x - 4)$

(d) $3(6 - d) + 4(2d + 3) = 50$

(e) $2(2x - 7) = 1 - (3 + 2x)$

(f) $5(p - 2) = 2(6p + 7) - 4(3p + 1)$

(g) $4x - 3(x + 1) = 0$

(h) $6(3m + 5) - 2(4m + 35) = 0$

(i) $5(2x - 5) + 2 = 2(8 - 2x) + x$

(j) $10(6f - 8) = 6(5f + 6) - 26$

(k) $3(x + 2) = 8 - 2(x - 4)$

(l) $2(c - 3) - 2 = 4(2c + 1)$

3 Solve:

(a) $4x - 2(1 - 3x) = 3$

(b) $8 - 2(p - 1) = 3(p + 2)$

(c) $4(y - 1) = 12 - 2(2y - 2)$

(d) $3(x + 2) = 8 - 2(x - 1)$

(e) $4(x - 3) = -5(x + 1)$

(f) $3(7 - 2t) = 3(t + 5) - 84$

9.8 Complex equations with algebraic fractions

Example 1

Solve $\dfrac{x}{3} = 2x - 5$

$$\dfrac{x}{3} = 2x - 5$$

$$3 \times \dfrac{x}{3} = 3(2x - 5) \quad \boxed{\text{Multiply by 3.}}$$

$$x = 6x - 15$$

$+15 \qquad\qquad +15$

$$15 + x = 6x$$

$-x \qquad -x$

$$15 = 5x$$

$\div 5 \qquad \div 5$

$$3 = x$$

$$x = 3$$

Example 2

Solve $\quad \dfrac{y}{2} \quad = \quad \dfrac{y + 1}{3}$

$$\dfrac{y}{2} = \dfrac{y + 1}{3} \quad \boxed{2 \times 3 = 6}$$

$$6 \times \dfrac{y}{2} = \dfrac{6(y + 1)}{3} \quad \boxed{\text{Multiply by 6.}}$$

$$3y = 2(y + 1)$$

$$3y = 2y + 2$$

$-2y \qquad -2y$

$$y = 2$$

Exercise 9.8

1 Solve each equation:

(a) $\dfrac{y}{2} = 2y - 18$

(b) $\dfrac{x}{4} = 3x - 11$

(c) $\dfrac{z}{3} = 4z + 22$

(d) $y - 16 = \dfrac{y}{5}$

(e) $\dfrac{x}{6} = 3x + 85$

(f) $\dfrac{x}{2} = \dfrac{x + 25}{3}$

(g) $\dfrac{y}{3} = \dfrac{y + 2}{4}$

(h) $\dfrac{z + 2}{5} = \dfrac{z}{4}$

(i) $\dfrac{x}{3} = \dfrac{x + 12}{6}$

2 Solve:

(a) $\dfrac{x}{2} = x - 5$

(b) $\dfrac{z}{3} = \dfrac{z - 4}{4}$

(c) $\dfrac{s}{10} = \dfrac{s - 14}{3}$

(d) $\dfrac{p}{3} = \dfrac{p - 2}{4}$

(e) $\dfrac{y}{5} = \dfrac{y + 1}{4}$

(f) $\dfrac{x - 6}{7} = \dfrac{x}{10}$

(g) $\dfrac{x - 3}{2} = \dfrac{x + 1}{3}$

(h) $\dfrac{y + 5}{6} = \dfrac{y + 4}{5}$

(i) $\dfrac{x + 2}{4} = \dfrac{x - 3}{6}$

(j) $\dfrac{y - 5}{5} = \dfrac{y + 1}{3}$

(k) $6m - 4 = \dfrac{m}{2}$

(l) $\dfrac{y}{3} = 2y - 1$

9.9 Factorising expressions

5 is a **common factor** of $15x + 35$ since 5 is a factor of both $15x$ and 35.

$$15x + 35$$
$$= 5(3x + 7)$$

Check this mentally by expanding the bracket.

This is called **factorising** or **factorisation**.
When factorising, the convention is to use the largest common factor.

Example

Factorise each expression using a common factor:

(a) $12y - 40$ (b) $7m + 14n - 21$

(a) $12y - 40$
   $= 4(3y - 10)$

(b) $7m + 14n - 21$
   $= 7(m + 2n - 3)$

Exercise 9.9

1 Write the largest common factor in each expression:

   (a) $8y + 16$ (b) $10m - 30$ (c) $5x + 25$ (d) $8a - 12b + 20c$

2 Factorise each expression:

   (a) $2x + 8$ (b) $3y + 21$ (c) $4y + 16$ (d) $5m - 35$
   (e) $8t + 36$ (f) $10t - 35$ (g) $20f + 50$ (h) $12s + 16t - 20$

3 Factorise where possible:

   (a) $4r + 2s - 8$ (b) $16x + 24$ (c) $30x + 15y - 25$
   (d) $18m + 9n$ (e) $20t + 16u - 36$ (f) $3 - 21g$
   (g) $6x + 30y$ (h) $4x + 32y - 36z$ (i) $18m - 27n + 81$
   (j) $20f - 17g$ (k) $28r + 49s - 21$ (l) $6f - 8g$
   (m) $30r + 45s - 15$ (n) $18m + 36n - 42$ (o) $-5f - 10g$

4 Factorise where possible:

   (a) $10m - 25n - 55$ (b) $20d + 28e - 12$ (c) $11r - 33s + 77$
   (d) $40x - 60y$ (e) $300f + 700g - 600$ (f) $13x - 26y + 39$
   (g) $16m + 24n$ (h) $24x + 36y - 2$ (i) $12b + 9c - 18$
   (j) $42m - 49n + 77p$ (k) $17x + 51y$ (l) $4g + 6h - 10i$
   (m) $16f - 24g$ (n) $20x + 50y$ (o) $70s + 35t$
   (p) $50x + 25y - 75$ (q) $32r + 40s$ (r) $33x - 55y + 88z$

9.10 Forming equations

Remember
An equation may be used to model a situation.

Example
Carmen thinks of a number. She adds 7 then doubles her answer.
Her total is 26.
What number did she start with?

My total is 26

Call her number n.

$$2(n + 7) = 26$$

Double   Add 7   Total 26

$$2n + 14 = 26$$
$$-14 \qquad -14$$

$$2n = 12$$
$$\div 2 \qquad \div 2$$

$$n = 6 \qquad \text{Carmen's number was } \mathbf{6}.$$

Exercise 9.10

For each question write an equation.
Solve your equation to answer the question.

1 Tim adds x to 5 then multiplies the total by 3. His answer is 27.
What number is x?

2 When three times y is added to 11 the answer is 38.
What number is y?

3 The sum of $2x$ and $7x$ is 45. Find x.

4 When 15 is added to four times x the total is 55. What number is x?

5 Five times x divided by 2 is 10. Find x.

6 The product of 9 and y and 2 is 36. What number is y?

7 Michael adds $2y$ to 7 then multiplies the total by 4. His answer is 52.
What number is y?

8 The quotient of $9x$ and 2 is -9. Find x.

9 For each shape find the value of x.

(a)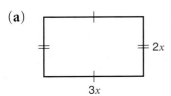

Perimeter = 50 cm

(b)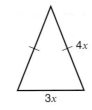

Perimeter = 66 m

(c)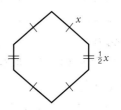

Perimeter = 75 cm

(d)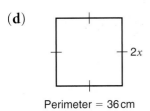

Perimeter = 36 cm

(e)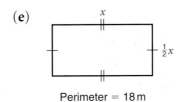

Perimeter = 18 m

9.11　Solving inequations

Example 1

Solve $3(2x + 5) > 24$

$$3(2x + 5) > 24$$
$$6x + 15 > 24$$
$$-15 \qquad -15$$
$$6x > 9$$
$$\div 6 \qquad \div 6$$
$$x > \frac{9}{6} \text{ or } \frac{3}{2}$$

Example 2

Solve $-56 \leqslant -2(1 - 3y) + 3y$

$$-56 \leqslant -2 + 6y + 3y$$
$$-56 \leqslant -2 + 9y$$
$$+2 \qquad +2$$
$$-54 \leqslant 9y$$
$$\div 9 \qquad \div 9$$
$$-6 \leqslant y$$
$$y \geqslant -6$$

Exercise 9.11

1 Solve the inequations:

(a) $3(x + 2) > 9$

(b) $2(x + 5) < 20$

(c) $4(y - 2) \leqslant 12$

(d) $5(x + 2) - 2x \geqslant 13$

(e) $4(y + 1) - 3y > 6$

(f) $2(y + 5) - y < 19$

(g) $3y + 2(y + 1) \leqslant 12$

(h) $2x - (x - 3) > 7$

(i) $5(y - 1) + 3y \geqslant 3$

(j) $5(v - 3) + 4v < 30$

(k) $8t + 2(1 + t) \leqslant 50$

(l) $5p + 3(2 + p) < 8$

2 Solve:

(a) $3(2n + 1) + 2(n + 6) < 47$

(b) $8(x - 2) \geqslant 3(x + 3)$

(c) $7(x + 1) + 3(x + 2) > 23$

(d) $\frac{1}{2}(8x + 6) \leqslant 7$

(e) $5(6 - p) \leqslant p$

(f) $3(7x - 5) - 2x \leqslant 4$

(g) $3(x + 1) > x + 5$

(h) $3(2x - 1) < 2(2x + 3)$

(i) $2(4 - 3x) < 4(x - 5)$

(j) $5t - 9(t - 1) \geqslant 3t + 5$

(k) $2(n + 1) + 3(2n + 3) \geqslant 18$

(l) $3(2x + 7) > 2(5x - 3)$

Review exercise 9

1 Simplify:

(**a**) $5m + 2m$ (**b**) $6p + 3p - p$ (**c**) $3m + 2n - m + 6n$

2 Solve:

(**a**) $5x + 3 = 13$ (**b**) $23 = 4n - 1$ (**c**) $7 = 11 - 2p$

3 Expand:

(**a**) $4(3y + 2)$ (**b**) $7(3r - 2s + t)$ (**c**) $-4(5f + 3g - h)$

4 Simplify:

(**a**) $2(3p + 7q) + 5p$ (**b**) $3(x - 4y) + 2(4x - y)$ (**c**) $5(m - n) - 2(2m - n)$

5 Solve:

(**a**) $6(2y + 1) = 42$ (**b**) $25 = 5(x - 3)$ (**c**) $-3(2p + 4) = -24$

6 Solve:

(**a**) $4x + 3 = 3x + 10$ (**b**) $5y - 2 = 7y + 2$ (**c**) $-4s - 1 = 3s - 71$

7 Solve:

(**a**) $3(2x + 4) = 2(x + 16)$ (**b**) $4(3x - 1) = -2(x + 16)$ (**c**) $\dfrac{x}{3} = \dfrac{x - 4}{2}$

8 Factorise:

(**a**) $8x + 10y$ (**b**) $18m - 42n$ (**c**) $9f - 15g + 21h$

9 For each description, form an equation and solve it.

(**a**) John thinks of a number. He adds 11 and doubles his answer. His total is 50. What is his number?

(**b**) The sum of $5y$ and $2y$ is -63. Find y.

10 Solve each inequation:

(**a**) $9p + 11 > 29$ (**b**) $-5 < 4m - 17$ (**c**) $3(2x - 1) \geqslant 4x - 2$

Summary

Simplify

$$4(7x + 2y - 3) - 2(x - 8) + 9$$
$$= 28x + 8y - 12 - 2x + 16 + 9$$
$$= 28x - 2x + 8y - 12 + 16 + 9$$
$$= \mathbf{26x + 8y + 13}$$

> Expand the brackets.

> Simplify

Solve equations

$$
\begin{aligned}
2(3x + 1) &= 4(2x + 3) - 18 \\
6x + 2 &= 8x + 12 - 18 \\
6x + 2 &= 8x - 6
\end{aligned}
$$

> Expand

> Simplify

$-6x$ $-6x$

$$2 = 2x - 6$$

$+6$ $+6$

$$8 = 2x$$

$\div 2$ $\div 2$

$$4 = x$$
$$\mathbf{x = 4}$$

Factorise

$$
\begin{array}{ll}
24y - 36z & 10f - 12g + 22h \\
= \mathbf{12(2y - 3z)} & = \mathbf{2(5f - 6g + 11h)}
\end{array}
$$

Solve inequations

$$
\begin{aligned}
7(6 - 2y) &\geqslant 81 - y \\
42 - 14y &\geqslant 81 - y
\end{aligned}
$$

$+14y$ $+14y$

$$42 \geqslant 81 + 13y$$

-81 -81

$$-39 \geqslant 13y$$

$\div 13$ $\div 13$

$$-3 \geqslant y$$
$$\mathbf{y \leqslant -3}$$

10 Enlarging and reducing

In this chapter you will enlarge or reduce shapes using a scale factor.

10.1 Enlargement and reduction

A shape may be enlarged or reduced using a **scale factor**.
A scale factor multiplies the length of every side of a shape.
A scale factor greater than 1 will **enlarge** a shape.
A scale factor between 0 and 1 will **reduce** a shape.

Example 1
Enlarge the blue shape by a scale factor of 3

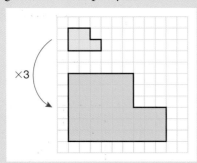

Example 2
Reduce the blue shape by a scale factor of $\frac{1}{2}$

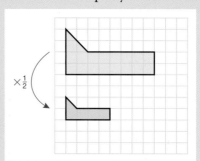

Exercise 10.1

1 (**a**) Copy each shape.

(**b**) Enlarge each shape by a scale factor of 2.

(**c**) Reduce each shape by a scale factor of $\frac{1}{2}$.

(**i**)
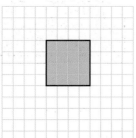

(**ii**)
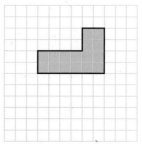

(**iii**)
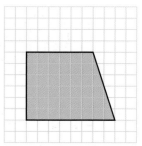

2 Enlarge each shape by a scale factor of 3.

(**a**)
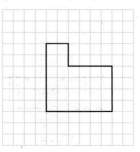

(**b**)
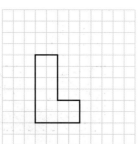

(**c**)
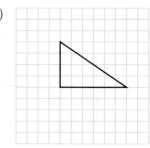

3 Reduce each shape by a scale factor of $\frac{1}{3}$.

(**a**)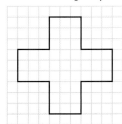

(**b**)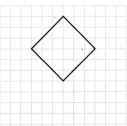

(**c**)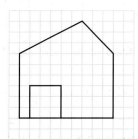

4 For each shape use the scale factor given to draw an enlargement or reduction.

(**a**)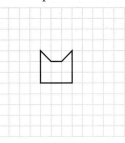

Scale factor 4

(**b**)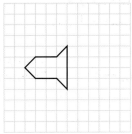

Scale factor 3

(**c**)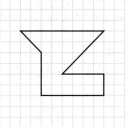

Scale factor $\frac{1}{2}$

(**d**)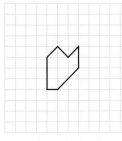

Scale factor 5

(**e**)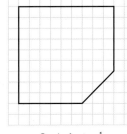

Scale factor $\frac{1}{3}$

(**f**)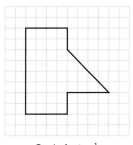

Scale factor $\frac{1}{4}$

5 For each sketch draw an enlargement or reduction using the given scale factor.

(**a**)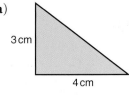

Scale factor 2

(**b**)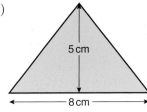

Scale factor $\frac{1}{2}$

(**c**)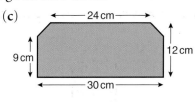

Scale factor $\frac{1}{3}$

6 Each **green** shape has been enlarged or reduced to form the **red** shape. Identify the scale factor used in each case:

(**a**)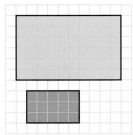

(**b**)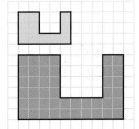

(**c**)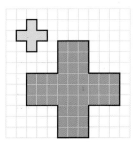

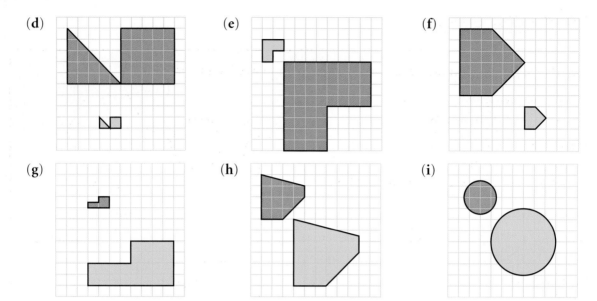

7 Each logo has been enlarged or reduced. Find the scale factor used in each case:

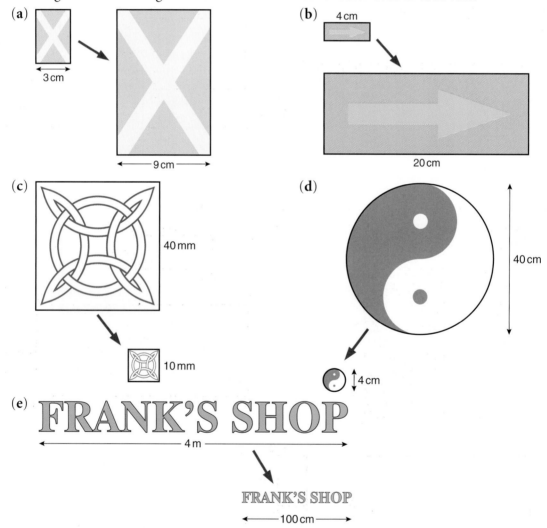

8 Would each scale factor enlarge or reduce a shape?

(**a**) 2 (**b**) 16 (**c**) $\frac{1}{3}$ (**d**) 3·5 (**e**) $\frac{2}{5}$ (**f**) $\frac{5}{2}$

10.2 Similar shapes

Objects are said to be **similar** if one is an enlargement or reduction of the other.

The regular hexagons shown have different sizes but are similar shapes.

For shapes to be similar they must be equiangular and have corresponding sides in proportion.

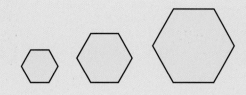

Example

Show that rectangles ABCD and PQRS are similar.

$$\frac{\text{length PQ}}{\text{length AB}} = \frac{10}{4} = \frac{5}{2}$$

$$\frac{\text{breadth PS}}{\text{breadth AD}} = \frac{7\cdot5}{3} = \frac{15}{6} = \frac{5}{2}$$

The shapes are equiangular (right angled) and corresponding sides are in proportion.

Hence rectangles are similar and the scale factor is 2·5.

Exercise 10.2

1 Which pairs of rectangles below are similar? Justify your answer.

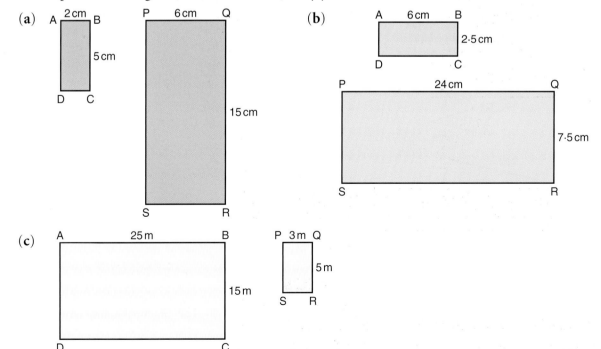

2 Which pairs of shapes are similar? Justify your answer.

(a)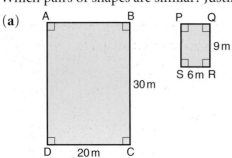

(b)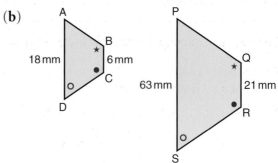

(c)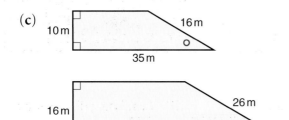

(d)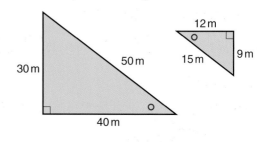

(e)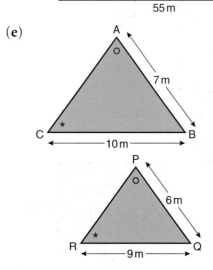

(f)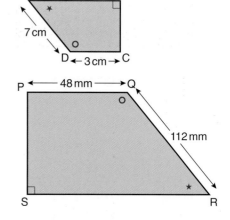

3 Find the scale factor in each pair of similar shapes:

(a)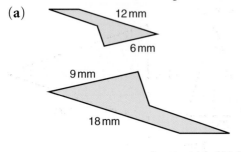

(b)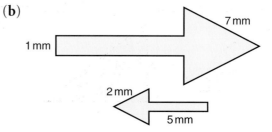

(c)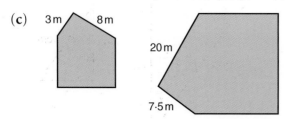

10.3 Calculating dimensions of similar shapes

For two similar shapes, the scale factor may be used to calculate the length of a side.

Example

Photographs A and B are similar.

Find the scale factor and calculate the breadth of photograph B.

$$\text{Scale factor} = \frac{\text{length of B}}{\text{length of A}} = \frac{21}{7} = 3$$

breadth B = 3 × breadth A

$x = 3 \times 4 = 12$ breadth of B is **12 cm**.

Exercise 10.3

1 For each pair of similar rectangles find **(i)** the scale factor   **(ii)** the missing dimension x.

(a)

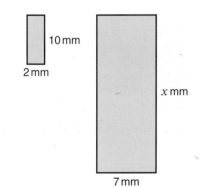

(b)

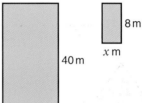

(c)

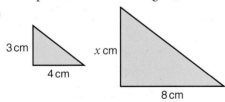

(d)

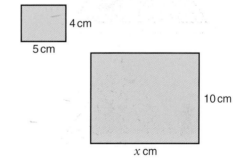

2 For each pair of similar triangles, find the missing dimension x:

(a)

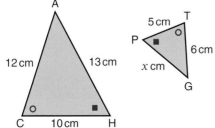

(b)

(c)

(d)

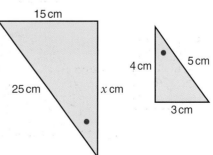

3 Each photograph is a reduction from an original.
For each (**i**) measure the height of the photograph
(**ii**) calculate the scale factor
(**iii**) measure the width of the photograph
(**iv**) calculate the width of the original.

(**a**)

Original height 54 cm

(**b**)

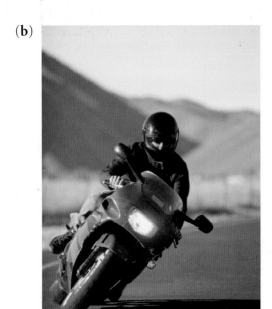

Original height 96 cm

(**c**)

Original height 65 cm

(**d**)

Original height 60 cm

(**e**)

Original height 77 cm

Review exercise 10

1 Would each scale factor enlarge or reduce a shape?

(**a**) 3 　　　　　　　　　(**b**) 12

(**c**) 0·9 　　　　　　　　(**d**) $\frac{1}{10}$

2 (**a**) Enlarge each shape by a scale factor of 3.

(**b**) Reduce each shape by a scale factor of $\frac{1}{2}$.

(**i**) 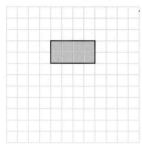 　　(**ii**) 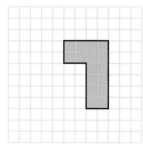 　　(**iii**)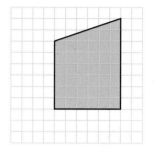

3 Find the scale factor used in reducing or enlarging each **red** shape to the **blue** shape:.

(**a**) 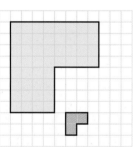 　　　　(**b**)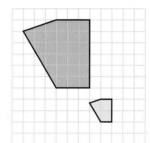

4 Show that each pair of rectangles is similar:

(**a**) 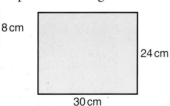 　　　　(**b**)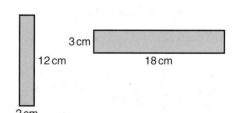

5 For each pair of similar shapes, find the scale factor and calculate *x*.

(**a**) 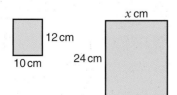 　　　　(**b**)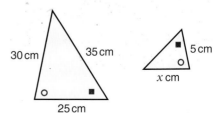

Summary

Enlargement and reduction

A shape may be enlarged or reduced using a scale factor.
A scale factor multiplies the length of every side of a shape.

A scale factor greater than 1 will enlarge a shape.
A scale factor between 0 and 1 will reduce a shape.

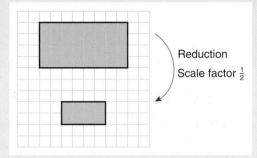

Reduction
Scale factor $\frac{1}{2}$

Similar shapes

Objects are said to be similar if one is an enlargement
or reduction of the other.

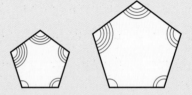

Similar shapes are equiangular and have corresponding sides in proportion.

The length of a side in a **similar** shape may be found using the scale factor.

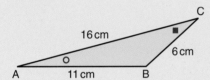

Scale factor $\dfrac{RQ}{BC} = \dfrac{15}{6} = \dfrac{5}{2}$

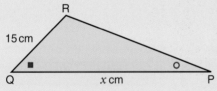

so $x = \dfrac{5}{2} \times 16 = 40$ cm

11 Circles

In this chapter you will learn how to calculate the circumference and area of a circle.

11.1 The circumference of a circle

Circumference – the distance around a circle.

Radius – the line from the centre of the circle to the circumference.

Diameter – the line across a circle from circumference to circumference, passing through the centre.

The circumference of a circle can be difficult to measure.

The diameter is often much easier to measure.

Throughout history mathematicians have looked for the relationship between the diameter and the circumference.

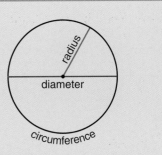

Exercise 11.1

You need five circular objects and a measuring tape.

1 (a) Copy the table below.

Object	Diameter (*d*)	Circumference (C)

(b) Measure the diameter and the circumference of each circle to the nearest centimetre and put your results in the table.

(c) What do you think the relationship is between the circumference and diameter?

2 For each circle estimate the circumference.

(**a**)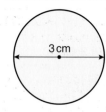

3 cm

(**b**)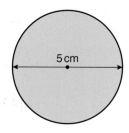

5 cm

(**c**)

20 mm

3 For each circle estimate the diameter.

(**a**)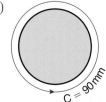

C = 90 mm

(**b**)

C = 45 mm

(**c**)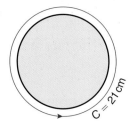

C = 21 cm

11.2 Circumference and diameter

Exercise 11.2

diameter 42 mm
circumference 132 mm

diameter 35 mm
circumference 110 mm

diameter 13·5 mm
circumference 42·4 mm

diameter 19·3 mm
circumference 60·6 mm

diameter 28·5 mm
circumference 89·4 mm

diameter 58 mm
circumference 182 mm

 1 Use the measurements from the diagrams above to copy and complete the table.

Item	Circumference (C)	Diameter (d)	Circumference ÷ Diameter	
			Calculator answer	Rounded to 2 d.p.

2 Copy and complete:
More accurately, the circumference of a circle is _____ times the diameter.

3 Throughout history there have been many approximations for this number. Excluding the 17th and 21st centuries, which of these is closest to today's value of π?

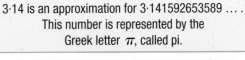

3·14 is an approximation for 3·141592653589 …. . This number is represented by the Greek letter π, called pi.

The Bible, Book of Kings

Babylon 2000 B.C.

Egypt 1650 B.C.

Greece 250 B.C.

China 480 A.D.

Pi computed to 35 decimal places. William Jones first used the symbol π in the 17th century.

4 There are a number of ways to find π.
This series gives a more and more accurate value for π.

$$\frac{4}{1} - \frac{4}{3} + \frac{4}{5} - \frac{4}{7} \ldots\ldots$$

(**a**) Copy and extend this series for ten terms.

(**b**) What value would you have after
  (**i**) ten terms   (**ii**) thirty terms?

11.3 Calculating the circumference

The formula **C = πd**, where π = 3·14 to 2 decimal places, can be used to calculate the circumference.

Example
Calculate the circumferences of each circle to 1 decimal place:

(a)
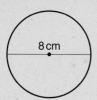
8 cm

(b)

30 mm

| The radius is 30 millimetres so the diameter is 60 millimetres. |

(a) C = πd

C = 3·14 × 8

C = **25·1** centimetres

$$\begin{array}{r} 3 \cdot 14 \\ \times \quad 8 \\ \hline 25 \cdot 12 \\ {\scriptstyle 1 \ 3} \end{array}$$

(b) C = πd

C = 3·14 × 60

C = **188·4** millimetres

| The π button on a scientific calculator may be used here. |

Exercise 11.3

In this exercise round answers appropriately.

1 Without using a calculator, use C = πd, where π = 3·14, to calculate the circumference of each circle.

(a)

9 mm

(b)

30 cm

(c)

500 mm

(d)

43 cm

Use 3·14 or the π button to answer the following questions.

2 Use the formula C = πd to calculate the circumference of each circle.

(a)

12 cm

(b)

19 cm

(c)
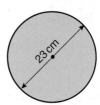
23 cm

3 Calculate the circumference of each circle.

(a)

16 cm

(b)

20 cm

(c)

13.5 cm

4 The diameter of the London Eye is 122 metres.
Calculate its circumference.

5 The radius of the earth is 6378 kilometres.
Calculate the distance around the equator.

6 (**a**) Find the length of lace needed to edge each of these cushions.

Diameter = 36 cm   Diameter = 0·8 m

(**b**) Lace can be bought in multiples of 10 centimetres.
What length of lace must be bought to edge **both** cushions?

7 Without using a calculator, use $\pi = \dfrac{22}{7}$ to calculate the

circumferences of the following circles:

(**a**) 70 cm

(**b**) 49 cm

(**c**) 84 cm

(**d**) 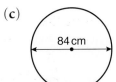 115·5 cm

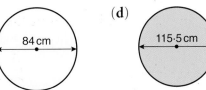

8 Without using a calculator, use $\pi = \dfrac{22}{7}$ to calculate the

circumferences of the following circles:

(**a**) 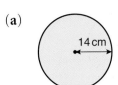 14 cm

(**b**) 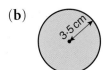 3·5 cm

(**c**) 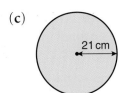 21 cm

(**d**) 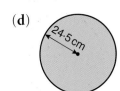 24.5 cm

11.4 Problems involving circumference

Example 1

Calculate how far this wheel will turn in 15 revolutions.

In one revolution the wheel will travel a distance equal to the circumference.

$$C = \pi d$$
$$C = 3{\cdot}14 \times 45$$
$$= 141{\cdot}3 \text{ cm}$$

15 revolutions = $15 \times 141{\cdot}3$
$$= 2119{\cdot}5$$
$$= \textbf{2120 cm} \text{ to 3 sig. figs.}$$

Example 2

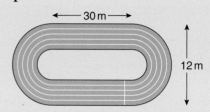

Calculate the perimeter of this sports track.

Perimeter = 2 semicircles + 2 straights

$$C = \pi d$$
$$C = 3{\cdot}14 \times 12$$
$$= 37{\cdot}68 \text{ m}$$

Perimeter = $37{\cdot}68 + 30 + 30$
$$= \textbf{97{\cdot}7 m} \text{ to 3 sig. figs.}$$

Exercise 11.4

In this exercise round answers appropriately.

1 Calculate how far this bicycle wheel will travel in
   (**a**) one revolution
   (**b**) fifty revolutions.

62 cm

2 A thread bobbin has diameter 2·5 centimetres.
   Thread wraps around the bobbin 330 times. How long is the thread?

3 The base tier of a cake has diameter 41·5 centimetres.
   The diameter of the middle tier is 8 centimetres smaller.
   The diameter of the top tier is 10 centimetres smaller than the middle.
   What length of ribbon is needed to go around all three tiers of this cake?

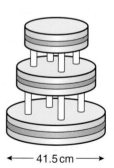

41.5 cm

4 The minute hand on a clock is 12·3 centimetres long.
   How far will the tip of the minute hand travel in:

   (**a**) one hour   (**b**) half an hour   (**c**) quarter of an hour?

5 A replica of Foucault's pendulum is to be constructed in a museum.
   The metal circular scale is to be fitted into a square hall of length
   45 metres. Calculate the circumference of the circular scale.

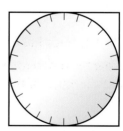

6 Calculate the perimeter of each athletics track.

(a)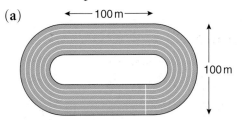

(b)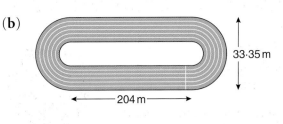

7 Rachel makes jewellery edged with silver wire.
Calculate the length of wire she needs for each item.

(a)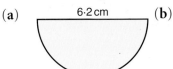

(b)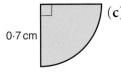

(c)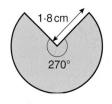

8 The front wheel of the world's largest bicycle has a diameter of 3·05 metres.

(a) How far will this wheel travel in 20 revolutions?

(b) How many times will this wheel revolve in 1 kilometre?

9 In 1999 a cyclist rode 4570 kilometres across America on one wheel of his bicycle. If the diameter of the wheel was 58 centimetres, how many revolutions did the wheel turn?

10 A tractor has large wheels of diameter 1·5 metres and small wheels of diameter 0·5 metres. Calculate:

(a) the circumference of a large wheel

(b) the circumference of a small wheel

(c) how far the tractor travels in 30 revolutions of the large wheel

(d) the number of revolutions made by the small wheel over the same distance.

11 Calculate the dimensions of the label for this tin.

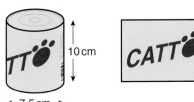

12 An athletics track has 6 lanes each 1·25 metres wide.

Calculate the difference in length between the inside and outside edges of the track.

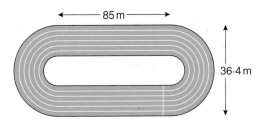

13 Ronald and Donald decide to measure the circumference of the earth. Ronald measures by putting his extra-long measuring tape at ground level. Donald measures one metre above the ground at all times. What is the difference between their measurements?

11.5 Finding the diameter

Example
Find the diameter of a circle which has circumference 148 centimetres.

diameter

$$C = \pi d$$
$$148 = \pi d$$
$$\frac{148}{\pi} = d$$
$$\frac{148}{3\cdot14} = d$$
$$d = 47\cdot1$$

The diameter is **47·1 centimetres** to 3 sig. figs.

Exercise 11.5

1 Find the diameter of each circle.

(a)

Circumference = 50 cm

(b)

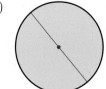

Circumference = 137 cm

(c)

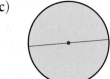

Circumference = 98 cm

2 Find the radius of each circle.

(a)

Circumference = 400 cm

(b)

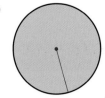

Circumference = 63 cm

(c)

Circumference = 12 cm

3 The circular boating pond in Galmerton park has a circumference of 140 metres. Calculate its diameter.

4 The traditional British golf ball had a circumference of 12·9 centimetres. In 1974 the American golf ball, with a circumference of 13·4 centimetres, replaced it. Calculate the diameters of the British and American golf balls correct to 3 significant figures.

5 Alison needs a card circle with a 1 metre circumference to make a trundle wheel. She can only buy square pieces of card. What are the dimensions of the smallest piece of card she will need to use, to the nearest centimetre?

6 The tunnel for the accelerator ring of CERN's particle accelerator is 27 kilometres in circumference.
Find its diameter to the nearest metre.

7 James is investigating the growth of a tree. In 1988 the circumference of the tree trunk was 120 centimetres. In 2005 the circumference was 190 centimetres.

(**a**) What was the increase in diameter?

(**b**) A tree trunk has a ring for every year. Calculate the average width of the rings which have been added since 1988.

8 Rosie had a piece of card 20 centimetres by 15 centimetres. If she rolls the card up to make a cylinder with no overlap, find

(**a**) the largest diameter of cylinder she could make

(**b**) the smallest diameter of cylinder she could make.

11.6 Area of a circle

Drawing circles on centimetre squared paper will give an approximate value for the area.

The approximate area of this circle is 12 squares.

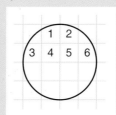

Exercise 11.6

You need centimetre squared paper and a pair of compasses.

1 (**a**) Copy the table opposite.

(**b**) Draw a circle with radius 2 centimetres.
Count the squares to find the approximate area and record your results in the table.

(**c**) Repeat for circles with radius 3 centimetres and 4 centimetres.

(**d**) Complete the table.

(**e**) Copy and complete: The area of a circle is about ☐ × r^2.

Radius (r)	r^2	Area (A)
2	4	
3		
4		
5		
6		

2 Estimate the area of these circles.

(**a**)

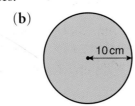

7 cm

(**b**)

10 cm

(**c**)

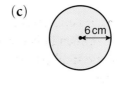

6 cm

11.7 Calculating the area of a circle

The formula $A = \pi r^2$, where $\pi = 3 \cdot 14$, can be used to calculate the area of a circle.

Example
Calculate the area of each circle.

(a)

12 cm

$A = \pi r^2$
$A = 3 \cdot 14 \times 12^2$
$A = 3 \cdot 14 \times 144$
$A = 452 \cdot 16$

The area is **452 cm²** to 3 sig. figs.

(b)

16 cm

$A = \pi r^2$
$A = 3 \cdot 14 \times 8^2$
$A = 3 \cdot 14 \times 64$
$A = 200 \cdot 96$

$d = 16$ cm
$r = 8$ cm

The area is **201 cm²** to 3 sig. figs.

Exercise 11.7

1 Without using a calculator, calculate the area of each circle.

(a) 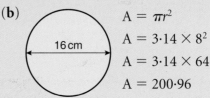 20 cm

(b) 10 cm

(c) 2 mm

(d) 4 cm

Use 3·14 or the π button to answer the following questions.

 2 Calculate the area of each circle.

(a) 68 cm

(b) 27 cm

(c) 23·7 cm

3 Calculate the area of each circle.

(a) 32 cm

(b) 57 cm

(c) 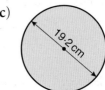 19·2 cm

4 The sweep on a radar screen is 15 centimetres. Calculate the area it sweeps out.

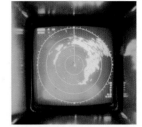

5 A circular area of grass underneath Mr Paterson's compost bin has been damaged. If the diameter of the base of the bin is 87 centimetres, calculate the area of damaged grass.

11.8 Problems involving area

Example 1
Calculate the area of this washer.

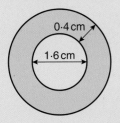

Small area $= \pi \times 0.8^2 = 2.0106$

Large area $= \pi \times 1.2^2 = 4.5239$

Area of washer $= 4.5239 - 2.0106$

$= 2.5133$

Area of washer $= \textbf{2.5 cm}^2$ to 2 sig. figs.

Example 2
Calculate the area of this tray.

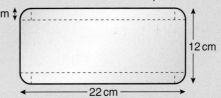

Area = 1 circle + 1 large rectangle
+ 2 small rectangles

$= (\pi \times 2^2) + (22 \times 8) + 2(18 \times 2)$

$= 12.56 + 176 + 72$

$= 260.56$

Area of tray $= \textbf{261 cm}^2$ to 3 sig. figs.

Exercise 11.8

1 A pond with diameter 3 metres has a path
60 centimetres wide around it. Calculate:

(**a**) the area of the pond

(**b**) the area of the path.

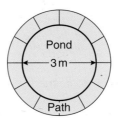

2 Raymond is planting a circular lawn of diameter 8 metres.

(**a**) Calculate the area of the lawn.

(**b**) 100 grammes of lawn seed are used per square metre. How many
kilogrammes of seed are needed for the whole lawn?

3 These table tops are made up from rectangles and semi-circles.
Calculate the area of each table top.

(**a**)

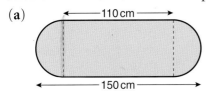

(**b**)

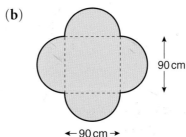

4 Calculate the total area of this tray. The corners form quarter circles.

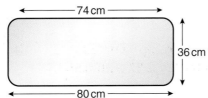

5 **(a)** In the diagrams below which shaded area do you think is greatest?

(a)

(b)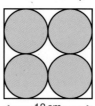

(c)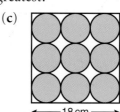

(b) For each diagram above, calculate the shaded area.

6 Lynn is making a cape for a fancy dress party.
Calculate the area of material used.

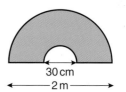

7 Pete is making a circular table top.
He thinks that if he doubles the diameter he
will double the area. Is he correct? Explain your answer.

11.9 Lengths of arcs

An **arc** is a section of the circumference of a circle.

The length of an arc is in direct proportion to the angle at the centre.

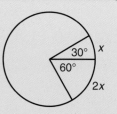

Example
Calculate the arc length in each circle.

(a)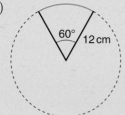

(b)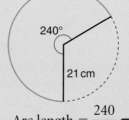

$$C = \pi d$$
$$= 3\cdot14 \times 24$$
$$= 75\cdot36$$

$$\text{Arc length} = \frac{60}{360} \times 75\cdot36$$
$$= \frac{1}{6} \times 75\cdot36$$
$$= \textbf{12·6 cm to 3 sig. figs.}$$

$$\text{Arc length} = \frac{240}{360}\pi d$$
$$= \frac{2}{3} \times \pi \times 42$$
$$= 87\cdot96\ldots$$
$$\text{Arc length} = \textbf{87·96 cm to 2 dec. pl.}$$

Exercise 11.9

1 Calculate the length of each arc:

(a)

15 cm

(b)

45°
7 cm

(c)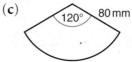

120° 80 mm

(d)

30°
12 cm

(e)
10·2 cm   72°

(f)
36°
20 cm

(g)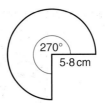
270°
5·8 cm

(h)
300°
6·3 mm

2 How far does the tip of the minute hand move in:
  (a) five minutes
  (b) 15 minutes?

3 Calculate the perimeter of these flower beds including the straight edges.

(a)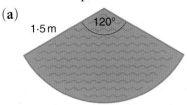
1·5 m   120°

(c)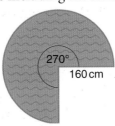
270°
160 cm

11.10 Area of sectors

A **sector** is a section of a circle enclosed
by two radii and an arc.
The area of a sector is in direct proportion to the angle at the centre.

Example
Calculate the area of the sector in each circle

(a)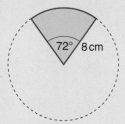
72°   8 cm

(b)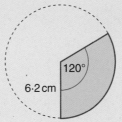
120°
6·2 cm

$A = \pi r^2$

$\quad = 3 \cdot 14 \times 8^2$

$\quad = 200 \cdot 96$

Sector area $= \dfrac{72}{360} \times 200 \cdot 96$

$\quad = \textbf{40·2 cm}^2$ to 3 sig. figs

Sector area $= \dfrac{120}{360} \, \pi r^2$

$\quad = \dfrac{1}{3} \pi \times 6 \cdot 2^2$

$\quad = 40 \cdot 25\ldots$

Sector area $= \textbf{40·3 cm}^2$ to 3 sig. figs

Exercise 11.10

1 Calculate the area of each sector.

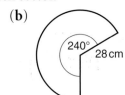
(a)
38 cm 60°

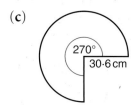
(b)
240° 28 cm

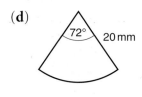
(c)
270° 30·6 cm

(d)
72° 20 mm

2 Richard buys a 12 inch diameter circular pizza. He shares it equally with 3 of his friends. What is the area of each slice?

3 Calculate the area of one cheese label

5 cm

4 A baby rattle is made up from sectors of circles. Calculate the area of each piece.

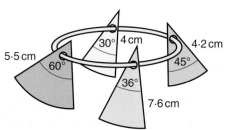
5·5 cm   30° 4 cm   4·2 cm
60°   45°
36°
7·6 cm

5 Calculate the area of the orange section of this javelin field.

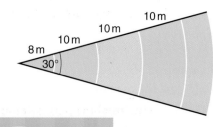
10 m
10 m
10 m
8 m
30°

6 **(a)** Calculate the area of the sector AOB.
(b) Calculate the area of the triangle AOB.
(c) Hence calculate the red area.

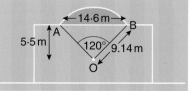
←14·6 m→ B
A
5·5 m   120° 9.14 m
O

7 Farmer McDonald attaches his goat to a fence post in the corner of the field using a 10 metre rope.

(a) Calculate the maximum area of grass the goat can graze.

(b) Farmer McDonald moves the goat to each corner post in turn, but each time he cannot untie the rope and has to cut 0·2 m from it. Calculate the area of the field on which the goat will not have been able to graze.

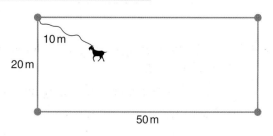
10 m
20 m
50 m

Draw a sketch to help

Review exercise 11

In this exercise, round the answers appropriately.

1 Calculate the circumference of each circle.

(a)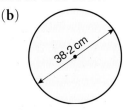
16 cm

(b)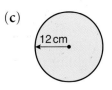
38.2 cm

(c)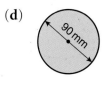
12 cm

(d)
90 mm

2 Calculate the area of each circle.

(a)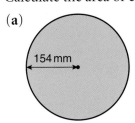
154 mm

(b)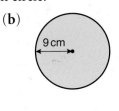
9 cm

(c)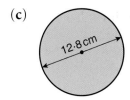
12.8 cm

(d)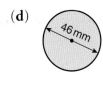
46 mm

3 A water pipe in John's house has a circumference of 17 centimetres. Calculate the diameter of the pipe giving your answer correct to one decimal place.

4 Emma is using a cylindrical washing up liquid bottle to make a boat. The circumference of the bottle is 30 centimetres. If she cuts the bottle in half lengthways to make the boat, what will the maximum depth be?

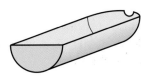

5 Calculate the total (a) perimeter and (b) area of this tray.

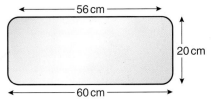
56 cm
20 cm
60 cm

6 Mr Parker is putting corrugated edging around **both** edges of his path.

(a) Calculate the length of edging he will need.

(b) Calculate the area of the path.

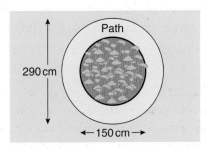
Path
290 cm
150 cm

7

40 cm

20 cm

Neon lighting is being used to make the above sign.
Calculate the total length of lighting required.

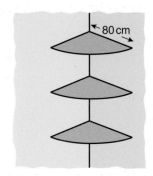

80 cm

8 Archie is making a corner unit with three shelves.
Each shelf forms a quarter circle.
Calculate the area of wood he needs to make the shelves.

9 Calculate the length of each arc.

(a)

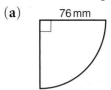

76 mm

(b)

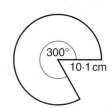

72° 8·2 cm

(c)

300° 10·1 cm

10 Calculate the area of each sector.

(a)

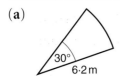

30° 6·2 m

(b)

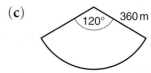

36° 4·3 cm

(c)

120° 360 m

11 A sprinkler jets water a distance of 2·5 m.
Calculate the area the sprinkler covers if the jet rotates 120°.

Summary

Circumference – the distance around a circle.

Radius – the line from the centre of the circle to the circumference.

Diameter – the line across a circle from circumference to circumference, passing through the centre.

$$\text{Circumference } C = \pi d$$

$$\text{Area} \qquad A = \pi r^2$$

where $\pi = 3\cdot14$ to 2 decimal places

Arc – a section of the circumference of the circle.

Sector – a section of the area of a circle enclosed by two radii and an arc.

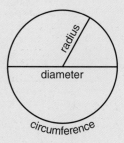

radius

diameter

circumference

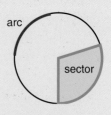

arc

sector

12 Time, distance and speed

In this chapter you will review calculations of speed, distance and time, and extend this knowledge to distance–time graphs.

12.1 Time – fractions and decimals

Remember

Example 1
Change 3·8 hours to hours and minutes.
0·8 × 60 = 48
Hence 3·8 hours = **3 hrs 48 mins**

Example 2
Change 2 hours 18 minutes to hours.
18 ÷ 60 = 0·3
Hence 2 hrs 18 mins = **2·3 hours**

Exercise 12.1

1 Change to hours and minutes:
   (**a**) 3·7 hours   (**b**) 3·3 hours   (**c**) 4·9 hours   (**d**) 10·2 hours
   (**e**) $1\frac{3}{10}$ hours   (**f**) $5\frac{7}{10}$ hours   (**g**) $1\frac{3}{5}$ hours   (**h**) $3\frac{5}{6}$ hours

2 Write in hours:
   (**a**) 2 hr 15 min   (**b**) 4 hr 30 min   (**c**) 18 minutes   (**d**) 1 hr 45 min
   (**e**) 1 hr 6 min   (**f**) 2 hr 42 min   (**g**) 1 hr 24 min   (**h**) 3 hr 54 min

12.2 Use of formulae to calculate speed, distance and time

During most journeys vehicles speed up, slow down and at times stop.
So for most journeys we should consider **average speed**.

Remember:
The three formulae to calculate speed, distance and time can be summarized in a diagram.

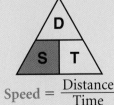

$$\text{Speed} = \frac{\text{Distance}}{\text{Time}}$$

$$\text{Distance} = \text{Speed} \times \text{Time}$$

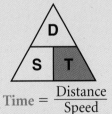

$$\text{Time} = \frac{\text{Distance}}{\text{Speed}}$$

Example 1
Calculate the average speed of a bus which takes 4 hrs 30 mins to travel 171 kilometres.

$$\text{Speed} = \frac{D}{T} = \frac{171}{4.5} = 38$$

Average speed = **38 km/h**

Example 2
How far can Joe walk in 5 hours 20 mins at an average walking speed of 3 miles per hour?

$$\text{Distance} = S \times T$$
$$= 3 \times 5\frac{1}{3} = 16$$

Jo can walk **16 miles**

Example 3
An Olympic cyclist recorded an average speed of 36 kilometres per hour. How long did he take for an 81 kilometre race?

$$\text{Time} = \frac{D}{S} = \frac{81}{36} = 2.25$$

He took $2\frac{1}{4}$ **hrs** or **2 hrs 15 mins**

Exercise 12.2

1 It took John 4 hours 30 minutes to cycle the 54 miles between
   Glasgow and Edinburgh. Calculate the average speed for the journey.

2 It took Tom 5 hours 20 minutes to drive from Edinburgh to
   Liverpool at an average speed of 45 miles per hour.
   How far is it from Edinburgh to Liverpool?

3 The distance from Inverness to Penzance is 725 miles.
   How long would a journey between the two towns take at an average
   speed of 50 miles per hour?

4 Owen is a long distance lorry driver. Here is his log for a trip from
   Cardiff to France. Calculate his average speed to the nearest
   kilometre per hour for each leg of the journey.

	Date	From / Departure time	To / Arrival time	Distance
	DRIVER'S LOG		**TRUCK No** _26_	
	Name _Owen Hughes_		Employee No _0068435_	
(a)	20/10/05	Cardiff / 0345	Portsmouth / 0730	210 km
(b)	20/10/05	Portsmouth / 0830 (ship)	Caen / 1315	160 km
(c)	20/10/05	Caen / 1500	Paris / 1820	240 km
(d)	21/10/05	Paris / 1100	Roscoff / 2215	585 km
(e)	21/10/05	Roscoff / 2330 (ship)	Plymouth / 0530	180 km
(f)	21/10/05	Plymouth / 0610	Cardiff / 0958	266 km

5 Emma works for a national haulage firm. She uses these estimates of
   average speeds.

> 50 mph on motorway journeys under 100 miles
> 46 mph on motorway journeys over 100 miles
> 40 mph on main roads
> 35 mph on minor roads

> M – motorway
> A – main road

For each journey calculate the estimated time in hours and minutes.
   (a) Edinburgh to Sunderland, 120 miles on the A1.
   (b) Carlisle to Shrewsbury, 184 miles on the M6 and M54.
   (c) London to Birmingham, 115 miles on the M40.
   (d) Bristol to Exeter, 75 miles on the M5.
   (e) Oxford to Southampton, 70 miles on the A34.
   (f) Cardiff to Swansea, 40 miles on the M4.
   (g) Llandovery to Oswestry, 77 miles on minor roads.
   (h) Exeter to Barnstaple, 42 miles on minor roads.

6 On a cycling holiday Adam averaged 48 kilometres per day.
He took three rest days during his two week holiday. Find the total
distance he cycled.

7 David drives a van from Cardiff to Edinburgh.
On one trip he picked up parcels at the towns on the map.
Journey times and average speeds are also shown for each section of
the journey.
Calculate the distance he travelled on each section.

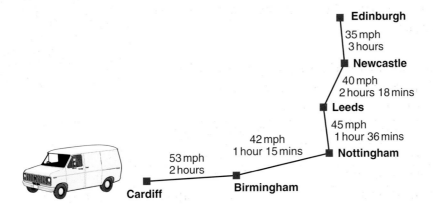

8 Hamish has to transport goods from Motherwell to Leeds,
a distance of 220 miles. He leaves at 11 am and the factory in Leeds
closes at 4.30 pm.
  (a) Calculate the average speed he must maintain to be able to
      deliver his load on time.
  (b) What speed must he maintain on the road if he takes a half hour
      lunch break?

9 A package has to be sent from Cardiff to Germany by the Harwich
ferry. It has to go by van to the ferry, a distance of 246 miles, and the
van is expected to average 50 miles per hour.
If the van leaves at 3 am will it arrive in Harwich in time for an
0745 departure? Explain.

10 The MacDonald family drove from Fort William to Plymouth.
They left at 1515 on Saturday and arrived in Plymouth at 0700 on
Sunday morning.
Mr MacDonald calculated the average speed for their journey as
38 miles per hour.
How far is it from Fort William to Plymouth?

12.3 Changing units of speed

Example 1

Change 72 kilometres per hour to metres per minute.

$$72 \text{ km/h} = 72 \times 1000 \text{ m/h}$$
$$= 72\,000 \div 60 \text{ m/min}$$
$$= \mathbf{1200 \text{ m/min}}$$

Example 2

Change 36 metres per second to kilometres per hour.

$$36 \text{ m/sec} = 36 \times 60 \text{ m/min}$$
$$= 2160 \times 60 \text{ m/hour}$$
$$= 129\,600 \div 1000 \text{ km/h}$$
$$= \mathbf{129 \cdot 6 \text{ km/h}}$$

Exercise 12.3

 1 Change each speed to metres per minute.

(**a**) 60 km/h   (**b**) 180 km/h   (**c**) 540 km/h   (**d**) 330 km/h

2 Change each speed to metres per second.

(**a**) 30 km/h   (**b**) 42 km/h   (**c**) 72 km/h   (**d**) 27 km/h

3 Change each speed to kilometres per hour.

(**a**) 12 m/s   (**b**) 18 m/s   (**c**) 28 m/s   (**d**) 72 m/s

4 (**a**) A lorry is travelling at 42 kilometres per hour.
How many metres will it go in one minute?

(**b**) A cyclist is moving at an average speed of 18 kilometres per hour.
Calculate his speed in metres per second.

(**c**) In a half marathon race John can average 15 kilometres per hour.
What is his average speed in metres/minute?

(**d**) The tug towed the crippled submarine at an average speed of
8 kilometres per hour.
Calculate this speed to the nearest metre per minute.

5 (**a**) The driver of a lorry travelling at 80 kilometres per hour sees a
crash ahead and takes 1 second to put his foot on the brake.
How far, in metres, does the lorry travel in this time?

(**b**) The driver of a van travelling at 100 kilometres per hour glances at
a road map for 2 seconds.
How far, in metres, does the van travel in this time?

(**c**) The driver of a car travelling at 120 kilometres per hour would lose
concentration for 3 seconds if he made a call on his mobile phone.
How many metres would the car travel in this time?

(**d**) The pilot of a jet travelling at 930 kilometres per hour glances at
his instruments for a second.
How many metres will the jet travel in this time?

12.4 Distance–time graphs

The graph illustrates a car journey which starts at Monmouth, goes through Newport and on to Cardiff.

The horizontal axis shows the time since leaving Monmouth.

The vertical axis shows distance in miles from Monmouth.

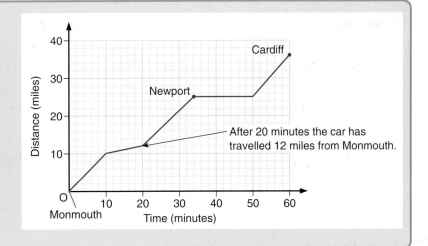

Exercise 12.4

1 From the graph above

(**a**) What is the distance between

    (**i**)   Monmouth and Newport

    (**ii**) Newport and Cardiff?

(**b**) How long is the stop at Newport?

(**c**) The car has to slow down for roadworks between Monmouth and Newport.
What distance do the roadworks cover?

(**d**) How long does it take to drive through the roadworks?

2 The Mackinnons drove from their home in Inverness to Kyle of Lochalsh.

The graph shows times and distances for their journey via Dingwall and Achnasheen.

(**a**) What is the distance between

    (**i**)   Inverness and Dingwall

    (**ii**)   Dingwall and Achnasheen

    (**iii**) Achnasheen and Kyle?

(**b**) Which part of the journey was the slowest?

(**c**) What distance did they cover in the first half hour?

(**d**) If they had not stopped in Achnasheen how long would the journey have taken?

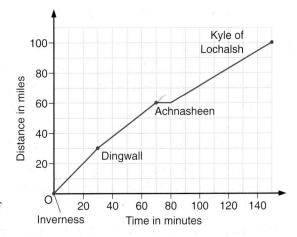

12.5 Calculating speed from graphs

Example

The graph shows the journey from Aberystwyth to Carnarvon.

Find the average speed from Dolgellau to Snowdon.

From Dolgellau to Snowdon

distance = 20 miles

time taken = 30 minutes

$$\text{Speed} = \frac{D}{T}$$

$$= \frac{20 \text{ miles}}{0 \cdot 5 \text{ hours}}$$

$$= 40 \text{ miles per hour}$$

Average speed = **40 miles per hour**

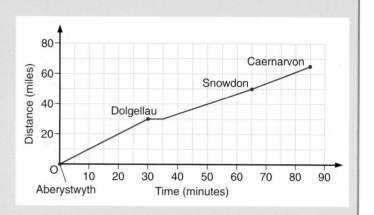

Exercise 12.5

1 For the journey from Aberystwyth to Dolgellau find:

   (**a**) the distance   (**b**) the time taken   (**c**) the average speed.

2 Repeat question **1** for the journey from Snowdon to Caernarvon.

3 From Aberystwyth to Caernarvon find:

   (**a**) the total distance

   (**b**) the journey time **excluding** stops

   (**c**) the average speed to the nearest mile per hour.

4 The graph shows the journey of a delivery van from Glasgow to Perth.

   (**a**) Copy and complete the table.

From	To	Distance miles	Time mins	Speed mph
Glasgow	Stirling			
Stirling	Perth			

   (**b**) If the van had not stopped in Stirling, what would the average speed have been, to the nearest mile per hour?

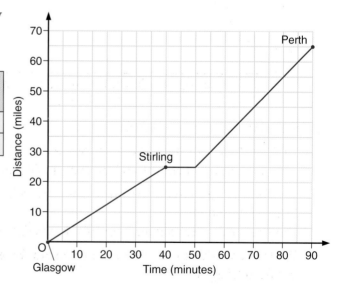

5 The graph shows Bill's drive from Glasgow to Wetherby in the north of England.

(**a**) How far is it from Glasgow to Penrith?

(**b**) How long did Bill stop in Penrith?

(**c**) Which stretch of the journey was the fastest?

(**d**) Did Bill speed up or slow down after he passed Scotch Corner?

(**e**) How far did Bill travel in the first 20 minutes of the journey?

(**f**) Describe the first 20 minutes of Bill's journey.

(**g**) Find:

    (**i**) the total distance from Bill's home to Wetherby

    (**ii**) the total time for Bill's journey including stops.

(**h**) Calculate Bill's average speed for the journey.

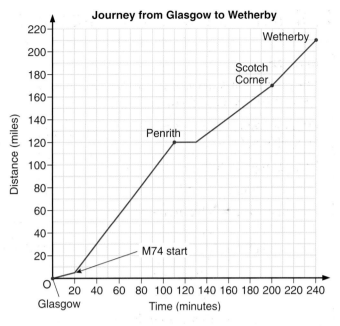

Journey from Glasgow to Wetherby

6 The graph shows Jim's car journey to Newcastle and back.

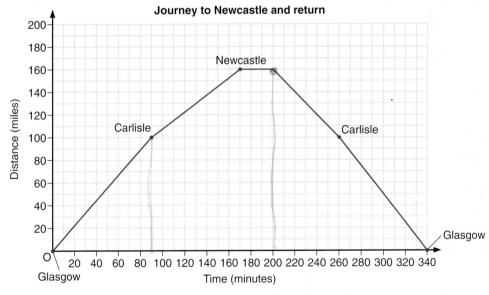

Journey to Newcastle and return

(**a**) Calculate the average speed for

    (**i**) the journey from Glasgow to Newcastle

    (**ii**) the return journey from Newcastle to Glasgow.

(**b**) The route from Glasgow to Carlisle has a speed limit of 70 miles per hour.
Did Jim break the speed limit for this stretch either going or returning?

(**c**) Jim left Newcastle to return home at 8.25 pm. When had he set out from Glasgow?

12.6 Distance charts

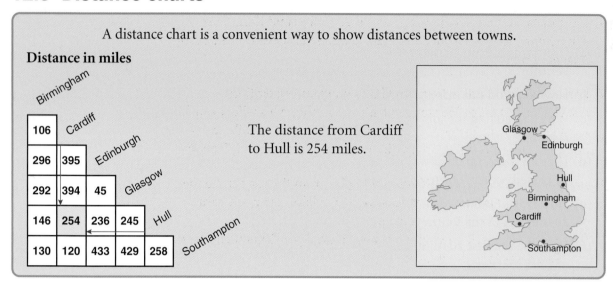

A distance chart is a convenient way to show distances between towns.

Distance in miles

The distance from Cardiff to Hull is 254 miles.

Exercise 12.6

1 Use the chart above to find the distances between:
  (**a**) Birmingham and Hull   (**b**) Edinburgh and Southampton
  (**c**) Glasgow and Hull   (**d**) Cardiff and Glasgow.

2 Use the chart above to calculate the average speed to the nearest mile per hour for each journey:
  (**a**) Glasgow and Southampton in 9 hours
  (**b**) Edinburgh to Hull in 4 hours 30 minutes
  (**c**) Birmingham to Glasgow in 5 hours 45 minutes.

3 Use the chart above to calculate the time for each journey:
  (**a**) Edinburgh to Glasgow at the average speed of 60 miles per hour
  (**b**) Southampton to Cardiff at the average speed of 50 miles per hour
  (**c**) Southampton to Hull at the average speed of 40 miles per hour.

4 Copy and complete this mileage chart using the map to find the shortest distances.

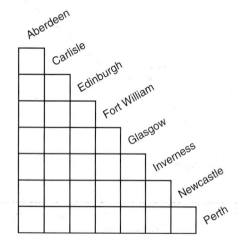
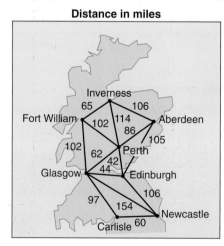

Review exercise 12

1 If the distance from Glasgow to Leeds is 230 miles and Karis takes 4 hr 30 mins for the journey, calculate her average speed to the nearest mile per hour.

2 Karim was driving back home to Hamilton from Wester Ross, a distance of 250 miles. He stopped half way to phone his wife saying he would be home in 2 hours 15 minutes. If he averaged 54 miles per hour for the rest of the journey, did he arrive home in time? Explain.

3 (**a**) Jim took 5 hours and 30 minutes to hike from the car park to the top of Ben Narnain. If the distance is 16·5 kilometres, what was his average speed on the way up?
(**b**) On the way back down Jim was able to average 4·5 kilometres per hour. How long did it take?

4 (**a**) Each morning Sylvie-Anne drives to the station to catch the 08 17 train into town. The distance from her house to the station is 8 kilometres and she averages 32 kilometres per hour. If she needs 4 minutes to park the car when does she have to leave her house?
(**b**) One morning she left at 4 minutes past 8. Did she have to break the 50 kilometres per hour speed limit to catch her train? Explain.

5 The high-speed train was travelling at 192 kilometres per hour. The waiter in the restaurant car took 4 seconds to pour Carole a glass of wine. How far in metres did they travel in this time?

6 The horse-drawn carriage was travelling at 9 kilometres per hour . Calculate this speed in metres per second.

7 Rachel drove from Ayr to Glasgow to pick up her husband before driving on to Inverness.The graph shows her journey.
(**a**) They stopped at Perth for a meal. How long was the stop?
(**b**) How long did Rachel drive before stopping for the meal?
(**c**) During the slowest part of the journey how far did she travel and how long did it take?
(**d**) How long did it take to get to Inverness after the stop?
(**e**) Calculate the average speed for the complete journey from Ayr to Inverness.

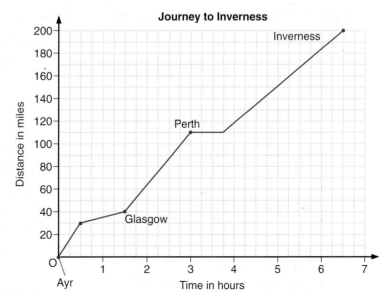

8 (a) How much further is it from Birmingham to Liverpool than from Birmingham to Manchester?

(b) Tom travelled from Edinburgh to Birmingham and then on to London. How much further was this than travelling directly to London?

Distance in miles

Aberdeen	Birmingham	Edinburgh	Liverpool	London	Manchester	Oxford
431						
125	298					
358	101	224				
545	120	412	215			
353	90	219	35	203		
503	68	370	173	56	161	

Summary

Converting units of time

Change 2·4 hours to hours and minutes.

$0·4 \times 60 = 24$

Hence 2·4 hours = **2 hrs 24 mins**

Change 4 hrs 18 minutes to hours.

$18 \div 60 = 0·3$

Hence 4 hrs 18 mins = **4·3 hours**

Formulae for speed, distance and time

$\text{Speed} = \dfrac{D}{T}$

$\text{Distance} = S \times T$

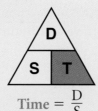

$\text{Time} = \dfrac{D}{S}$

Changing units of speed

Change 72 kilometres per hour to metres per minute

$72 \text{ km/h} = 72 \times 1000 \text{ m/h}$

$= 72\,000 \div 60 \text{ m/min}$

$= \textbf{1200 m/min}$

Change 36 metres per second to kilometres per hour

$36 \text{ m/sec} = 36 \times 60 \text{ m/min}$

$= 2160 \times 60 \text{ m/hour}$

$= 129\,600 \div 1000 \text{ km/h}$

$= \textbf{129·6 km/h}$

Distance–time graphs

Distances and times for a journey are illustrated by the graph.

Horizontal sections show a stop.

Faster sections of the journey have steeper lines.

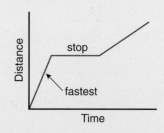

13 Pythagoras' theorem

13.1 Investigating triangles

To investigate the connection between sides of a triangle, squares can be drawn on each side.

Example

Calculate the area of the squares on the sides of this triangle.

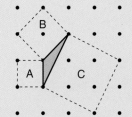

Area of square A = 1 cm^2

Area of square B = 2 cm^2

Area of square C = area of (2 yellow triangles
$\qquad$ + 2 green triangles
$\qquad$ + centre square)
$\qquad$ = 2 cm^2 + 2 cm^2 + 1 cm^2
$\qquad$ = 5 cm^2

> The squares can be split to make the calculation easier.

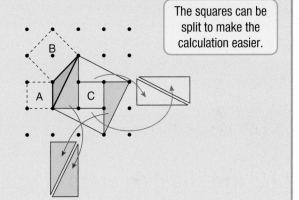

Exercise 13.1

1 (**a**) Copy the table.

Triangle	Area of square A	Area of square B	Area of square C
P			
Q			
R			
S			

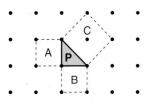

(**b**) Find the areas of each of the squares in the following diagrams and complete the table.

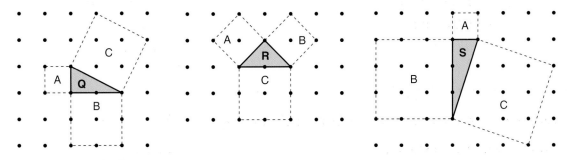

(**c**) What do you notice about the areas of the squares for each right angled triangle above?

2 (**a**) Find the areas of the squares in the following diagrams and complete the table.

Triangle	Area of square A	Area of square B	Area of square C
T			
V			

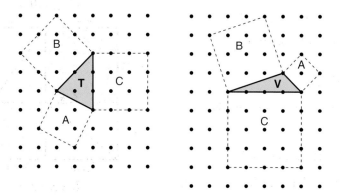

(**b**) What do you notice about the areas of the squares for each triangle above?

(**c**) How do these triangles differ from the triangles in question **1**?

13.2 Investigating areas of squares

For the right angled triangles in section 13.1

Area of square C = area of square A + area of square B

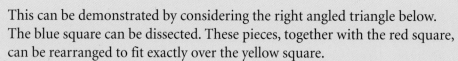

This can be demonstrated by considering the right angled triangle below. The blue square can be dissected. These pieces, together with the red square, can be rearranged to fit exactly over the yellow square.

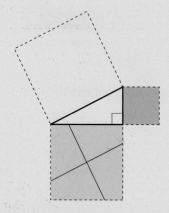
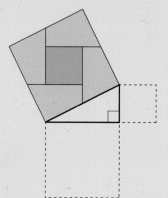

This shows:

Area of yellow square = area of blue square + area of red square

Exercise 13.2

You need centimetre squared paper, a ruler and a pair of scissors.

Diagram 1

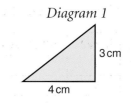

1 To find the longest side in the triangle in *Diagram 1* follow the steps below.

(a) • Accurately draw a square of side 7 centimetres.
   • Divide the square into the sections as shown in *Diagram 2*.
   • Cut the square into six sections.

Diagram 2

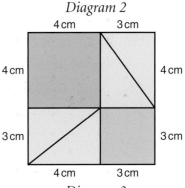

(b) Calculate the total area of the red square and the blue square.

(c) Using only the triangles, construct *Diagram 3*.

(d) For *Diagram 3* calculate the area of the unshaded shape.

(e) What do you notice about your answers to (b) and (d)?

(f) What shape is the unshaded area? Explain your answer.

(g) What is the length of a side of the unshaded shape?

(h) What is the length of the longest side of each yellow triangle?

Diagram 3

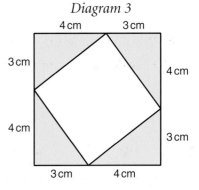

2 Assuming that the **area of square C = area of square A + area of square B**, find the area of square C in each case.

(a)

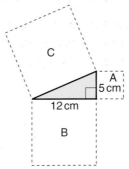

(b)

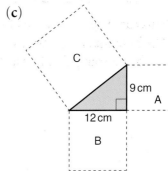

(c)

3 Find the area of the pink square in each case.

(a)

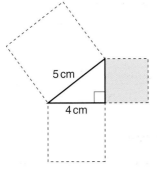

(b)

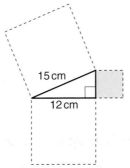

(c)

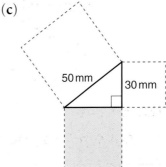

13.3 The hypotenuse

In a right angled triangle the longest side is called the **hypotenuse**.

The hypotenuse is the side opposite the right angle.

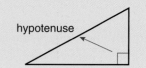

Exercise 13.3

1 Name the hypotenuse in each triangle.

(a) 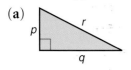 (b) 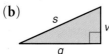 (c) 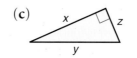 (d) 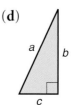 (e)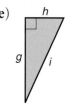

2 Name the hypotenuse in each triangle.

(a) 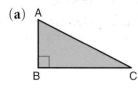 (b) 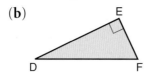 (c) 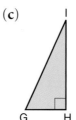 (d)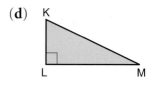

13.4 Pythagoras' theorem

Pythagoras of Samos lived around 500 BC and was a renowned early mathematician. He was also an astronomer and music theorist. He led a society which was half religious and half scientific which followed a code of secrecy. He believed all reality was mathematical in nature: that each number had its own personality – masculine or feminine, perfect or incomplete, beautiful or ugly. Ten was the very best number; it contained in itself the first four integers $1 + 2 + 3 + 4 = 10$.

Pythagoras is mainly remembered today for his famous geometry theorem. Although this is now known as Pythagoras' theorem, it was known to the Babylonians 1000 years earlier. He may have been the first to prove it.

Pythagoras' theorem states:

If a triangle is right angled
then the square on the hypotenuse is equal to the sum of the squares on the other two sides.

$$c^2 = a^2 + b^2$$

This can be used to calculate the length of the hypotenuse if the other two sides are known.

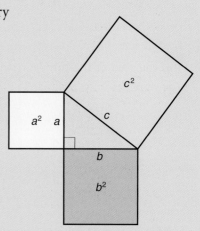

Example   Find the length of each hypotenuse.

(a)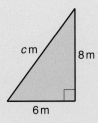

(b)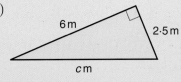

(c)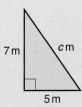

(a)
$$c^2 = a^2 + b^2$$
$$c^2 = 6^2 + 8^2$$
$$c^2 = 36 + 64$$
$$c^2 = 100$$
$$c = \sqrt{100}$$
$$c = \mathbf{10}$$

The hypotenuse is 10 m

(b)
$$c^2 = a^2 + b^2$$
$$c^2 = 2{\cdot}5^2 + 6^2$$
$$c^2 = 6{\cdot}25 + 36$$
$$c^2 = 42{\cdot}25$$
$$c = \sqrt{42{\cdot}25}$$
$$c = \mathbf{6{\cdot}5}$$

The hypotenuse is 6·5 m

(c)
$$c^2 = a^2 + b^2$$
$$c^2 = 5^2 + 7^2$$
$$c^2 = 25 + 49$$
$$c^2 = 74$$
$$c = \sqrt{74}$$
$$c = 8{\cdot}6023$$
$$c = \mathbf{8{\cdot}6} \text{ to 1 d.p.}$$

The hypotenuse is 8·6 m

Exercise 13.4

1 Find the length of the hypotenuse in each right angled triangle.

(a)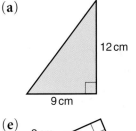

(b)

(c)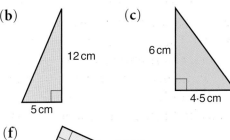

(d)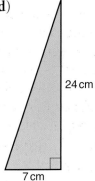

(e)

(f)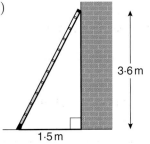

2 Calculate the length of each ladder:

(a)

(b)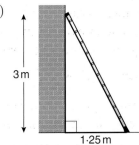

(c)

3 Calculate the length of the hypotenuse in each triangle. Give your answer correct to 1 decimal place.

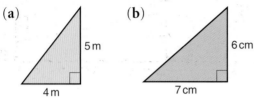
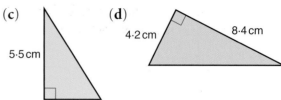

(**a**) 5 m, 4 m

(**b**) 6 cm, 7 cm

(**c**) 5·5 cm, 3·5 cm

(**d**) 4·2 cm, 8·4 cm

4 A skateboard ramp is shown in the diagram.

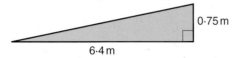

0·75 m

6·4 m

Calculate the length of the sloping edge to the nearest centimetre.

5 The size of a television is given as the length of the diagonal across the screen.
Calculate the size of each television.

size

(**a**) 12 inches, 16 inches

(**b**) 18 inches, 24 inches

(**c**) 13·5 inches, 18 inches

(**d**) 24 inches, 32 inches

6 The height of the mast in this dinghy is 5 metres.
The wire stay is attached to the boat 1·5 metres from the foot of the mast.
Calculate the length of the stay.

stay

1·5 m

7 The length of a farmer's rectangular field is 75 metres. It is 50 metres wide. How long is the path across the diagonal of the field?

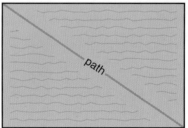

path

8 Khalid wants to cover the roof of his shed with felt.

(**a**) Calculate the length of the sloping edge of the roof of this garden shed.

(**b**) Calculate the area of the sloping roof.

(**c**) Roof felt costs £5 per square metre. If Khalid has £35 to spend on the roof, does he have enough money to pay for the felt? Explain your answer.

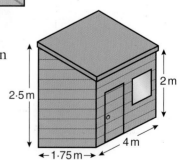

2 m

2·5 m

4 m

1·75 m

9 The diagram shows part of the plan of an artificial canoe slalom course. Distances are measured along the river bank and from the edge of the bank. Calculate the shortest distance between gate 2 and gate 3.

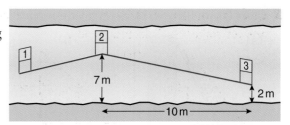

13.5 Calculating a shorter side

Example 1 Calculate the value of x in this triangle.

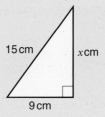

The hypotenuse is 15 cm

$$c^2 = a^2 + b^2$$
$$15^2 = x^2 + 9^2$$
$$225 = x^2 + 81$$
$$225 - 81 = x^2$$
$$144 = x^2$$
$$x = \sqrt{144}$$
$$x = 12$$

Example 2 For safety reasons this 4 metre ladder must be placed at least 2 metres from the foot of the wall. What is the maximum height which the ladder can reach?

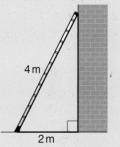

Draw a sketch and fill in the values.

$$c^2 = a^2 + b^2$$
$$4^2 = h^2 + 2^2$$
$$16 = h^2 + 4$$
$$16 - 4 = h^2$$
$$12 = h^2$$
$$h = \sqrt{12}$$
$$h = 3.46 \text{ to 2 dp}$$

The maximum height is **3·46 metres**

Exercise 13.5

1 Calculate the value of x in each right angled triangle.

(**a**)
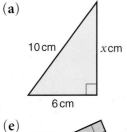
10 cm x cm   6 cm

(**b**)
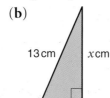
13 cm x cm   5 cm

(**c**)

x cm   6·5 cm   2·5 cm

(**d**)
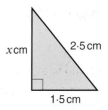
x cm   2·5 cm   1·5 cm

(**e**)
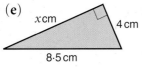
x cm   4 cm   8·5 cm

(**f**)
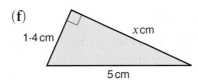
1·4 cm x cm   5 cm

2 How far up the wall does each ladder reach?

(a)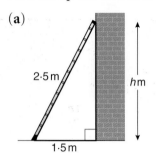

(b)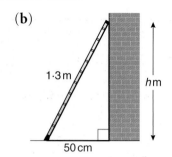

(c)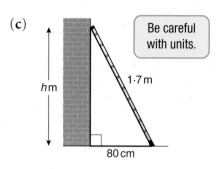

Be careful with units.

3 Find the value of x in each triangle. Give your answer correct to 1 decimal place.

(a)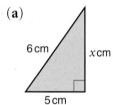

(b)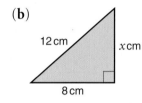

(c)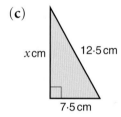

(d)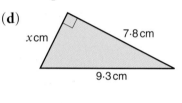

4 Joe makes timber roof frames.

(a) What lengths should Joe make the vertical straps p and q.

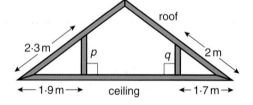

(b) Find the length of support y.

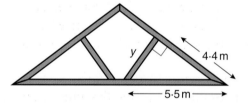

5 A garden gate is constructed with dimensions shown in the diagram. Calculate w, the width of the gate.

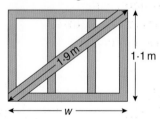

6 A support wire 4·5 metres long is fixed to the ground 2·5 metres from the foot of a telegraph pole. Calculate the height of the pole.

13.6 Applications

Example

The diagram shows the penalty spot and the goals on a
High School football pitch.
Calculate the distance from the spot to the foot of the goal post.

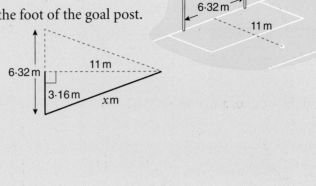

Step 1   Draw a sketch of the
right angled triangle.

Step 2   Use Pythagoras' theorem here.

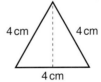

$$c^2 = a^2 + b^2$$
$$x^2 = 11^2 + 3 \cdot 16^2$$
$$x^2 = 121 + 9 \cdot 9856$$
$$x^2 = 130 \cdot 9856$$
$$x = \sqrt{130 \cdot 9856}$$
$$x = 11 \cdot 44489$$
$$x = 11 \cdot 4 \text{ to 1 dp}$$

The distance to the post is **11·4 metres.**

Exercise 13.6

1 Calculate the height of this equilateral triangle.

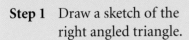

2 From Scrabster a fishing boat sails 30 kilometres
due north then 40 kilometres due west. How far
would it have to travel to return directly to Scrabster?

3 Two dinghies start from the same position. After 5 minutes one has
travelled 500 metres due south and the other has travelled 400
metres due west. How far apart are the dinghies at this point?

4 A new mathematics room should have a rectangular floor, with
dimensions 6·3 metres and 8·4 metres. A builder wants to check that
the floor is a perfect rectangle and measures the diagonals of the
floor. How long should each diagonal be?

5 As part of her training sessions Louise either runs along
two edges of the pitch or diagonally across the pitch. The
pitch measures 80 metres by 60 metres. How much
further does she run if she follows the edge of the pitch?

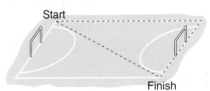

6 For the isosceles triangle opposite, calculate
(**a**) the height h
(**b**) the area of the triangle.

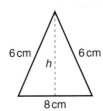

7 Calculate the perimeter of the isosceles triangle shown opposite. Give your answer correct to 1 decimal place.

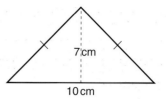

7 cm

10 cm

8 Which of these rectangles has the longer diagonals?

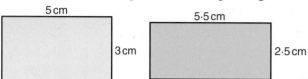

5 cm

3 cm

5·5 cm

2·5 cm

9 Use Pythagoras' theorem to find the distance between A and B in this coordinate diagram.

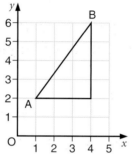

10 For each pair of points
(**i**) plot them on a coordinate diagram
(**ii**) calculate the distance between them.

(**a**) C (2, 3) and D(8, 11)   (**b**) E(−4, 1) and F(8, 6)
(**c**) G(−5, −2) and H(7, 7)   (**d**) I(−4, 4) and J(8, −1)

11 The length of the diagonal of a square is 10 centimetres. How long are the sides of the square?

12 A bookcase has the dimensions shown in the diagram. Kausar wants to move it from a narrow hallway and thinks it would be easier to move if it was turned to the carrying position shown. If the ceiling of the hallway is 2·7 metres high, will she be able to turn the bookcase to their preferred carrying position?

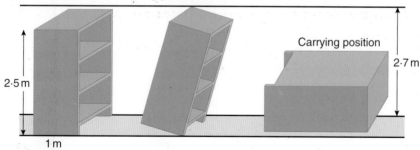

Carrying position

2·7 m

2·5 m

1 m

13 (**a**) Copy and complete this table to produce the squares of whole numbers from 1 to 30.

(**b**) Look at the square numbers in your table. Notice

$$25 + 144 = 169$$

so $5^2 + 12^2 = 13^2$

5, 12, 13 is called a **Pythagorean triple**.

Use your table to find eight other Pythagorean triples.

Number	1	2	3	4
Square number	1	4	9	16

13.7 The converse of Pythagoras' theorem

Pythagoras' theorem states for any triangle:

if a triangle is right angled

then the square on the longest side is equal to the sum of the squares on the other two sides.

The **converse** of Pythagoras' theorem states for any triangle:

if the square on the longest side is equal to the sum of the squares on the other two sides

then the triangle is right angled.

Example 1   Is this triangle right angled?

If $c^2 = a^2 + b^2$ then the triangle is right angled

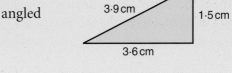

$$3 \cdot 9^2 = 15 \cdot 21$$
$$3 \cdot 6^2 + 1 \cdot 5^2 = 12 \cdot 96 + 2 \cdot 25$$
$$= 15 \cdot 21$$

Since $3 \cdot 9^2 = 3 \cdot 6^2 + 1 \cdot 5^2$ the triangle is right angled.

Example 2   A joiner wanted to make a rectangular frame with sides of 1·5 metres and 2 metres. To check this he measured the diagonal. This was 2·6 metres long. Is the frame rectangular?

If $c^2 = a^2 + b^2$ then the triangle is right angled.

$$2 \cdot 6^2 = 6 \cdot 76$$
$$2^2 + 1 \cdot 5^2 = 4 + 2 \cdot 25$$
$$= 6 \cdot 25$$

Check that the sides are at right angles.

Since $2 \cdot 6^2 \neq 2^2 + 1 \cdot 5^2$ the triangle is not right angled and the frame is not rectangular.

Exercise 13.7

1 Which of these triangles are right angled? Explain fully.

(a)
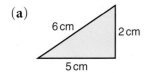

(b)

(c)
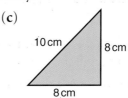

(d)
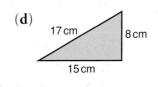

2 Firaz is building a garage with a rectangular floor.
The dimensions of the floor are 2·7 metres by 3·6 metres.
To check this he measured the diagonal. This was 4·5 metres long.
Is the floor rectangular?

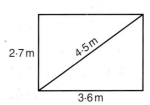

3 Charlie is creating a formal lawn and has marked out what she thinks is a rectangle. The sides of the lawn measure 18 metres and 24 metres. The diagonal measures 30 metres. Is the lawn rectangular?

4 An isosceles triangle has two sides of 8 centimetres and one of 11 centimetres.

Is the triangle right-angled?

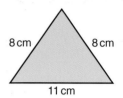

5 Builders used to check whether their work was right angled using a loop of rope with twelve equally spaced knots as shown. Would this form a right angled triangle?

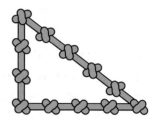

Review exercise 13

1 Find the length of the hypotenuse in each right angled triangle.

(a) 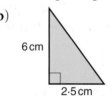   6 cm   8 cm

(b) 6 cm   2·5 cm

(c) 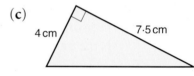 4 cm   7·5 cm

2 Find the length of the missing side in each right angled triangle.

(a) 15 cm   9 cm

(b) 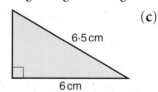 6·5 cm   6 cm

(c) 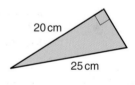 20 cm   25 cm

3 Calculate the length of the sides marked x. In each case give your answer to 1 decimal places.

(a) 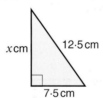 x cm   5 cm   4 cm

(b) x cm   12·5 cm   7·5 cm

(c) 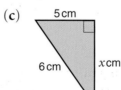 5 cm   6 cm x cm

(d) 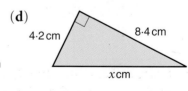 4·2 cm   8·4 cm x cm

4 Calculate the length of the diagonal of this rectangle.

2·75 m

50 cm

5 In a sailing regatta, buoys are placed so that Buoy A is 500 metres south of the starting buoy and 400 metres west of Buoy B. How far would a boat have to travel to return directly to the start if it was at Buoy B?

6 The bracket shown is used to support a hanging basket.

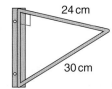

(**a**) Calculate the length of the section placed against the wall.

(**b**) The holes for mounting the bracket on the wall are drilled at positions one quarter and three quarters of the distance along this edge. How far apart are the holes?

7 For the isosceles triangle shown opposite calculate,

(**a**) the height of h (**b**) the area of the triangle.

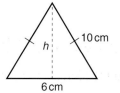

8 Domhnall wants to edge his kite with new tape. The diagram shows a sketch of his kite with the lengths of the diagonals marked.

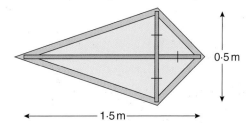

How much tape does he require to edge his kite?

9 Which of these triangles are right angled? Explain fully.

(**a**)

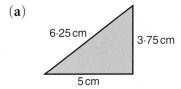

(**b**)

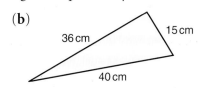

10 Janice makes timber frames for garden sheds. Each side of the shed must be rectangular. The sides of the frame measure 2·25 metres and 3 metres. The diagonal of the frame measures 3·75 metres. Is the frame rectangular? Explain your answer.

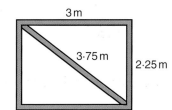

Summary

Pythagoras' theorem states:

If a triangle is right angled
then the square on the hypotenuse is equal to the sum
of the squares on the other two sides.

$$c^2 = a^2 + b^2$$

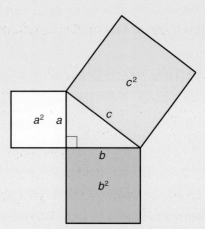

Calculating the hypotenuse

Find the length of the hypotenuse.

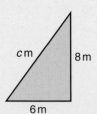

$$c^2 = a^2 + b^2$$
$$c^2 = 6^2 + 8^2$$
$$c^2 = 36 + 64$$
$$c^2 = 100$$
$$c = \sqrt{100}$$
$$c = \mathbf{10}$$

The hypotenuse is 10 cm

Calculating a shorter side

Calculate the value of x in this triangle.

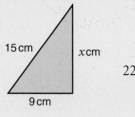

$$c^2 = a^2 + b^2$$
$$15^2 = x^2 + 9^2$$
$$225 = x^2 + 81$$
$$225 - 81 = x^2$$
$$144 = x^2$$
$$x = \sqrt{144}$$
$$x = \mathbf{12}$$

Converse of Pythagoras' theorem

The converse of Pythagoras' theorem states that:

if the square on the longest side is equal to the sum of the squares on the other two sides
then the triangle is right angled.

If $c^2 = a^2 + b^2$ then the triangle is right angled

$$3{\cdot}9^2 = 15{\cdot}21$$
$$3{\cdot}6^2 + 1{\cdot}5^2 = 12{\cdot}96 + 2{\cdot}25$$
$$= 15{\cdot}21$$

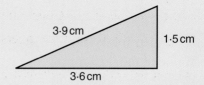

Since $3{\cdot}9^2 = 3{\cdot}6^2 + 1{\cdot}5^2$ the triangle is right angled.

14 Probability

In this chapter you will learn about probability and expectation.

14.1 Simple probability

A square spinner has four equal sections coloured red, blue, green and yellow.

When spun, each coloured edge has the same chance of landing on the table.

The red edge should land on the table once in every four spins. The probability of landing on red is 1 out of 4:

$$P(\text{red}) = \tfrac{1}{4}$$

Probability is often expressed as a fraction.

Probability (event) = $\dfrac{\textbf{number of favourable outcomes}}{\textbf{total number of possible outcomes}}$

Example
A dart is thrown at this board. If it lands on the board, find the probability it will hit:

(**a**) a 5   (**b**) an even number

(**c**) a factor of 16   (**d**) a prime number.

(**a**) $P(5) = \tfrac{1}{20}$ (**b**) $P(\text{even}) = \tfrac{10}{20} = \tfrac{1}{2}$

(**c**) $P(\text{factor of } 16) = \tfrac{5}{20} = \tfrac{1}{4}$ (**d**) $P(\text{prime}) = \tfrac{8}{20} = \tfrac{2}{5}$

> 1, 2, 4, 8, 16 are factors of 16

> 2, 3, 5, 7, 11, 13, 17, 19 are prime

Exercise 14.1

1 A die is rolled. Find the probability of getting

(**a**) a 5   (**b**) an odd number

(**c**) a number divisible by 3   (**d**) a prime number.

2 Find the probability of winning a prize at a raffle if there are:

(**a**) 2000 tickets with 50 winning numbers

(**b**) 5000 tickets with 20 winning numbers.

3 This 7-sided spinner is spun and its number noted. Find the probability it stops at

(**a**) a 3   (**b**) a square number

(**c**) a number less than 6   (**d**) a multiple of 3

(**e**) a factor of 12.

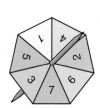

4 A bag has 3 red, 6 green and 9 blue marbles.
If a marble is picked at random, find the probability that it will be
  (**a**) red   (**b**) green   (**c**) blue   (**d**) orange.

5 One of the letters of the word MISSISSIPPI is chosen at random.
Find the probability that it is:
  (**a**) P   (**b**) M   (**c**) I   (**d**) a letter other than S.

6 Last year a garage sold 13 red cars, 9 silver cars and 5 black cars.
Carole bought one of these cars. What is the probability that the car
she bought was
  (**a**) silver   (**b**) not silver?

7 The number of each colour in a box of assorted paper clips is shown.

Colour	blue	pink	purple	yellow
Frequency	6	3	7	5

If one is chosen at random, find the probability that it is:
  (**a**) purple   (**b**) blue   (**c**) not yellow.

8 In a survey of 50 families, the number of children in each was recorded.

Number of children	0	1	2	3	4
Frequency	4	21	16	8	1

Calculate the probability that a family, chosen at random has:
  (**a**) 2 children
  (**b**) less than 2 children
  (**c**) 2 or more children.

9 A mini lottery game uses red, green, blue and orange balls.
There are 10 of each colour, numbered 1 to 10. They are all placed in
a drum and one is drawn out. Find the probability that it is:
  (**a**) a 7   (**b**) blue   (**c**) a blue 7.

10 A 12-sided spinner is spun and its number noted. Find
  (**a**) P (less than 3)   (**b**) P (multiple of 4)   (**c**) P (prime)
  (**d**) P (factor of 20)   (**e**) P (prime factor of 12).

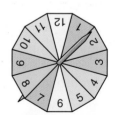

11 A pack of cards contains 52 cards divided into 4 suits.
Each suit contains 13 cards: ace, king, queen, jack,
10, 9, 8, 7, 6, 5, 4, 3, 2. A card is drawn from a shuffled pack.
Find
  (**a**) P (red card)   (**b**) P (face card)
  (**c**) P (black queen)   (**d**) P (a five)
  (**e**) P (heart)   (**f**) P (a club less than 7)
  (**g**) P (a card bigger than 9)   (**h**) P (ace of spades)

Spades   Clubs

Hearts   Diamonds

12 (**a**) Write all the ways that the 3 letters R, T and A can be arranged.

(**b**) If the 3 letters are written down at random, find the probability that they will:
(**i**) spell RAT   (**ii**) spell a word   (**iii**) be in alphabetical order.

13 (**a**) Write all the three-figure numbers that can be made from the digits 3, 4 and 5 without repeating.

(**b**) If one of these numbers is selected at random, find the probability that the number is
(**i**) less than 400   (**ii**) greater than 500
(**iii**) less than 300   (**iv**) odd
(**v**) a multiple of 6   (**vi**) prime.

14 (**a**) Write all the four-figure numbers that can be made from the digits 1, 2, 5 and 7 without repeating.

(**b**) If one of these numbers is selected at random, find the probability that the number is
(**i**) less than 5000   (**ii**) greater than 2000
(**iii**) even   (**iv**) a multiple of 5
(**v**) a multiple of 25   (**vi**) a square number.

14.2 Two-way tables

Example
One weekend Sue sorted her CDs and classified them in a table.
If she selects a CD to listen to, at random, find
(**a**) P (instrumental)   (**b**) P (jazz)
(**c**) P(rock and vocal)   (**d**) P (not rock)

	Rock	Jazz	Classical	Total
Instrumental	4	3	2	9
Vocal	6	8	7	21
Total	10	11	9	30

(**a**) P (instrumental) $= \frac{9}{30} = \frac{3}{10}$ (**b**) P (jazz) $= \frac{11}{30}$
(**c**) P(rock and vocal) $= \frac{6}{30} = \frac{1}{5}$ (**d**) P (not rock) $= \frac{20}{30} = \frac{2}{3}$

Exercise 14.2

1 In a health promotion campaign, fifty people were asked whether or not they smoked cigarettes. The table shows their responses. Find the probability that a person chosen at random from this group is

(**a**) female

(**b**) a non-smoker

(**c**) a male smoker.

	Smoker	Non Smoker
Male	5	15
Female	12	18

2 A garage carried out a survey on 300 cars.
The results are shown in the table.

| | Engine size (cc) | | | |
	0–1000	1001–1500	1501–2000	2001+
less than 3 years	35	40	90	15
3 years or more	20	50	40	10

Age

Find the probability that a car, chosen at random:

(**a**) is 3 or more years old

(**b**) has engine size greater than 2000 cc

(**c**) has engine size 1001–1500 cc and is less than 3 years old.

3 Two different spinners are used for a game.
The scores from each spinner are added together
and all possible totals are shown in the table.

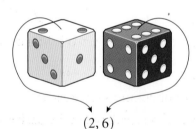

Spinner 1

	1	2	3	4	5
2	3	4	5	6	7
3	4	5	6	7	8
4	5	6	7	8	9
5	6	7	8	9	10
6	7	8	9	10	11

Spinner 2

Find the probability of scoring a total of:

(**a**) 11   (**b**) 7   (**c**) more than 8.

4 Two dice are rolled for a game and the scores are added together.
(**a**) Make a table to show all possible totals.
(**b**) Find
    (**i**) P (double 6)
   (**ii**) P (any double)
  (**iii**) P (odd total)
  (**iv**) P (7)
   (**v**) P (at least 7)
  (**vi**) P (square number).

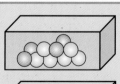

(2, 6)

14.3 Further probabilities

Example
There are 4 red beads and 6 blue beads in a box.
What is the probability that:

(**a**) without looking, you choose a red one?

(**b**) having removed a red one, you take a second one which is red?

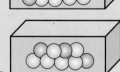

(**a**) P (first bead red) $= \frac{4}{10} = \frac{2}{5}$ (**b**) P (second bead red) $= \frac{3}{9} = \frac{1}{3}$

Exercise 14.3

1 There are 6 white and 2 red napkins in a pile.
What is the probability that:

(**a**) without looking, a white napkin is chosen

(**b**) having removed a white one, a red one is now chosen?

2 David has a bag of sweets. It holds 6 yellow, 4 green, 2 red and
3 orange sweets. The corner of the bag is torn and a sweet falls out.

(**a**) What is the probability that this sweet is orange?

(**b**) The sweet that fell out was orange and he put it in the bin.
What is the probability that the next sweet to fall out is also orange?

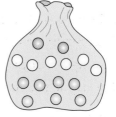

3 A box contains 8 plain chocolates and 28 milk chocolates.
Find the probability that:

(**a**) without looking, Kate takes out a milk chocolate

(**b**) after eating it, the next one taken is a plain chocolate?

4 In a car park there are 17 saloon cars, 12 estate cars and 4 four-wheel
drive cars.

(**a**) Find the probability that the first car to leave is an estate car.

(**b**) If the first car was an estate car, find the probability that the next
car to leave will be a four-wheel drive.

5 A cool box holds 10 cans of cola and 6 cans of iron brew.
What is the probability that:

(**a**) a can of cola is selected at random

(**b**) after drinking the cola, the next can selected is iron brew?

6 A card is drawn from a standard pack of 52 cards.

(**a**) What is the probability of obtaining a red queen?

(**b**) If a red queen is drawn, and not replaced in the pack and then a
second card is drawn, what is the probability of drawing a club?

7 There are 3 blue, 4 red and 1 yellow counters in a bag.

(**a**) A counter is removed. What is the probability that the counter is
blue?

(**b**) The counter is replaced in the bag and 2 green counters are also
added. If a counter is now taken from the bag find the
probability that it is not red.

8 Jack has 6 copper and 4 silver coins in his pocket. Find the
probability of taking out:

(**a**) a copper coin

(**b**) a second copper coin if you replace the first copper one

(**c**) a second copper coin if you do not replace the first copper one?

9 Gail has a bag of marbles. It contains 5 green, 6 red, 4 blue and 1 yellow marbles. Without looking she picks one for her friend Anne.

(**a**) Find the probability that the marble she gives to Anne is yellow.

(**b**) If Anne did get a yellow one, find the probability of the next one chosen by Gail being

   (**i**) green   (**ii**) blue   (**iii**) yellow.

10 A bag contains 6 yellow and 3 green balls. Zelada takes two balls out in turn without looking. Find the probability of the second ball being yellow if:

(**a**) Zelada replaced the first ball

(**b**) Zelada did not replace the first ball which was yellow

(**c**) Zelada did not replace the first ball which was green?

14.4 Expectation

Probability can be used to make predictions.

Example

Three out of five people use shampoo for normal hair.

If 100 people are interviewed how many would you expect to use 'normal' shampoo?

$$P(\text{normal shampoo}) = \tfrac{3}{5}$$

$$\text{Expected users} = \tfrac{3}{5} \times 100 = 60$$

You would expect **60** to use normal shampoo.

Exercise 14.4

1 Two out of five housewives use Amino soap powder. If 300 housewives are interviewed how many are expected to use Amino?

2 Five out of eight car-owners have a saloon car. If 200 car-owners are asked, how many are expected to own a saloon car?

3 A choice of English or Latin was given for their new school motto. Five pupils out of six voted for English. In a class of 30, how many would you expect to have voted for Latin?

4 Find the expected number of

(**a**) heads in 80 tosses of a coin   (**b**) tails in 500 tosses

(**c**) sixes in 300 rolls of a die   (**d**) twos in 150 rolls of a die.

5 Mr Golden buys 15 apples and discovers that 6 are bruised.

   (**a**) What is the probability of getting a bruised apple?

   (**b**) How many bruised apples can we expect in a further 40 apples?

6 How many pupils in a class of 28 would be expected to be born on a Friday?

7 In 130 draws from a shuffled pack of cards (with replacement), how many times might Brian expect to obtain

   (**a**) a red card   (**b**) a red seven   (**c**) an ace

   (**d**) a face card   (**e**) a red queen   (**f**) an even number

   (**g**) a black four?

8 An English Literature exam is taken by 200 candidates who answer one question from a choice of four.

Question	novel	play	poem	short story
Frequency	75	40	61	24

   (**a**) An examiner picks a paper at random. What is the probability that it will be
       (**i**) a poem   (**ii**) a novel   (**iii**) not a short story?

   (**b**) If another 50 candidates take the exam, how many papers can be expected to be:
       (**i**) a short story   (**ii**) a play   (**iii**) neither a play nor short story?

Review exercise 14

1 A die is rolled. Find the probability of getting

   (**a**) a 6   (**b**) an even number

   (**c**) a square number   (**d**) a factor of 30

2 A bag has 8 red, 5 blue, 3 green and 2 yellow marbles. If a marble is picked at random, find the probability it will be

   (**a**) blue   (**b**) green

   (**c**) red or yellow   (**d**) not red

3 In a health promotion campaign, forty people were asked whether or not they took sugar in their coffee. The table shows their responses.
What is the probability that a person chosen at random from this group

	Sugar	Non Sugar
Male	7	15
Female	5	13

   (**a**) is male   (**b**) takes sugar   (**c**) is a female who takes sugar?

4 A bag of sweets contains 12 orange and 9 lemon flavours. Find the probability that:

   (**a**) without looking, Mike takes out a lemon sweet

   (**b**) after eating it, the next one he takes is also lemon?

5 Find the expected number of:

(**a**) tails in 50 tosses of a coin

(**b**) sixes in 150 rolls of a dice

(**c**) hearts in 20 draws from a pack of cards.

6 The choices made by 180 pupils in an option column are shown in the table

Option	Biology	Chemistry	Physics	Science
Frequency	40	45	23	72

(**a**) If a pupil is picked at random, what is the probability that the choice made is:

  (**i**) physics

 (**ii**) chemistry or physics

(**iii**) not science?

(**b**) In next year's group of 200 pupils, how many can be expected to take

  (**i**) science

 (**ii**) chemistry

(**iii**) biology or physics?

Summary

$$\text{Probability (event)} = \frac{\text{number of favourable outcomes}}{\text{total number of possible outcomes}}$$

Expected value = number of events $\times$ probability

15 Introduction to straight line graphs

In this chapter you will learn about straight line equations and their graphs.

15.1 Lines on coordinate diagrams

The graph of an equation may be drawn on a coordinate diagram.

Example

Draw a graph of the equation $y = 2x + 3$.

When $x = 0$ When $x = 1$ When $x = 3$
$y = 2x + 3$ $y = 2x + 3$ $y = 2x + 3$
$y = 2 \times 0 + 3$ $y = 2 \times 1 + 3$ $y = 2 \times 3 + 3$
$y = 3$ $y = 5$ $y = 9$

The coordinates for several points may be shown in a table.

x	0	1	3
y	3	5	9

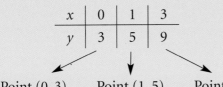

Point $(0, 3)$ Point $(1, 5)$ Point $(3, 9)$

When these points are plotted and joined up they form the graph of $y = 2x + 3$

$y = 2x + 3$ is the equation of this line.

A **linear equation** has a straight line graph.

Exercise 15.1

1 For each equation
- copy and complete the table
- plot the points and join them
- label each graph with its equation.

   (**a**) $y = x + 3$ (**b**) $y = 3x + 1$

x	0	2	5
y	3	5	

x	0	3	5
y	1		

2 For each equation, the given points lie on a straight line graph.
Write the coordinates of the points.

   (**a**) $y = 4x$ A(1,)   B(3,)   C(5,)
   (**b**) $y = 2x + 5$ P(0,)   Q(2,)   R(4,)
   (**c**) $y = x + 4$ K(2,)   L(5,)   M(7,)
   (**d**) $y = 5x + 1$ S(0,)   T(1,)   U(6,)

3 For each equation
- make a table to show the values of y when x is 0, 1, 2, 3, 4 and 5
- draw a graph and label it.

(**a**) $y = x + 1$ (**b**) $y = x$

(**c**) $y = x + 2$ (**d**) $y = x + 5$

(**e**) $y = 3x + 2$ (**f**) $y = 2x + 1$

(**g**) $y = 3x$ (**h**) $y = 2x + 4$

15.2 Families of lines

Exercise 15.2

1 (**a**) Draw a coordinate diagram with the axes as shown.

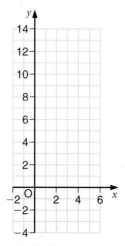

(**b**) On the same diagram draw the graphs of each equation and label them.

$y = 3x + 3$
$y = 3x + 1$
$y = 3x$
$y = 3x - 2$

> The number in front of x is the **coefficient**.

(**c**) What do you notice about:
(**i**) the lines
(**ii**) the **coefficient** of x in the equation?

2 Repeat question **1** for each of these families of linear equations.

(**a**) $y = x + 3$ (**b**) $y = 4x + 2$ (**c**) $y = 2x + 5$
      $y = x + 1$ $y = 4x$ $y = 2x$
      $y = x - 1$ $y = 4x - 3$ $y = 2x - 3$

15.3 Equations of parallel lines

Lines which are parallel have the same **slope** or **gradient**.

The **coefficient** of x is a measure of the gradient of the line.

When the **coefficients** of x are **equal**, lines are **parallel**.

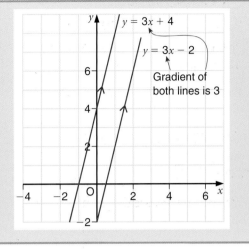

$y = 3x + 4$

$y = 3x - 2$

Gradient of both lines is 3

Exercise 15.3

1 For each equation write:
  (i) the coefficient of x
  (ii) the gradient of the line.

  (a) $y = 5x + 3$ **(b)** $y = 3x - 4$

  (c) $y = 8x$ **(d)** $y = 3x - 9$

  (e) $y = 8x + 7$ **(f)** $y = x + 4$

  (g) $y = \frac{1}{2}x - 6$ **(h)** $y = x$

2 Which pairs of lines in question **1** are parallel?

3 Match equations which give parallel lines.

$y = x + 10$ $y = 4x + 6$ $y = 3x - 8$ $y = 10x$

$y = 9x + 3$

$y = 2x$ $y = 5x - 7$ $y = 6x - 12$

$y = 4x - 7$ $y = 3x$ $y = x + 8$

$y = 9x$ $y = 5x - 5$ $y = 2x - 6$ $y = 10x + 3$

$y = 6x + 10$

4 Which lines in question **3** do you think are steepest?
  Explain why you think so.

15.4 The *y*-intercept

The **y-intercept** of a line is where it **cuts the y-axis**.

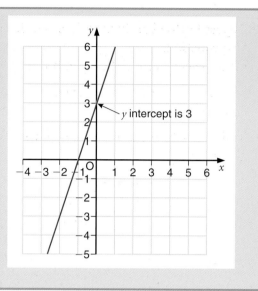

y intercept is 3

Exercise 15.4

1 (a) Draw a coordinate diagram with the axes as shown.

(b) On the same diagram draw the graph of each equation and label it.

$$y = x + 3$$
$$y = 2x + 3$$
$$y = 3x + 3$$

(c) What do you notice about the *y*-intercept?

(d) Where would the line $y = 5x + 3$ cut the *y*-axis?
Check your answer.

2 (a) On the same diagram draw the graphs of this family of linear equations.

$$y = x + 1$$
$$y = 2x + 1$$
$$y = 3x + 1$$

(b) What do you notice about the *y*-intercept?

(c) Where would the line $y = 5x + 1$ cut the *y*-axis?
Check your answer.

3 Draw graphs for each family of equations and state the *y*-intercept for each.

(a) $y = x + 2$ (b) $y = x - 1$ (c) $y = x$
$\quad\;\; y = 2x + 2$ $y = 2x - 1$ $y = 2x$
$\quad\;\; y = 3x + 2$ $y = 3x - 1$ $y = 3x$

15.5 The *y*-intercept and linear equations

It is possible to identify the *y*-intercept from the linear equation.
This is the **constant** in the equation.

The line $y = 4x + 3$ crosses the *y*-axis at $(0, 3)$.
The *y*-intercept is 3.

The line $y = 4x - 5$ crosses the *y*-axis at $(0, -5)$.
The *y*-intercept is -5.

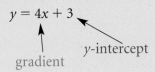

Example
Write the equation of the line with gradient 5 crossing the *y*-axis at $(0, -4)$

$$y = 5x - 4$$

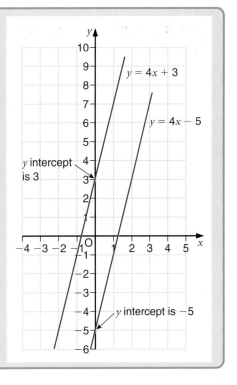

Exercise 15.5

1 Write the coordinates of the point where each line cuts the *y*-axis.

(**a**) $y = 4x + 7$ (**b**) $y = 6x + 5$ (**c**) $y = 4x - 7$ (**d**) $y = 2x - 9$

2 For each line write the *y*-intercept.

(**a**) $y = 5x + 9$ (**b**) $y = 3x + 7$ (**c**) $y = 3x - 4$ (**d**) $y = x + 1$
(**e**) $y = 6x - 1$ (**f**) $y = x - 9$ (**g**) $y = 7x + 8$ (**h**) $y = 6x$

3 For each line write: (**i**) the gradient
                           (**ii**) the *y*-intercept.

(**a**) $y = 2x + 3$ (**b**) $y = 4x + 9$ (**c**) $y = x + 5$ (**d**) $y = 3x + 1$
(**e**) $y = 7x - 2$ (**f**) $y = 10x - 3$ (**g**) $y = 8x - 11$ (**h**) $y = x - 1$
(**i**) $y = x - \frac{1}{2}$ (**j**) $y = 5x$ (**k**) $y = \frac{1}{4}x + 1$ (**l**) $y = 12x - \frac{5}{8}$

4 Write equations for the following lines:

(**a**) gradient 2, *y*-intercept 4
(**b**) gradient 7, *y*-intercept 3
(**c**) gradient 5, *y*-intercept 8
(**d**) gradient 1, *y*-intercept 9
(**e**) gradient 3, *y*-intercept -6
(**f**) gradient 4, *y*-intercept -2
(**g**) gradient 9, *y*-intercept -9
(**h**) gradient 1, *y*-intercept -5

5 Write equations for the lines with the given gradients and passing through the given points.

(**a**) 6, (0, 2)   (**b**) 8, (0, 7)   (**c**) 3, (0, 0)   (**d**) 1, (0, 6)

(**e**) 1, (0, 0)   (**f**) 10, (0, −2)   (**g**) 5, (0, −12)   (**h**) 0, (0, −3)

6 Write the equation of the line parallel to $y = 9x - 2$ and passing through $(0, 7)$.

Review exercise 15

1 (**i**) Copy and complete the table for each equation.

   (**ii**) Draw the graph of each equation and label it.

     (**a**) $y = 2x + 5$ (**b**) $y = 3x - 4$

x	0	3	5
y	5		

x	0	2	5
y	−4		

2 For each linear equation, the given points lie on the graph.
Write the coordinates of the points.

(**a**) $y = 3x$ A(1,)   B(4,)   C(9,)

(**b**) $y = 5x - 3$ P(0,)   Q(2,)   R(10,)

3 State the gradient of the graph of each linear equation:

(**a**) $y = 6x + 5$ (**b**) $y = 9x - 4$ (**c**) $y = -2x + 7$ (**d**) $y = -8x$

4 Match the equations which give parallel lines.

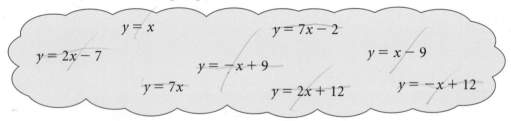

$y = x$ $y = 7x - 2$

$y = 2x - 7$ $y = x - 9$

$y = -x + 9$

$y = 7x$ $y = 2x + 12$ $y = -x + 12$

5 Write the coordinates of the point where each line cuts the y-axis.

(**a**) $y = 6x + 3$ (**b**) $y = 9x + 9$ (**c**) $y = 3x$ (**d**) $y = x - 8$

6 (**a**) A line has y-intercept 2 and gradient 7. Write the equation of the line.

   (**b**) Write the equation of the line which passes through the origin and has gradient 5.

   (**c**) A line is parallel to $y = 2x + 5$. State the gradient of this line.

   (**d**) Write the equation of the line parallel to $y = 2x + 5$ which has y-intercept 4.

Summary

Linear equations

The graph of a linear equation is a straight line.

$$y = 3x + 2$$

x	1	2	3
y	5	8	11

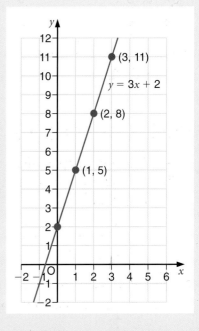

Gradient

The coefficient of x is a measure of the gradient of a line.
Parallel lines have the same gradient.

- $y = 2x + 5$ has gradient 2.
- $y = 4x - 1$ and $y = 4x + 3$ are parallel.

y-intercept

The y-intercept is found where the line cuts the y-axis.

The constant in the equation gives the y-intercept.

$y = 3x + 2$ cuts the y-axis at $(0, 2)$.

coefficient   constant

$$y = 3x + 2$$

gradient y-intercept

16 Problem solving

Exercise 16.1

1 (**a**) The number of my house and the one next door multiply to give 483.
What are these house numbers?

(**b**) Two houses on the other side of the street have numbers which multiply to give 624.
One of these houses is directly opposite mine.
What are these house numbers?

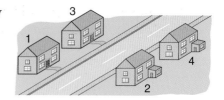

2 Three brothers, Craig, Andrew and Seamus have a total age of 39 years.

(**a**) Write a possible age for each brother in the first line of a table like this.

(**b**) Use the clues to find each brother's age.
Clue 1 Craig, the eldest, is 11 years older than Andrew.
Clue 2 There are 4 years between Andrew and Seamus.

(**c**) In how many years will Craig's age be double Andrew's age?

	Craig	Andrew	Seamus
Guess 1			
Guess 2			
Guess 3			

3 These crowns represent **odd** numbers.

The sum of the **first three** odd numbers is

$$1 + 3 + 5 = 9 \text{ or } 3^2$$

(**a**) Copy and complete the table.

(**b**) Describe the pattern in your table.

(**c**) Use the pattern to find the sum of
(**i**) the **first seven** odd numbers
(**ii**) the **first ten** odd numbers
(**iii**) the **first twenty** odd numbers.

(**d**) We describe $1 + 3 + 5$ as the sum of the first three odd numbers.
Describe and find
(**i**) $1 + 3 + 5 + 7 + 9$
(**ii**) $1 + 3 + 5 + 7 + \ldots + 17 + 19$
(**iii**) $1 + 3 + 5 + 7 + \ldots + 27 + 29$
(**iv**) $1 + 3 + 5 + 7 + \ldots \quad 97 + 99$

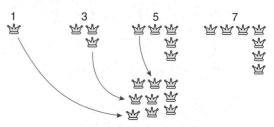

Sum of odd numbers	Total
1	1 or 1^2
1 + 3	4 or 2^2
1 + 3 + 5	9 or 3^2
1 + 3 + 5 + 7	
1 + 3 + 5 + 7 + 9	
1 + 3 + 5 + 7 + 9 + 11	

4 Class 3 at Ionnsachadh School is collecting 20p coins for a local charity. They have chosen different fund raising activities.

Work in a group

For each activity

- discuss how to solve the problem
- list the equipment you will need
- estimate how much money they should collect.

5 You need centimetre square dot paper.

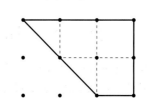

This shape has
- 8 dots on its boundary
- 1 dot inside
- an area of 4 cm².

(**a**) Draw at least 4 different shapes each with only one dot inside.

(**b**) Copy and complete the table for your shapes.

(**c**) Describe the pattern in your table.

(**d**) What is the area of a shape with 16 dots on its boundary and 1 dot inside?

Number of dots on boundary	Area of shape in cm²
8	4

6 This shape has
- 8 dots on its boundary
- 2 dots inside the boundary
- an area of 5 square units.

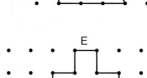

(**a**) (**i**) Copy and complete the table for each of these shapes.

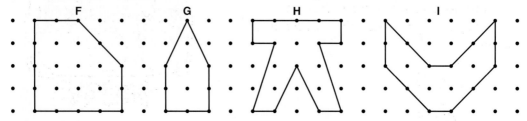

Shape	Number of dots on boundary (*b*)	Number of dots inside boundary (*i*)	$\frac{1}{2}b + i$	Area (*A*) in square units
A	8	1		
B				
C				

(**ii**) Draw some shapes of your own and add the information to your table.

(**iii**) Look at the last two columns in your table. What do you notice?

(**iv**) Copy and complete the formula $A = \frac{1}{2}b + i - \square$.

This is called Pick's Formula.

(**b**) Use the formula to find the area of each of these shapes.

(**c**) Use Pick's formula to find the shaded area in each of these shapes.

7 At Jordan Stadium the floodlights consist of rows of lamps.
Each lamp can be

[Off]　or　[On]

Natasha operates the lights. She can arrange a row of three lights in
eight different ways. Here are two of them:

[On]　　[On]　　[On]　and　[Off]　　[On]　　[Off]

(**a**) Draw sketches to show all eight arrangements.

(**b**) Draw sketches to show all the different ways Natasha can arrange a row of

　　1 lamp　　2 lamps　　4 lamps.

(**c**) Copy and complete this table:

Number of lamps in a row	1	2	3	4
Number of possible arrangements	2		8	

(**d**) Without drawing, how many different ways can Natasha arrange a row of
　　(**i**) 5 lamps　　(**ii**) 10 lamps?
　　Explain your answers.

8 (**a**) Here are the entrance gates to
　　Jordan Stadium.
　　Each gate can be open or shut.
　　How many different arrangements of
　　the gates are possible?

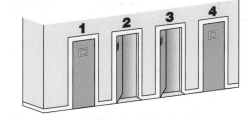

(**b**) For this floodlight, how many different
　　possible arrangements are there with four
　　lamps on?

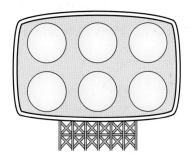

(**c**) Here is a block of eight seats in the
　　grandstand.
　　Each seat can be up or down.
　　How many different arrangements
　　of the seats are possible?

9 A minibus takes people from the station to the Custom
Car Exhibition.

These groups of people are at the station waiting to go to
the exhibition.

(**a**) How many people altogether are waiting?

(**b**) The minibus can seat 12 passengers.
How many trips does the minibus have to make?

(**c**) Each group wants to stay together on the way to the exhibition.
How many trips must the minibus make now? Explain your answer.

10 Val uses a transporter to bring cars to
the exhibition.

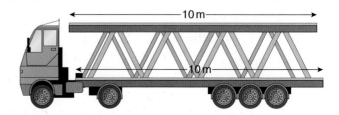

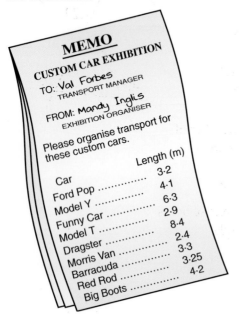

MEMO

CUSTOM CAR EXHIBITION

TO: Val Forbes
TRANSPORT MANAGER

FROM: Mandy Inglis
EXHIBITION ORGANISER

Please organise transport for
these custom cars.

	Length (m)
Car	3·2
Ford Pop	4·1
Model Y	6·3
Funny Car	2·9
Model T	8·4
Dragster	2·4
Morris Van	3·3
Barracuda	3·25
Red Rod	4·2
Big Boots	

(**a**) Write the names of the cars in order of length,
starting with the shortest.

(**b**) Val puts the two longest cars on the transporter.
Which others **cannot** be loaded at the same time?

(**c**) What is the greatest number of cars that Val can
load at any one time? Name them.

(**d**) The transporter needs three trips to bring all the
cars. Explain why.

11 Alan designs road systems. All the streets in this new town are to be straight lines. At each crossroads a control box will be needed to operate the traffic lights.
Three roads **could** cross in the following ways.

1 control box
is needed.

2 control boxes
are needed.

3 control boxes
are needed.

The **maximum** number of control boxes needed for 3 roads is **3**.

(a) Draw a diagram to show the maximum number of control boxes needed for a design with
　　(i) 2 roads　　(ii) 4 roads.

(b) Copy this table. Record the maximum number of control boxes needed for designs with 2, 3 and 4 roads.

Number of roads	1	2	3	4	5	6
Maximum number of control boxes	0					

(c) (i) What do you think is the maximum number of control boxes needed for 5 roads?
　　　 Check by drawing a diagram.
　　(ii) Complete your table.

(d) Alan's design has 8 roads in the centre of the new town. What is the greatest number of control boxes needed for the town centre?

(e) (i) Look at the diagram for 3 roads.
　　　 There are 2 control boxes on each road.
　　　 How many control boxes are there altogether?
　　(ii) Look at **your** diagram for 4 roads.
　　　 How many control boxes are there on **each** road?
　　　 How many control boxes are there altogether?
　　(iii) Repeat (i) for 5 roads.
　　(iv) Describe how Alan could find the maximum number of control boxes when he knows the number of roads.

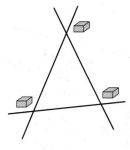

(f) There are to be 20 roads in the new town.
What is the greatest number of control boxes needed?

(g) Write a formula to find the maximum number of control boxes needed for a design with n roads. Check your formula.

Answers

Chapter 1

Exercise 1.1

1 (a) {0, 1, 2, 3, 4, 5} **(b)** {−1, 0, 1, 2, 3}
(c) 1, 2, 3, 4, 5 **(d)** −9, −8, −7, −6, −5, −4

2

	Natural N	Whole W	Integer Z	Rational Q
7	✓	✓	✓	✓
6.3				✓
12	✓	✓	✓	✓
−6			✓	✓
0.7				✓
$\frac{1}{4}$				✓
0		✓	✓	✓

3 (a) {1, 2, 3, 4, 5} **(b)** {... −2, −1, 0, 1, 2, 3, 4, 5}
(c) {4, 5, 6 ...} **(d)** {0, 1, 2, 3, 4}
(e) {1, 2, 3, 4, 5, 6} **(f)** {−2, −1, 0, 1 ...}

Exercise 1.2

1 (a) −4 **(b)** −5 **(c)** 4 **(d)** −8 **(e)** −3
(f) −6 **(g)** 3 **(h)** −9 **(i)** −3 **(j)** 0
2 (a) −1 **(b)** 8 **(c)** 3 **(d)** 11
(e) 21 **(f)** 17 **(g)** −22 **(h)** −13
(i) −22 **(j)** −2 **(k)** −5 **(l)** 10
3 (a) 7 **(b)** −1 **(c)** −21
(d) 26 **(e)** 24 **(f)** −1
(g) 5 **(h)** 27 **(i)** −63
4 1 °C
5 (a) A′(−12, 10), B′(−10, 8), C′(−13, 5), D′(−15, 7)
(b) A″(5, 10), B″(7, 8), C″(4, 5), D″(2, 7)
(c) A‴(0, −1), B‴(2, −3), C‴(−1, −6), D‴(−3, −4)
(d) A⁗(0, 24), B⁗(2, 22), C⁗(−1, 19), D⁗(−3, 21)

Exercise 1.3

1 −12
−30
−24
−12
−35
2 Multiplying a positive number by a negative number gives a negative number.
3 (a) −35 **(b)** −18 **(c)** −90 **(d)** −28 **(e)** −40
(f) −96 **(g)** −120 **(h)** −130 **(i)** −36 **(j)** −144
4 −6 −9 −12
−4 −6 −8
−2 −3 −4
0 0 0
2 3 4
4 6 8
6 9 12
5 Multiplying a negative number by a negative number gives a positive number.
6 (a) 20 **(b)** 18 **(c)** 18 **(d)** 56
(e) 80 **(f)** 156 **(g)** 33 **(h)** 16
(i) 48 **(j)** 18 **(k)** 22·5 **(l)** 150
7 (a) −84 **(b)** −42 **(c)** 63 **(d)** −66
(e) −80 **(f)** −104 **(g)** 120 **(h)** 75
(i) −12·5 **(j)** 6 **(k)** 12·8 **(l)** −240
8 Wick −6°C, Faroe Islands −12°C
9 −27°C

Exercise 1.4

1 (a) $\frac{-35}{5} = -7$ or $\frac{-35}{-7} = 5$ **(b)** $\frac{-42}{6} = -7$ or $\frac{-42}{-7} = 6$
(c) $\frac{24}{-3} = -8$ or $\frac{24}{-8} = -3$ **(d)** $\frac{36}{-4} = -9$ or $\frac{36}{-9} = -4$
2 (a) −5 **(b)** −5 **(c)** −3 **(d)** −3 **(e)** −3
3 (a) 8 **(b)** 8 **(c)** 5 **(d)** 41 **(e)** 12
4 (a) −3 **(b)** 17 **(c)** −5 **(d)** −8 **(e)** 4
5 £155

Exercise 1.5

1 (a) −90 **(b)** −72 **(c)** 80 **(d)** 120 **(e)** −70
(f) 120 **(g)** −126 **(h)** −1600 **(i)** −1350
2 (a) −12 **(b)** 27 **(c)** 2 **(d)** −24
(e) −4 **(f)** 9 **(g)** −28 **(h)** −14
(i) −40·5 **(j)** 11·2 **(k)** −48 **(l)** 27
3 (a) −6 **(b)** 21 **(c)** −25 **(d)** 8 **(e)** −8
(f) 3 **(g)** −4 **(h)** −82 **(i)** 23
4 (a) $K = -15$ **(b)** $F = -33$ **(c)** $P = -28\cdot8$ **(d)** $V = 11\cdot5$
(e) $T = 42$ **(f)** $S = 70$ **(g)** $X = 12$

Exercise 1.6

1 (a) 64 **(b)** 25 **(c)** 36 **(d)** 100 **(e)** 1
(f) 144 **(g)** 121 **(h)** 400 **(i)** 81 **(j)** 900
2 (a) 225 **(b)** 324 **(c)** 360 000 **(d)** 1·44 **(e)** 30·25
(f) 5·29 **(g)** 0·01 **(h)** 1156 **(i)** 46·24 **(j)** 0·25
3 (a) 10 000 **(b)** 1 000 000
4 (a) 5 mm **(b)** 13 cm **(c)** 20 cm
5 (a) 4 **(b)** 9 **(c)** 10 **(d)** 12 **(e)** 14
6 (a) 5 **(b)** 6 **(c)** 20 **(d)** 13 **(e)** 10
(f) 100 **(g)** 1 **(h)** 300 **(i)** 12 **(j)** 1000

7

n	1	2	3	4	5	6	7	8	9	10	11	12	13	14	15
n^2	1	4	9	16	25	36	49	64	81	100	121	144	169	196	225

8 $\sqrt{1024} = 32$ $\sqrt{361} = 19$ $\sqrt{625} = 25$
$\sqrt{1089} = 33$ $\sqrt{1681} = 41$ $\sqrt{784} = 28$
$\sqrt{576} = 24$ $\sqrt{1600} = 40$ $\sqrt{729} = 27$
$\sqrt{1296} = 36$
9 32
10 63
11 16
12 7
13 (a) (i) 25 **(ii)** 169 **(iii)** 100
(b) Square numbers
14 1225, 1296
15 1, 4, 9, 16, 25, 36, 49, 64, 81, 100, 121, 144, 169, 196

Exercise 1.7

1 (a) 4 and 5 **(b)** 4 and 5 **(c)** 2 and 3 **(d)** 4 and 5
(e) 5 and 6 **(f)** 7 and 8 **(g)** 11 and 12 **(h)** 10 and 11
(i) 2 and 3 **(j)** 9 and 10
2 (a) 5·2 **(b)** 9·1 **(c)** 10·9 **(d)** 16·5 **(e)** 32·4
(f) 29·2 **(g)** 17·9 **(h)** 44·7 **(i)** 61·4 **(j)** 49·6
3 (a) 8·4 cm **(b)** 15·5 mm **(c)** 7·3 cm
4 DR = $4\cdot8^2$ m
5 KL = 2·23 m
6 (a) 19·1 m **(b)** 364·8 m²

Exercise 1.8

1 (a) 4^3 **(b)** $(-9)^2$ **(c)** 5^6 **(d)** 15^3 **(e)** 1^3
(f) 3^8 **(g)** $(-10)^3$ **(h)** $(-5)^2$ **(i)** $(-1)^5$
2 (a) 8 **(b)** 64 **(c)** 81
(d) 64 **(e)** 1 **(f)** 243
(g) 1 **(h)** 12 **(i)** 100 000
(j) 8000 **(k)** 1 **(l)** −1
(m) 16 **(n)** −27 **(o)** −100 000
3 (a) 2^3 **(b)** 2^1 **(c)** 2^5 **(d)** 2^7 **(e)** 2^8
4 (a) 3^3 **(b)** 3^2 **(c)** 3^4 **(d)** 3^1 **(e)** 3^5

5 (a) 10^2 (b) 10^3 (c) 10^5 (d) 10^6 (e) 10^9
6 (a) $2^5 = 32$ (b) $5^3 = 125$
  (c) $3^6 = 729$ (d) $4^5 = 1024$
  (e) $2^{10} = 1024$ (f) $10^6 = 1\,000\,000$
7 4^6
8 128
9 2
10 Sum of rows 2, 4, 8, 16, 32, 64, 128, 256 ….
   Powers of two
11 (a) (i) 32   (ii) 16   (iii) 256   (iv) 128   (v) 4
   (b) Add powers in question for power in answer.

Exercise 1.9

1 2, 17, 29, 37, 73
2 (a) 2×5 (b) 2^4
  (c) 3×2^4 (d) $3^2 \times 2^2$
  (e) $2 \times 7 \times 13$ (f) $2 \times 3 \times 5^2$
  (g) $2 \times 3 \times 5$ (h) 3×29
  (i) $2^3 \times 3^2 \times 5^2$ (j) $2^2 \times 3^2 \times 5^2 \times 7$
3 (a) $3 + 5$ (b) $3 + 17$ (c) $7 + 31$
  (d) $7 + 43$ (e) $17 + 29$

4

n	$n^2 - n + 41$	Prime number
0	$0^2 - 0 + 41$	41
1	$1^2 - 1 + 41$	41
2	$2^2 - 2 + 41$	43
3	$3^2 - 3 + 41$	47
4	$4^2 - 4 + 41$	53
5	$5^2 - 5 + 41$	61
6	$6^2 - 6 + 41$	71
7	$7^2 - 7 + 41$	83
8	$8^2 - 8 + 41$	97
9	$9^2 - 9 + 41$	113
10	$10^2 - 10 + 41$	131
11	$11^2 - 11 + 41$	151
12	$12^2 - 12 + 41$	173
13	$13^2 - 13 + 41$	197
14	$14^2 - 14 + 41$	223
15	$15^2 - 15 + 41$	251

Exercise 1.10

1 (a) 1072, 756, 404, 1002   (b) 3465, 756, 57, 1002
  (c) 1072, 756, 404   (d) 3465, 756
2 2, 6
3 (a) 0 or 5   (b) 0
  (c) 2   (d) 1 or 3 or 5 or 7 or 9
  (e) 4   (f) 1
  (g) 1 or 5 or 9   (h) 1 or 4 or 7
4 28 $(1 + 2 + 14 + 4 + 7 = 28)$
5 Pupils investigate 341652, 143652, 361254, 321654, 163254, 123654,
  341256, 143256

Exercise 1.11

1 (a) 4×10^4 (b) 6×10^3 (c) 2×10^5 (d) 5×10^7
  (e) 6×10^2 (f) 1×10^6 (g) 8×10^1 (h) 9×10^{10}
2 (a) 2.3×10^2 (b) 1.6×10^3 (c) 7.8×10^4 (d) 1.5×10^8
  (e) 9.6×10^5 (f) 5.5×10^4 (g) 4.5×10^1 (h) 3.4×10^{10}
3 (a) 2.58×10^5 (b) 3.32×10^4
  (c) 4.05×10^2 (d) 9.01×10^3
  (e) 2.84×10^1 (f) 1.4623×10^2
  (g) 2.0602×10^3 (h) 5.04×10^7
4 (a) 1000   (b) 100 000   (c) 1 000 000
  (d) 10 000 000   (e) 9 000 000   (f) 500
  (g) 800 000   (h) 60
  (i) 400 000 000   (j) 20 000
5 (a) 2300   (b) 5 870 000   (c) 720 000
  (d) 50 000   (e) 12 400 000   (f) 12·4
  (g) 208   (h) 3 450 000 000   (i) 10 200

6 (a) 6×10^9 (b) 1.5×10^8
  (c) 2.48×10^{13} (d) 1.311×10^8
7 (a) 300 000 000
  (b) 4 370 000
  (c) 6 000 000 000 000 000 000 000 000

Exercise 1.12

1 (a) 10^{-6} (b) 10^{-4} (c) 10^{-9} (d) 10^{-1}
2 (a) 7×10^{-2} (b) 6×10^{-5} (c) 1×10^{-6}
  (d) 9×10^{-1} (e) 2×10^{-3} (f) 3.4×10^{-3}
  (g) 5.9×10^{-8} (h) 3.2×10^{-5} (i) 1.24×10^{-1}
  (j) 1.38×10^{-4} (k) 5.06×10^{-3} (l) 6.67×10^{-7}
3 (a) 0·002   (b) 0·000 000 008
  (c) 0·000 000 000 005   (d) 0·000 069
  (e) 0·000 000 11   (f) 0·000 002 7
  (g) 0·000 361   (h) 0·000 000 000 000 070 2
  (i) 0·000 000 000 711
4 (a) 3×10^{-9} (b) 3.169×10^{-8}
  (c) 7.53×10^{-10}
5 (a) 0·000 000 000 000 000 000 000 000 001 63
  (b) 0·000 000 000 000 000 000 160 2
  (c) 0·000 000 000 052 9

Exercise 1.13

1 (a) 8×10^5 (b) 2.4×10^8 (c) 2.5×10^8
  (d) 2.7×10^{16} (e) 8.32×10^3 (f) 1.56×10^{21}
  (g) 7.82×10^{25} (h) 1.056×10^9 (i) 1.525×10^6
2 (a) 600 000 000   (b) 5600
  (c) 360 000 000   (d) 335 000 000
  (e) 173 400   (f) 85 100 000 000
  (g) 1 288 000   (h) 136 000 000
  (i) 757·5
3 (a) 1.8×10^9 metres   (b) 4.5×10^9 metres

Review exercise 1

1 (a) {0, 1, 2, 3, 4, 5, 6, 7, 8}   (b) {−3, −2, −1, 0, 1}
2 (a) {1}   (b) {… −2, −1, 0, 1, 2, 3, 4}
3 (a) 14   (b) 18   (c) −22   (d) 17
4 (a) −45   (b) 7·2   (c) 105   (d) −162
5 (a) −8   (b) 5   (c) −13   (d) −16   (e) 4
6 (a) −4   (b) 24   (c) 3   (d) −28
7 (a) −10   (b) 31   (c) −64
  (d) −4   (e) −4   (f) −8
8 (a) $K = -21$ (b) $F = -79$ (c) $P = -51$
9 (a) 5   (b) 10   (c) 3   (d) 30   (e) 12
10 (a) 2·8   (b) 4·1   (c) 11·6   (d) 5·4   (e) 31·6
11 (a) 3^3 (b) -6^2 (c) 7^6
12 (a) 27   (b) 32   (c) 1
   (d) 1   (e) 14   (f) 10 000 000
13 43, 3, 71, 19
14 (a) 2×3^2 (b) 2×13 (c) 2×3^3
   (d) 5×3^3 (e) $2 \times 7 \times 13$
15 (a) 1 or 3 or 5 or 7 or 9   (b) 2 or 5 or 8
16 (a) 3×10^5 (b) 2.7×10^2
   (c) 2.8×10^7 (d) 6.24×10^7
   (e) 1.82×10^1 (f) 4×10^{-8}
   (g) 5.6×10^{-3} (h) 1.89×10^{-1}
   (i) 3.48×10^{-2} (j) 7.08×10^{-1}
17 (a) 30 000
   (b) 4500
   (c) 116
   (d) 10·2
   (e) 0·000 000 009
   (f) 0·000 007 2
   (g) 0·000 000 000 000 000 004 6
   (h) 0·000 000 000 000 003 1
18 (a) 4.5×10^{17} (b) 7.5×10^{29}
   (c) 2.295×10^{25}

Chapter 2

Exercise 2.1

1 (a) 6   (b) 16   (c) 102   (d) 1
   (e) 6   (f) 1040   (g) 1000   (h) 33
2 (a) 25·7   (b) 13·2   (c) 6·1   (d) 52·0
   (e) 0·1   (f) 3·0   (g) 12·4   (h) 0·4
3 (a) 3·46   (b) 21·07   (c) 0·91   (d) 120·66
   (e) 302·46   (f) 33·43   (g) 45·01   (h) 0·03
4 (a) 35·6   (b) 15·07   (c) 4·1   (d) 0·23   (e) 43·556
   (f) 2·01   (g) 32·11   (h) 7·406   (i) 533·13
5

House	Car	Holiday	Food	Petrol
15·6	3·1	7·0	2·3	8·0

Exercise 2.2

1 (a) 3   (b) 2   (c) 4   (d) 3
   (e) 1   (f) 1   (g) 3   (h) 4
   (i) 4   (j) 4   (k) 5   (l) 4
   (m) 4   (n) 7   (o) 3   (p) 2
2 (a)

Firhill	Hampden	Cappielow	Pittodrie	Rugby Park	Love Street
1	3	2	4	3	2

(b) Firhill's
3

75C	89A	36C	82C	55D
1	2	3	1	1

4 (a) 7, 0·5, 0·004
   (b) 52, 4·6, 0·10, 3·2
   (c) 901, 206, 0·0500
   (d) 326·9, 530·6, 6901
5 (a) 60   (b) 4   (c) 0·07   (d) 500
   (e) 700   (f) 80   (g) 4000   (h) 8
   (i) 400   (j) 80 000   (k) 0·008   (l) 800 000
   (m) 7   (n) 50 000   (o) 9   (p) 400
6 (a) 360   (b) 7·3   (c) 1600   (d) 0·098
   (e) 55 000   (f) 1·2   (g) 45   (h) 2·1
   (i) 2300   (j) 46 000 000   (k) 1·6   (l) 0·091
   (m) 14   (n) 0·20   (o) 65   (p) 2·9
7 (a) 2350   (b) 1·26   (c) 32 600   (d) 0·0589
   (e) 3·00   (f) 305 000   (g) 12·1   (h) 34·6
   (i) 0·0111   (j) 123 000 000   (k) 23·2   (l) 45·0
   (m) 3010   (n) 40 500   (o) 3 570 000   (p) 7·01
8

Number	1 sig fig	2 sig figs	3 sig figs
5263	5000	5300	5260
4872	5000	4900	4870
3·201	3	3·2	3·20
0·023 51	0·02	0·024	0·0235
54 657	50 000	55 000	54 700
4·609	5	4·6	4·61
4·5000	5	4·5	4·50
3 349 000	3 000 000	3 300 000	3 350 000
4 568 954	5 000 000	4 600 000	4 570 000
0·005 409	0·005	0·0054	0·005 41
20·033	20	20	20·0

9 (a) 600   (b) 0·005   (c) 350
   (d) 45·0   (e) 14·01   (f) 100
   (g) 0·0079   (h) 5 700 000   (i) 0·0020
   (j) 326 000 000   (k) 34·7   (l) 50·1
10 (a) 29   (b) 9·5   (c) 0·0021
   (d) 0·30   (e) 2·9   (f) 2·3
11 1·2 m
12 (a) 4 kg
   (b) 8 kg
   (c) 9 kg
13 10 000, 8100, 30 000, 36 000
14 20 m

Exercise 2.3

1 24·6   2 6·9   3 −13·2   4 51
5 45·5   6 0·6   7 4·1   8 0·06
9 5·2   10 0·41   11 23   12 347
13 −2   14 1   15 44·5   16 340
17 90   18 −620   19 103   20 0·2
21 −3410   22 89   23 21 100   24 3
25 4500   26 −0·34   27 0·041   28 23·4
29 0·123   30 −0·0004   31 0·034   32 0·45
33 0·0078   34 0·0008   35 8·76   36 0·056
37 0·0348   38 0·000 07   39 −0·000 005 7   40 0·102
41 −4   42 14   43 57·6   44 −8·1
45 78   46 9   47 900   48 0·67
49 0·023   50 0·002   51 −13   52 −10
53 22   54 8·1   55 23   56 2·1
57 300   58 0·009   59 0·012   60 7·6 kg
61 £3.40   62 29·4 m

Exercise 2.4

1 16·35   2 24·481   3 308·74   4 24·89
5 12·108   6 7·6   7 0·65   8 0·907
9 1·68   10 122·01   11 18   12 0·21
13 0·81   14 108   15 276·06   16 0·48
17 58·7   18 0·197   19 0·668   20 9·34
21 3·09   22 0·21   23 6·232   24 5·85
25 0·4325   26 0·005   27 0·61   28 42·64
29 23·499   30 0·32   31 92   32 3660
33 250

Exercise 2.5

1 128·78   2 13·357   3 2·1252   4 152·55
5 13·043   6 144·59   7 8·38   8 1·176
9 129·007   10 44·93

Exercise 2.6

1 (a) (i) €76.96   (ii) €361.12   (iii) €666
   (b) (i) £43.24   (ii) £68.92   (iii) £233.78
2 (a) (i) €92.43   (ii) 105.3 SFr   (iii) $100.62
   (b) (i) £45.57   (ii) £105.81   (iii) £117.78
3 1·1 cm
4 (a) $387.20   (b) £221.25 ± 0.01
5 (a) Ian   (b) 0·48 sec   (c) 15·338 sec
6 (a) 54·3 secs   (b) 2·16 secs   (c) 3
7 (a) Flour 0·125 kg, Sugar 0·085 kg, Butter 0·075 kg
   (b) Flour 2·25 kg
     Sugar 1·53 kg
     Butter 1·35 kg
8 4·15 m
9 (a) (i) 24·3 kg   (b) (i) 21·7 kg   (c) (i) 25·6 kg
     (ii) Yes   (ii) Yes   (ii) No
10 (a) 33·4 kg   (b) 33 kg
11 (a) £81.40   (b) Doughnuts

Review exercise 2

1 (a) 34·7   (b) 6·1   (c) 4·6   (d) 102·2   (e) 0·0
2 (a) 3·26   (b) 13·1   (c) 0·046
   (d) 405·67   (e) 0·50   (f) 56·00
3 (a) 3   (b) 4   (c) 5   (d) 2   (e) 3
4 (a) 240   (b) 4700   (c) 0·032
   (d) 8·0   (e) 2 600 000
5 (a) 24   (b) 3·46   (c) 0·06
   (d) 3·7   (e) 15   (f) 2 348 000
6 (a) 5·6   (b) 12·5   (c) −5·5   (d) 6·17
   (e) 9   (f) 30·2   (g) −3·58   (h) 0·0076
   (i) 102   (j) −87   (k) 0·2345   (l) 0·000 51
   (m) 6750   (n) 1500   (o) 0·023   (p) 0·0006

7 (a) 19·18   (b) 46·82   (c) 27·145
   (d) 224·5   (e) −0·807   (f) 42·245

8 (a) 25·88   (b) 48·55   (c) 3·377
   (d) 3·929   (e) 70·92   (f) 3·256 25

9 (a) (i) $94.50   (ii) $1155   (iii) $219.63
   (b) (i) £200   (ii) £262.86   (iii) £481.14

10 (a) 131·9 mins   (b) 2·1 mins   (c) 32·975 mins

Chapter 3

Exercise 3.1

1 $a = 27, b = 31, c = 159, d = 88, e = 108$

2 (a) 34   (b) 84   (c) 60   (d) 26
   (e) 36   (f) 54   (g) 21

3 $a = 73, b = 81, c = 14, d = 90, e = 90, f = 18, g = 76, h = 44, i = 71,$
$j = 38, k = 13, l = 107, m = 60$

4 $a = 58, b = 37, c = 85, d = 95, e = 95, f = 85, g = 70, h = 140,$
$i = 65, j = 65, k = 50, l = 35, m = 120, n = 30, p = 25, q = 65,$
$r = 38, s = 38, t = 104, u = 104, v = 104, w = 38$

5 (a) (i) $x = 18$ (ii)

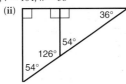

  (b) (i) $x = 18$
  (ii)

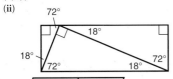

6

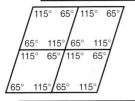

7

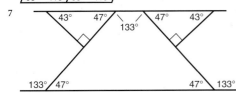

Exercise 3.2

1 (a) 60°, 120°   (b) 120°, 60°   (c) 108°, 72°   (d) $154\frac{2}{7}°, 25\frac{5}{7}°$

2 (a) 140°, 40°   (b) 144°, 36°   (c) 150°, 30°

Exercise 3.4

1 (a) 1·75 km   (b) 1·35 km   (c) 1·95 km   (d) 3·00 km

2 6 km

3 2·625 km

4 Yes, it is 48 km from the port.

5 Yes, it is 29·9 km.

6 (a) (i) 30 cm long 25 cm wide
     (ii) 12 cm long 10 cm wide
     (iii) 6 cm long 5 cm wide
   (b) Scale (ii). Diag. would be too small for scale (i).
   (c) 11 cm

7 15 cm

8 40 cm

Exercise 3.5

1 (a) Scale 1 : 10   Height = 45 cm
   (b) Scale 1 : 20   Width = 110 cm
   (c) Scale 1 : 5   Height = 20·5 cm

2 (a) Scale 1 : 75   (b) 3 m

3 Scale for length = 1 : 55
   Scale for wing span = 1 : 50 i.e. model is not to scale.

Exercise 3.6

1 $h = 20$ m

2 (a) 160 m   (b) 300 m

3 (a) Pupil's scale drawing   (b) 225 m

4 53 m

5 Height = 64 m

6 (a) 12 m   (b) 4·8 m

Exercise 3.7

1 13 km

2 (a) Pupil's scale drawing
   (b) (i) 6 miles   (ii) 8 miles
   (c) (i) 050°   (ii) 140°

3 (a) Pupil's scale drawing
   (b) (i) 70 km   (ii) 20 km

Exercise 3.8

1 $\angle$ALB = 105°, $\angle$ABL = 35°

2 $\angle$PQR = 20°, $\angle$PRQ = 110°

3 105°

4 20°

5 (a)

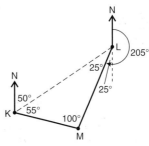

   (b) $\angle$KLM = 25°, $\angle$KML = 100°

Review exercise 3

1 (a) $a = 90, b = 90, c = 90, d = 23, e = 157, f = 157, g = 77, h = 75,$
$i = 62$
   (b) $j = 37, k = 37, l = 72, m = 71, n = 71, p = 109, q = 72, r = 71,$
$s = 72$

2 (a) (i) $x = 72$ (ii) $y = 108$ (iii) $z = 72$
   (b) (i) $x = 36$ (ii) $y = 144$ (iii) $z = 36$

3 12 km

4 17.5 cm

5 Yes. Each dimension is in the ratio 1:50.

6 (b) (i) 44 km   (ii) 28·5 km

Chapter 4

Exercise 4.1

1 (a) (i)

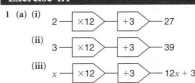

   (b) C = $12x + 3$

2 (a) (i)

   (b) C = $2·5x + 3$

3 (a) (i)

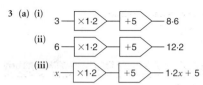

$3 \xrightarrow{\;\times 1\cdot 2\;} \xrightarrow{\;+5\;} 8\cdot 6$

(ii)

$6 \xrightarrow{\;\times 1\cdot 2\;} \xrightarrow{\;+5\;} 12\cdot 2$

(iii)

$x \xrightarrow{\;\times 1\cdot 2\;} \xrightarrow{\;+5\;} 1\cdot 2x + 5$

(b) $C = 1\cdot 2x + 5$

4 (a) Wayfarer £35   Laser £43   Topper £16
(b) Wayfarer $C = 10x - 5$ Laser $C = 7x + 15$ Topper $C = 5x - 4$

5 (a)

$x \xrightarrow{\;\times 5\cdot 2\;} \xrightarrow{\;-3\;}$ Cost, where $x \geqslant 5$

(b) (i) £28.20
(ii) £43.80
(iii) $5\cdot 2x - 3$ where $x \geqslant 5$
(c) $C = 5\cdot 2x - 3$

6 (a)

weight $\xrightarrow{\;\times 2\cdot 5\;} \xrightarrow{\;+15\;}$ Total length

(b) (i) 35 cm   **(ii)** 65 cm   **(iii)** $2\cdot 5x + 15$
(c) $L = 2\cdot 5x + 15$

7 (a) (i) 42 800 cm³   **(ii)** 46 800 cm³
(b) $V = 80x + 42\,000$
(c) 100 seconds (1 min 40 secs)

Exercise 4.2

1 (a)

$31 \xrightarrow{\;-3\;} \xrightarrow{\;\div 4\;} x$

$x = 7$

(b)

$75 \xrightarrow{\;-12\;} \xrightarrow{\;\div 9\;} x$

$x = 7$

(c)

$95 \xrightarrow{\;+5\;} \xrightarrow{\;\div 10\;} x$

$x = 10$

(d)

$39 \xrightarrow{\;-7\;} \xrightarrow{\;\times 8\;} x$

$x = 256$

(e)

$65 \xrightarrow{\;+12\;} \xrightarrow{\;\div 11\;} x$

$x = 7$

(f)

$39 \xrightarrow{\;+25\;} \xrightarrow{\;\div 8\;} x$

$x = 8$

(g)

$42 \xrightarrow{\;-16\;} \xrightarrow{\;\times 20\;} x$

$x = 520$

(h)

$72 \xrightarrow{\;+25\;} \xrightarrow{\;\times 9\;} x$

$x = 873$

2 (a)

Number of CDs $\xrightarrow{\;\times 12\;} \xrightarrow{\;+7\;}$ Cost

(b)

Cost $\xrightarrow{\;-7\;} \xrightarrow{\;\div 12\;}$ Number of CDs

(c) (i) 3   **(ii)** 7   **(iii)** $(c - 7) \div 12$

3 (a)

Cost $\xrightarrow{\;-4\;} \xrightarrow{\;\div 2\cdot 5\;}$ Number of hours parked

(b) (i) 3 hours   **(ii)** 8 hours   **(iii)** $(c - 4) \div 12$

Exercise 4.3

1 (a) 48   **(b)** 133   **(c)** 37   **(d)** 11·6
(e) 14·3   **(f)** 21·5   **(g)** 12·4   **(h)** 42·7
2 (a) £50   **(b)** £32·50   **(c)** £43·75   **(d)** £56·75
3 (a) (i) 77°F   **(ii)** 122°F   **(iii)** 149°F   **(iv)** 107·6°F
(b) 98·6°F
(c) 51·8°F, 53·6°F, 57·2°F, 62·6°F, 66·2°F
4 (a) 12·4   **(b)** 90   **(c)** 43·2   **(d)** −32
(e) 10   **(f)** 6   **(g)** 0·6   **(h)** 0·56

5 (a) (i) 10°C   **(ii)** 20°C   **(iii)** 50°C   **(iv)** −5°C
(b) 100°C
(c) 0°C

Exercise 4.4

1 (a) 42 m²   **(b)** 45 m²   **(c)** 38·5 m²
2 (a) (i) 145   **(ii)** 9·6
(b) (i) 230   **(ii)** 134
(c) (i) 612   **(ii)** 97·9
(d) (i) 1000   **(ii)** 208
(e) (i) 701   **(ii)** 48·2
(f) (i) 122   **(ii)** 51·35
(g) (i) 999   **(ii)** 72·8
3 (a) 180 mins = 3 hours
(b) A. 296 mins   B. 220 mins   C. 210 mins
    = 4 h 56 min   = 3 h 40 min   3 h 30 min
4 (a) 45 m   **(b)** 500 m   **(c)** 180 m   **(d)** 11·25 m
5 (a) 18   **(b)** 36   **(c)** 54   **(d)** 144
(e) 490   **(f)** 43·2   **(g)** 121   **(h)** 289
6 (a) Lee 19·8   Shirley 29·4   Liz 18·5
(b) Liz is the marathon runner – light body weight
    Lee is the sprinter – medium body weight
    Shirley is the hammer thrower – high body weight
(c) Shirley

Exercise 4.5

1 (a) $65 = 8h + 25$ $h = 5$
(b) $78 = 12h + 18$ $h = 5$
(c) $240 = 5 \times R$ $R = 48$
(d) $100 = 2\cdot 5 \times a$ $a = 40$
(e) $72 = 6 \times u$ $u = 12$
(f) $540 = 240 + 3q$ $q = 100$
(g) $42 = 24 + 0\cdot 1h$ $h = 180$
(h) $60 = 32 + 2b$ $b = 14$

2 (a) 9 sides   **(b)** 11 sides
3 (a) (i) 2 hours   **(ii)** 10 hours   **(iii)** 20 hours
(b) (i) 3 hours   **(ii)** 9 hours   **(iii)** 14 hours
(c) (i) Better Bikes   **(ii)** Boneshakers
(d) For £55:   Both give 5 hours
4 (a) $l = 8$ cm
(b) $b = 14$ cm
5 (a) $h = 3$ cm
(b) $b = 5$ cm
(c) $l = 4\cdot 5$ cm

Review exercise 4

1 (a) (i)

$5 \xrightarrow{\;\times 10\;} \xrightarrow{\;+120\;} 170$

(ii)

$x \xrightarrow{\;\times 10\;} \xrightarrow{\;+120\;} 10x + 120$

(b) $t = 10x + 120$
2 (a) $V = 405$ **(b)** $m = 37\cdot 4$ **(c)** $F = 167°$
(d) $x = 18\cdot 3$ **(e)** $s = 252$ **(f)** $C = 35$
3 (a)

Number of bags $\xrightarrow{\;\times 3\cdot 5\;} \xrightarrow{\;+5\;}$ Cost

(b)

Cost $\xrightarrow{\;-5\;} \xrightarrow{\;\times 3\cdot 5\;}$ Number of bags

(c) (i) 10 bags   **(ii)** 20 bags
4 (a) Otter 4 hours
(b) Lazer 4 hours
(c) Otter 2·5 hours Lazer 1 hour 40 mins.
(d) 5 hours

Chapter 5

Exercise 5.1

1 (a) $\frac{7}{20}$ (b) $\frac{3}{5}$ (c) $\frac{33}{50}$ (d) $\frac{6}{25}$ (e) $\frac{3}{8}$
   (f) $\frac{2}{5}$ (g) $\frac{2}{7}$ (h) $\frac{3}{11}$ (i) $\frac{41}{222}$ (j) $\frac{1}{3}$
   (k) $\frac{11}{20}$ (l) $\frac{81}{100}$ (m) $\frac{19}{50}$ (n) $\frac{1}{20}$ (o) $\frac{1}{200}$
2 (a) £7.20   (b) 30 kg   (c) 45 cm
   (d) 310 l   (e) 24p   (f) $35
3 12 tonnes
4 Prize B

Exercise 5.2

1 (a) £2.25   (b) 45 g   (c) 24·5 cm
   (d) 3·2 mm   (e) 16 ml   (f) £2.10
2 (a) £2   (b) 12€   (c) £5.25
3 (a) 165 kg   (b) 96 m   (c) £21
   (d) 12p   (e) £108   (f) 67·5 l
4 (a) £12   (b) 13·5 kg   (c) $0·30   (d) £2·80
5 (a) £22   (b) £61.25   (c) £14
6 (a) £52.50   (b) £7.35   (c) £2.63   (d) £21
7 (a) 330€   (b) 78 kg   (c) £9
   (d) $139.50   (e) 5040 mm   (f) £6.93

Exercise 5.3

1 (a) £64.80   (b) 92.50€   (c) £9.72
   (d) £0.27   (e) $22   (f) £55
2 (a) £29   (b) £46.40   (c) £301.60
3 £26
4 lemonade   4·48 l
   orange   1·76 l
   pineapple   1·12 l
   grapefruit   0·64 l
5 (a) £43.55   (b) £93.80   (c) £52.93
6 (a) £52.87   (b) £148.05   (c) £4418
7 £465.75
8 (a) BST since it give the highest rate.
   (b) City Bank   £164
       P.O. Account   £266.50
       Hullifax   £143.50
       B.S.T.   £287
   (c) £143.50
9 £33.75
10 (a) £998.75   (b) £10 105   (c) £15 040

Exercise 5.4

1 (a) 68%   (b) 85%   (c) 75%   (d) 82·22%
2 (a) Maths 78%   English 85%   French 77%
   (b) English, Maths, French
3 62·5%
4 20%
5 (a) 40%   (b) 10%
6 (a) 22%   (b) 17%   (c) 1%   (d) 27%   (e) $33\frac{1}{3}$%

Exercise 5.5

1 10·5%
2 30%
3 (a) Plant 1 25%   Plant 2 66·67%   Plant 3 6·25%
   (b) Plant 2
4 (a) 23·5%   (b) 23%   (c) 41·2%

Exercise 5.6

1 (a) £60   (b) £250   (c) £180   (d) £12 000
2 (a) £50   (b) £300   (c) £220   (d) £640
3 (a) £30 000   (b) £16 000   (c) £21 000
4 (a) £235.29   (b) £150.59   (c) £88.24
5 45·8% decrease

6 The scarf has the greater percentage reduction.
7 Percentage decrease in area = 9·75%

Exercise 5.7

1 (a) £449.95   (b) £49.95
2 (a) £286.23   (b) £723.52   (c) £8837.34   (d) £1059.25
3 Lindsay
4 (a) £3001.13   (b) £6001.13

Review exercise 5

1 (a) $\frac{57}{100}$, 57%, 0·57   (b) $\frac{1}{4}$, 25%, 0·25
   (c) $\frac{69}{100}$, 69%, 0·69   (d) $\frac{3}{100}$, 3%, 0·03
   (e) $\frac{1}{10}$, 10%, 0·1
2 (a) £50   (b) 220 kg   (c) $112   (d) 9 cm
3 (a) 172.50€   (b) £474   (c) £138.40   (d) £15.20
4 (a) £164.50   (b) £1459.35
5 (a) Local Bank   (b) £13
6 (a) £37.95   (b) £14.38
7 (a) 80%   (b) 55%   (c) 75.6%
8 72·2%
9 (a) £48   (b) £6800
10 £3937.02

Chapter 6

Exercise 6.1

1 (a)

Minutes	1	2	3	4	5	6	7	8
Words	50	100	150	200	250	300	350	400

   (b) (i) Words doubled
       (ii) Words trebled
       (iii) Words quadrupled

2 (a)

Hours worked	1	2	3	4	5	6	7	8
Wage (£)	6	12	18	24	30	36	42	48

   (b) (i) Doubled   (ii) Halved   (iii) Quartered

3 (a)

Petrol (litres)	1	2	3	4	5	6	7	8
Cost (£)	0·80	1·60	2·40	3·20	4·00	4·80	5·60	6·40

   (b) (i) Doubled   (ii) Halved   (iii) Trebled

4 (a)

Sweets (g)	100	200	300	400	500	600	700
Cost (£)	0·99	1·98	2·97	3·96	4·95	5·94	6·93

   (b)

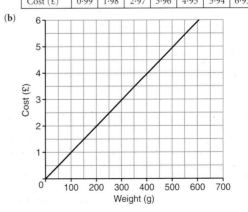

5 (a)

Length (min)	1	2	3	4	5	6
Cost (p)	5	10	15	20	25	30

(b)

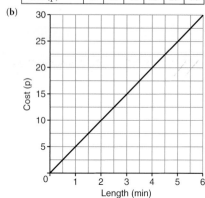

6 They are straight lines through the origin.

7 (a) Straight line through the origin

(b) … direct proportion …

(c) (i) cost halves   **(ii)** cost trebles

(iii) cost quarters   **(iv)** cost multiplies by 5

8 (a) Graph R

(b) The others are not straight lines through the origin.

9 (a)

Distance (km)	1	2	3	4	5	6	7
Cost (£)	0·90	1·30	1·70	2·10	2·50	2·90	3·30

(b)

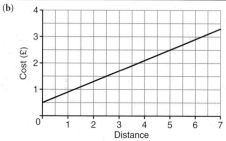

(c) No. Hire charge of 0·50 is added to what would otherwise be directly proportional. Graph is a straight line but does not go through O.

10 (a)

Length	1	2	3	4	5	6	7
Area	1	4	9	16	25	36	49

(b) No. Area is the length squared.

Exercise 6.2

1 £26.75

2 £108

3 (a) £1078   **(b)** £231   **(c)** £770

4 (a) (i) 6   **(ii)** 45   **(iii)** 63

     (b) (i) 9   **(ii)** 14   **(iii)** 20

5 Dried fruit – 300 g, Boiling water – 1000 ml, S.R. flour – 750 g, Caster sugar – 350 g, Butter – 200 g, Eggs – 5

6 (a) 96 miles   **(b)** 9 gallons

7 36 minutes

8 67.20€

9 10 l (9·6 l)

10 1666·67 g (9 boxes)

11 21p

12 (a) 200   **(b)** 30   **(c)** 45

13 (a) €87   **(b)** €210·25   **(c)** €261

14 (a) Packet – 11.8p   Loose – 9.67p   **(b)** Loose

15 £67.42

16 200 g

17 £30

18 £240

19 £5953.19

Exercise 6.3

1 (a)

Length (metres)	Sections
1	120
2	60
4	30
6	20
12	10

(b) Halved

2 (a) (i) 100   **(ii)** 50   **(iii)** 25

(b) Halved

3 (a)

Length (min)	Programmes
10	48
20	24
30	16
40	12
60	8
120	4
240	2

(b)

(c) Curve decreasing from left to right

4 (a) Time is doubled   **(b)** Time is halved

(c) Time is reduced to $\frac{1}{3}$

5 (a) 12 days   **(b)** 6 days   **(c)** 18 days

Exercise 6.4

1 18 hours

2 16 minutes

3 (a) 3 hr   **(b)** 5 hr   **(c)** 4 hr

4 (a) 15 hrs   **(b)** 12 hrs   **(c)** 10 hrs   **(d)** $7\frac{1}{2}$ hrs

5 40 days

6 (a) 280   **(b)** 175

7 24

8 (a) $4\frac{1}{2}$ hrs   **(b)** 2 hrs   **(c)** 3 hr 36 min

9 90

10 54

11 6 pages

Exercise 6.5

1 420 miles

2 7·2 metres

3 35

4 500

5 30 kph

6 15 km, not in proportion

7 4 hrs 12 minutes (4·2 hr)

8 8 minutes (unless they are being boiled individually)

9 195 km

10 Values not in proportion!

11 £58 500

12 £46.67

13 £350 000

Review exercise 6

1 98 pence

2 315 g butter, 700 ml milk, 840 g flour, 367·5 g sugar, 35 g coffee, 7 eggs

3 (a) 11·07p at Saveways, 11·75p at Scoop A Mix

(b) Saveways

4 (a) 8 hr   **(b)** 12 hr

(c) 2·4 hr (ie 2 hr 24 min)   **(d)** $6\frac{2}{3}$ hr (6 h 40 min)

5 31·5 days

6 (a) 270   **(b)** 90 boxes

Chapter 7

Exercise 7.1

1 (a) 40 cm²   (b) 36 cm²   (c) 42 mm²
   (d) 160 cm²   (e) 44 m²   (f) 72 cm²
   (g) 60·5 cm²   (h) 28 cm²   (i) 73·5 cm²
   (j) 800 mm²   (k) 1200 mm²   (l) 900 mm²

2

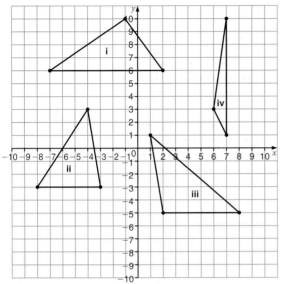

   (b) (i) 15 sq. units   (ii) 18 sq. units
       (iii) 18 sq. units   (iv) 4·5 sq. units
3 75·5 m²
4 73·5 m²
5 (a) 14 cm   (b) 9 cm

Exercise 7.2

1 (a) 72 cm²   (b) 48 cm²   (c) 80 mm²
   (d) 40 cm²   (e) 400 mm²   (f) 81 mm²
   (g) 320 cm²   (h) 250 m²   (i) 240 mm²
   (j) 45 cm²   (k) 49·5 cm²   (l) 325·5 mm²

2

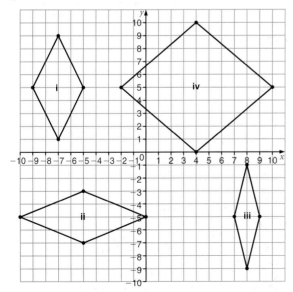

   (b) (i) 16 sq. units   (ii) 20 sq. units
       (iii) 8 sq. units   (iv) 60 sq. units

3 1000 cm², 1875 cm²
4 (a) 3·84 m²
   (b) 3·12 m²
5 (a) x = 60 cm
   (b) x = 30 cm
   (c) x = 8 cm

Exercise 7.3

1 (a) 56 cm²
   (b) 80 cm²
   (c) 480 mm²
   (d) 72 m²
   (e) 72 cm²
   (f) 48 mm²
2 (a) 60 cm²
   (b) 40 cm²
   (c) 20 cm²
   (d) Yes
3 (d) 48 cm²
   (e) 54 mm²
   (f) 28 cm²
4 (a)

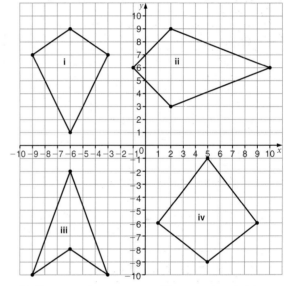

   (b) (i) 24 sq. units   (ii) 33 sq. units
       (iii) 18 sq. units   (iv) 32 sq. units
5 7150 cm² (71·5 mm²), 5250 cm² (5·25 mm²)
6 2700 mm², 440 mm²
7 (a)
   (i)   (ii)   (iii)

   (b) (ii), (i), (iii)
8 (a) 12 cm
   (b) 14 cm
   (c) 10 cm
   (d) 8 mm
   (e) 15 cm
   (f) 11·5 cm

Exercise 7.4

1 (a) 30 cm²   (b) 54 cm²   (c) 44 cm²
   (d) 40 cm²   (e) 36 nm²   (f) 56 m²
   (g) 96 cm²   (h) 35 m²   (i) 84 cm²
   (j) 3·6 cm²   (k) 24 cm²   (l) 99 cm²

2 (a)

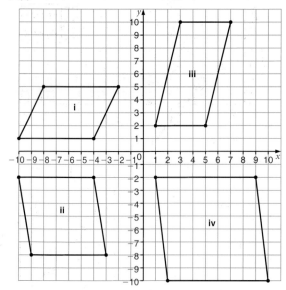

(b) (i) 24 sq. units   (ii) 36 sq. units
     (iii) 32 sq. units   (iv) 64 sq. units
3   77 m², 108 m², 52 m²
4 (a) (i) 100 cm², (ii) 144 cm², (iii) 88 cm²
    (b) (iii), (i), (ii)
5 (a) 12 cm
    (b) 13 cm
    (c) 2·5 m

Exercise 7.5

1 (a) 30 cm²   (b) 36 cm²   (c) 130 cm²
    (d) 25 cm²   (e) 800 mm²   (f) 35 mm²
    (g) 80 cm²   (h) 144 m²   (i) 90 cm²
2 (a)

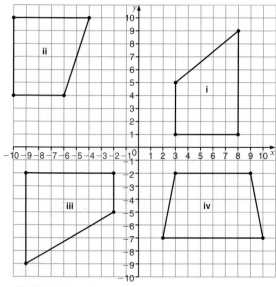

(b) (i) 30 sq units   (ii) 30 sq units
     (iii) 35 sq. units   (iv) 35 sq units

Exercise 7.6

1 (a) 52 cm²   (b) 78 cm²   (c) 59 cm²
    (d) 100 cm²   (e) 88 cm²   (f) 70 m²
    (g) 94 m²   (h) 76 m²   (i) 204 cm²
    (j) 112 cm²   (k) 104·5 mm²   (l) 286 cm²

2 (a)

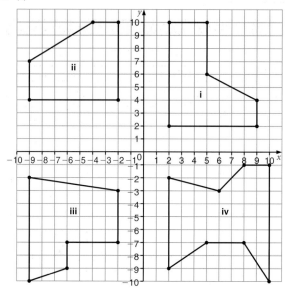

(b) (i) 36 sq. units   (ii) 34·5 sq. units
     (iii) 39 sq. units   (iv) 46 sq. units
3 (a) $x = 4$ cm
    (b) $x = 2$ cm
    (c) $x = 3$ cm

Review exercise 7

1 (a) 30 cm²   (b) 66 mm²   (c) 44 cm²
2 (a) 45 cm²   (b) 90 mm²
3 (a) 198 cm²   (b) 24 cm²
4 (a) 176 cm²   (b) 270 m²   (c) 35 cm²
5 (a) 12 cm   (b) 22 cm   (c) 22 mm
6 (a) 72 cm²   (b) 165 cm²
7 (a) 172 cm²   (b) 126 cm²
8 (a)

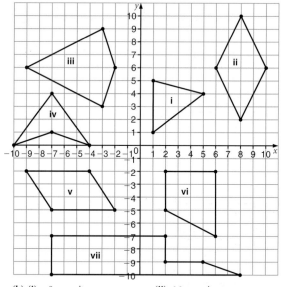

(b) (i) 8 sq. units   (ii) 16 sq. units
     (iii) 21 sq. units   (iv) 9 sq. units
     (v) 15 sq. units   (vi) 16 sq. units
     (vii) 31·5 sq. units
9 (a) Roses = 6 m²   Tulips = 3·6 m²   Carnations = 0·225 m²
    (b) Carnations, Tulips, Roses

Chapter 8

Exercise 8.1

1 (b)

Categorical	Numerical	
	Discrete	Continuous
Favourite TV channel	Children in family	Time watching TV
Favourite style of music	TV's in household	Length of words
	T shirt size	Life expectancy
	A round of golf	
	Audience viewing figures	
	No of leaves on a plant	
		Time to eat a cream cracker
		Fat content
		Height of trees
		Rainfall

(c) Many of the numerical statements could go in either column, e.g. life expectancy in years would be discrete; length of word in cm. rather than number of letters would be continuous.

Exercise 8.2

1 (a)

Fledglings	Tally	Frequency
2	|	1
3	|	1
4	|||	3
5	||||	4
6	|||	3
7	|||	3
8	|	1

(b)

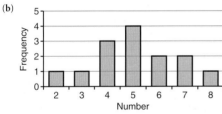

(c) Pupils' own answers, e.g. the fledgling population has stayed approximately the same; there are slightly fewer in 2003; average number per nest has increased slightly.

2 Round 1

Shots	Tally	Freq.
2	|	1
3	||	2
4	||||	4
5	|||	3
6	|||	3
7	||||	4
8	|	1

Round 2

Shots	Tally	Freq.
2		
3	||	2
4	|||| |||	8
5	||||	4
6	|	1
7	|	1
8		
9	|	1
10	|	1

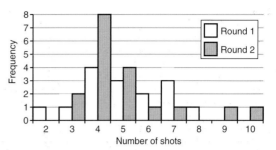

(c) Pupils' own answers.

3 Rural

Cans	Tally	Freq
0	|||| |||| |||| |||| |||| |	26
1	|||| |||	8
2	|||| |	6
3	|||	3
4	||	2
5	|	1
7	|	1
10	|	1
12	||	2

Urban

Cans	Tally	Freq
0	|||| |||| |||	13
1	|||| |||	8
2	|||| ||||	10
3	|||| |	6
4	||||	4
5	|||	3
6	|	1
7	|	1
8	|	1
10	|	1
11	|	1
12	|	1

Drinks consumed in rural area

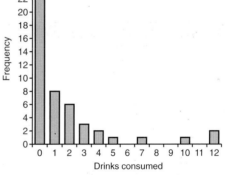

Drinks consumed in rural area

Exercise 8.3

1 (a) Max. 48   Min 18

(b) (c)

1	8
2	6
3	3 6 6 7 7
4	2 7 8

(d) Yes, at least 3

2 (a) Max. 79   Min 31

(b)

```
3 | 1 8 8 9 9
4 | 0 2 3
5 | 0 0 1 2 3 7
6 | 0 3 5
7 | 5 6 9
```

(c) 3

3 (a) Max. 203   Min. 101

(b)

```
10 | 1 4 5 8
11 | 8
12 | 2 4
13 | 2 4 5 9
14 | 7 8
15 | 0 6 7
16 | 4
17 | 7
18 | 4
19 |
20 | 3
```

(c) A lot of time spent watching TV. Is it too high?

(d) Pupils' surveys

4 (a) Max. 6·7 kg   Min. 0·6 kg

(b)

```
0 | 6 8
1 | 1 2 5 6 7
2 | 3 3 5 6 8
3 | 1 2
4 | 3
5 | 1 4
6 | 7
```

(c) Yes. Most fish had higher weights than average.

Exercise 8.4

1 (a) Max. 50.9   Min. 35.6

(b)

```
          M          F
                35 | 6 7
          6 8  36 |
      9 4 3 1  37 | 5 5
          5 4  38 | 7
                39 | 4 7 9
                40 |
            7  41 | 4
      7 6 5 2  42 |
          9 6  43 |
            4  44 | 2
      9 8 2 0  45 | 5 5
            6  46 | 3
            6  47 | 0 0
            0  48 | 2 3 4 6 6
                49 | 7
                50 | 9
```

Key 8 | 36 = 36·8 years   **Key** 41 | 4 = 41·4 years

(c) LE generally lower in Africa. There is not such a marked difference between male and female in Africa

2 (a) Max 269 lb   Min 172 lb

(b)

```
      Backs      |     Forwards
          8 2 | 17 |
          6 1 | 18 |
      6 4 0 0 | 19 |
          8 7 1 | 20 |
          8 0 0 | 21 | 0 4 7
            4 0 | 22 | 4
                | 23 | 4 8 8
                | 24 | 1 2 2 3 5 5 5 8 9
                | 25 | 4 4 6
                | 26 | 2 5 9
```

Key 2 | 17 = 172 lb   **Key** 21 | 7 = 217 lbs

(c) In general, the weight does determine the position played, although there is some overlap. Forwards are heavier than backs.

3 (a)

1983/84	*2003/04*
Max. – 80	Max. – 90
Min. – 29	Min. – 33

(b)

```
            1983/84 |   | 2003/4
                9 | 2 |
                  | 3 | 3 3 3 9
              8 1 | 4 | 1 4 5 5 7 8
  7 3 2 1 1 1 1 0 0 | 5 | 0 2 3 3 6 6
        3 2 1 0 0 | 6 | 0
            7 4 4 3 | 7 | 5 9
                0 | 8 |
                  | 9 | 0
```

Key 9 | 2 = 29 points   **Key** 7 | 5 = 75 points

(c) Fewer 'outliers' and main group in the higher range. More competitive.

Exercise 8.5

1 (a) Hearts scored

Time (mins)	Tally	Freq.
$0 \leqslant t < 15$	|||	3
$15 \leqslant t < 30$	|||	3
$30 \leqslant t < 45$	⩕ ||||	9
$45 \leqslant t < 60$	⩕ ⩕ |||	13
$60 \leqslant t < 75$	⩕ ⩕	10
$75 \leqslant t \leqslant 90$	⩕ ⩕ ⩕ |||	18

(b) Hearts conceded

Time (mins)	Tally	Freq.
$0 \leqslant t < 15$	||||	4
< 30	⩕ ⩕		11
< 45	⩕ ⩕	10
< 60	⩕	5
< 75	⩕ ⩕	10
$\leqslant 90$	⩕ ⩕	10

(c) (d) Hibs scored   Hibs conceded

	Tally			
$t < 15$	⩕		6	⩕ |||	8
< 30	⩕		6	||||	4
< 45	⩕ ⩕		10	⩕ ⩕	10
< 60	⩕ ||	7	⩕ ||||	9
< 75	⩕ ||	7	⩕ ⩕		11
$\leqslant 90$	⩕ ⩕ ⩕ ⩕ ⩕	25	⩕ ⩕		11

(e)

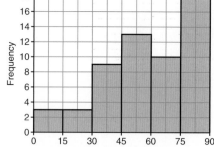

Hearts Scored

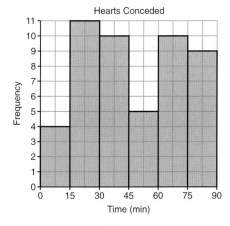

Hearts Conceded

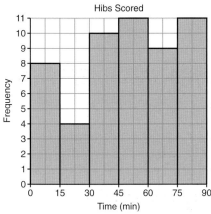

Hibs Scored

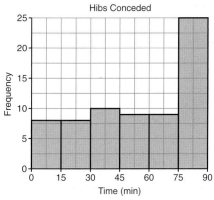

Hibs Conceded

2

Salt, s, grammes	Tally	Frequency
$0 < s < 0.2$	|||	3
$0.2 < s < 0.4$	||	2
$0.4 < s < 0.6$	||||	4
$0.6 < s < 0.8$	||| |||	8
$0.8 < s < 0.1$			1
$1.0 < s < 1.2$	||	2
$1.2 < s < 1.4$		0
$1.4 < s < 1.6$		0
$1.6 < s < 1.8$			1

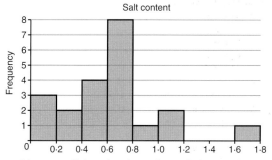

Salt content

3 Pupils' answers will depend on choice of intervals, for example:

River Inver

Rainfall, r (mm)	March		May		Aug		Nov	
$0 \leqslant r < 50$		0	|||	5		0		0
$50 \leqslant r < 100$	|||	3	||| |||	10	|||	7			1
$100 \leqslant r < 150$	||||	4	||| ||	7	||| |||	10	||||	4
$150 \leqslant r < 200$	|||	3	|||	3	||	2	||||	4
$200 \leqslant r < 250$	||| ||	7		0	|||	3	|||	3
$250 \leqslant r < 300$	|||	5		0	|||	3	|||	3
$300 \leqslant r < 350$			1		0		0	|||	3
$350 \leqslant r < 400$			1		0		0	||||	4
$400 \leqslant r < 450$		0		0		0	||	2
$450 \leqslant r < 500$		0		0		0		0
$500 \leqslant r < 550$			1		0		0			1

River Almond

Rainfall, r (mm)	March		May		Aug		Nov	
$0 \leqslant r < 50$	||	2	||| ||| ||	12	||| ||	7	||	2
$50 \leqslant r < 100$	||| ||| ||| |||	18	||| |||	10	||| ||||	9	||| ||||	9
$100 \leqslant r < 150$	||||	4	|||	3	||| |||	8	||| ||| |||	13
$150 \leqslant r < 200$			1		0			1			1
$200 \leqslant r < 250$		0		0		0		0
$250 \leqslant r < 300$		0		0		0		0
$300 \leqslant r < 350$		0		0		0		0
$350 \leqslant r < 400$		0		0		0		0
$400 \leqslant r < 450$		0		0		0		0
$450 \leqslant r < 500$		0		0		0		0
$500 \leqslant r < 550$		0		0		0		0

(d)

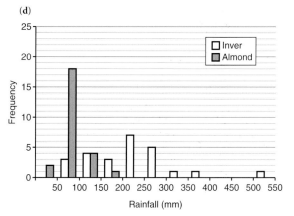

(e) Rainfall lighter in the west as demonstrated by histogram.

Exercise 8.6

1 (a)

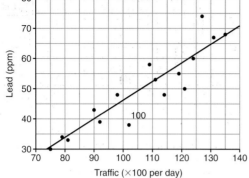

(b) Positive correlation
(c) (i) 37 ppm
  (ii) 10 900 vehicles

2 (a)

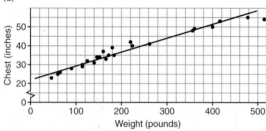

(b) Positive correlation
(c) (i) 310 pounds
  (ii) 48 inches

3 (a)

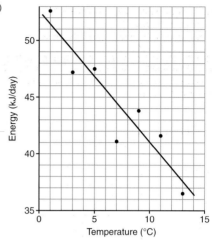

(b) No correlation obvious, so no line of best fit

4 (a)

(b) Negative correlation
(c) (i) 8·5°C   **(ii)** 41 kJ

5 (a)

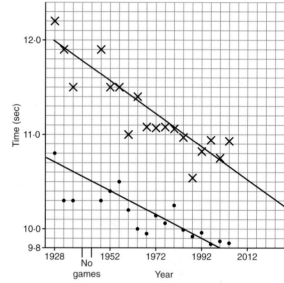

(c) 9·8 seconds
(d) 10·7 seconds
(e) Best fit lines running almost parallel therefore the answer is *NO*

Exercise 8.7

1 (a) 6   **(b)** 10   **(c)** 43·8   **(d)** 66·625   **(e)** 28
2 (a) 7·1875   **(b)** 5·5   **(c)** 58   **(d)** 158   **(e)** 2858
3 (a) 14   **(b)** 19   **(c)** $\dfrac{x+y}{2}$
4 23
5 (a) 67   **(b)** 66   **(c)** 3·02   **(d)** 7·14   **(e)** 856·5
  (f) 15·9   **(g)** 15·9   **(h)** £30.44   **(i)** £30.44
6 Nothing
7 377 kg
8 37·6 kg
9 (a) (i) Various answers
    (ii) 5, 7, 10, 13, 15
    (iii) 5, 6, 11, 13, 15
  (b) 6, 9, 14, 15, 16   6, 10, 13, 15, 16   6, 11, 13, 14, 16
    6, 9, 14, 15, 16
10 (a) mean £11 400, median £6000, modal range £4000
  (b) (i) Modal wage of £4000   **(ii)** Mean at £11 400
11 (a) 4
  (b) 6·44 (6)
  (c) Most people require that size.

12 (a) Mean = £308.57, Median £90, Modal wage £90
   (b) Unhappy and underpaid
   (c) Mean drops to £249.05, others remain the same.

Review exercise 8

1 (a) Numerical and continuous, or numerical and discrete
   (b) Numerical and discrete
   (c) Categorical
   (d) Categorical
   (e) Numerical and continuous
   (f) Numerical and continuous

2 (a)

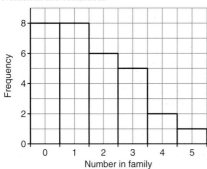

   (iii) 1·6
   (iv) Population falling. Number of children less than adults in the family.

3 (a) Max BBC1 18m   ITV 16·8m
       Min BBC1 6·3m   ITV 6·3m
   (b)

BBC1		ITV
9 8 8 7 6 5 4 3 3	6	3 6 8 9
9 9 8 5 1 0	7	0 0 3 3 8 8
9 8 8 7 6 4 2 1	8	1 2 4 5 9
8 3 1	9	3 5 6
	10	1 4 8
	11	4 7
	12	2 3
	13	4 7
	14	
	15	6 6
8	16	8
8 8	17	
0	18	

   (c) ITV is more popular

4 Frequency tables and histograms will depend on class intervals chosen. For example:

Time, t	Boys		Girls	
$0 \le t < 10$	|||	3	ⅢⅢ|	11
$10 \le t < 20$	||	2	ⅢⅠ	5
$20 \le t < 30$	|||	3	||	2
$30 \le t < 40$	||||	4		0
$40 \le t < 50$	|	1	||	2
$50 \le t < 60$	||	2		0
$60 \le t < 70$	|	1		0
$70 \le t < 80$	||	2		0
$80 \le t < 90$	|	1		0
$90 \le t < 100$		0		0
$100 \le t < 110$		0		0
$110 \le t < 120$		0		0
$120 \le t < 130$	|	1		0

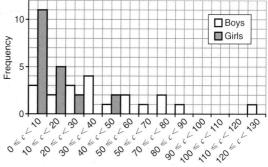

   (c) The girls spend less time than the boys playing computer games.

5 (a) Mean consumption 2503, Mean prod. 2120
   (b) Median consumption 1335, Median prod. 815
   (c) Largest consumer and largest user/head is USA. Japan is the 2nd largest consumer and 2nd largest/head. India consumes more than UK but much less than anybody else/head.

6

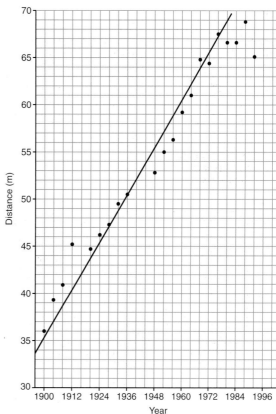

   (b) Positive correlation
   (c) Values between 65 m and 70 m.   (d) No

Chapter 9

Exercise 9.1

1 (a) $7p$ (b) $5c$ (c) $19q$
  (d) $12z$ (e) $11e + 9f$ (f) $5y + 4g$
  (g) $15x - 16y$ (h) $19p + 7q$ (i) $23f + 4g$
  (j) $8a + 3b$ (k) $6s + 5c$ (l) $15s + 9$
  (m) $3p + 1$ (n) $4 + 2p$ (o) $p + 2q$
2 (a) $7p + 11$ (b) $t + 14$ (c) $5x + 1$
  (d) $11y + 15$ (e) $3a + 13b$ (f) $2q + 4$
  (g) $k + 2l$ (h) $11b + 5a$ (i) $4x + 4$
  (j) $15y + 25$ (k) $50z - 13w$ (l) $11p - 17q$

3 (a) $15a - 6b$ (b) $17n + 11m$ (c) $8s - 12r$
(d) $5s - 15t$ (e) $10f - 10g$ (f) $x + y$
(g) $12y - 2x$ (h) $32a - 8b$ (i) $3y - x - 5z$
(j) $29m - 19p$ (k) $-8k - 4j$ (l) $5f - 5g - 6h$

Exercise 9.2

1 (a) $x = 7$ (b) $p = 20$ (c) $b = 7$
(d) $r = 10$ (e) $g = 1$ (f) $t = -10$
(g) $a = 2$ (h) $w = 9$ (i) $g = 7$
2 (a) $x = 10$ (b) $p = 10$ (c) $e = 4, t = 4$
(d) $y = 3$ (e) $s = 5$ (f) $y = 4$
(g) $p = -2$ (h) $s = -1$ (i) $t = -2$
(j) $w = -7$ (k) $x = -2$ (l) $y = -2$
3 (a) $x = 5$ (b) $p = 3$ (c) $c = 2$
(d) $m = 4$ (e) $s = 3$ (f) $x = 5$
(g) $x = -3$ (h) $y = -2$ (i) $c = -5$
4 (a) $p = 5$ (b) $x = 2$ (c) $x = 1$
(d) $t = 3$ (e) $y = 2$ (f) $m = -5$
(g) $p = -4$ (h) $v = -1$ (i) $q = -2$
5 (a) $x = 4$ (b) $y = 6$ (c) $a = 4$
(d) $b = 3$ (e) $t = -3$ (f) $p = -2$
(g) $s = 5$ (h) $x = 1$ (i) $x = \frac{1}{2}$
(j) $x = \frac{7}{2}$ (k) $y = -\frac{1}{3}$ (l) $m = -\frac{2}{3}$

Exercise 9.3

1 (a) $x = 3$ (b) $y = 4$ (c) $z = 2$
(d) $x = 6$ (e) $m = 5$ (f) $v = -5$
(g) $w = 6$ (h) $y = 4$ (i) $r = 5$
(j) $x = 6$ (k) $y = -2$ (l) $f = -7$
(m) $q = -10$ (n) $t = 1$ (o) $y = 7$
(p) $t = -1$ (q) $s = -7$ (r) $t = 2$
2 (a) $r = 6$ (b) $y = 4$ (c) $k = 5$
(d) $b = 10$ (e) $s = -3$ (f) $b = -2$
(g) $x = -1$ (h) $a = 5$ (i) $z = 7$
(j) $x = 3$ (k) $x = 4$ (l) $x = 3$
(m) $x = -1$ (n) $x = -3$ (o) $x = 0$
3 (a) $x = 3$ (b) $p = 2$ (c) $p = 2$
(d) $t = -2$ (e) $x = -2$ (f) $p = 2$
(g) $y = -\frac{3}{2}$ (h) $m = \frac{2}{3}$ (i) $x = 3\frac{1}{2}$
(j) $p = 5\frac{1}{2}$ (k) $x = \frac{1}{2}$ (l) $x = -\frac{2}{3}$
(m) $x = -\frac{1}{2}$ (n) $t = \frac{14}{9}$ (o) $x = \frac{14}{15}$

Exercise 9.4

1 (a) $3x + 6$ (b) $42 + 24f$ (c) $9r + 18p + 6$
(d) $6z - 8$ (e) $72y - 16$ (f) $35q - 10w + 5$
(g) $54e - 18$ (h) $4x + 24$ (i) $16t + 80s - 40$
(j) $3y - 12$ (k) $21r - 28s$ (l) $55 - 22d + 66e$
(m) $50y - 80$ (n) $24 - 40y$ (o) $12x - 2y - 6$
2 (a) $2x + 11$ (b) $5y + 12$ (c) $13x + 20y - 5z$
(d) $12m - 6$ (e) $12 - 18p$ (f) $22a + 33b + 14c$
(g) $8f - 24g$ (h) $32x + 40y$ (i) $12p + 2q - 28$
(j) $9x - 6y$ (k) $12f + 24$ (l) $6 + 11e - 3f$
(m) $6x + 6$ (n) $8y + 30$ (o) $15y + 10 - 5x$
3 (a) $-4q - 12$ (b) $-6p - 21$ (c) $-2p - 6q - 10$
(d) $-3y + 21$ (e) $-3w + 2z$ (f) $-28j + 35k - 14$
(g) $-10y - 25$ (h) $-12x - 15$ (i) $-12n + 28m + 20$
(j) $-12m + 12$ (k) $-64d + 48f$ (l) $-24m + 16m + 8$
4 (a) $-4y - 21$ (b) $-32n + 3$ (c) $8x + 8y - 6z$
(d) $-28x - 40y$ (e) $-15x + 11y$ (f) $12a + 24b - 14c$
(g) $-12f + 64$ (h) $-17m + 10n$ (i) $36d - 12c + 10$
(j) $-80g + 30$ (k) $-27w + 24v$ (l) $-11x - 10y - 10z$
(m) $90g - 16f$ (n) $28e - 8f$ (o) $-4x + 5y$
(p) $1 - 2a$ (q) $b + 3$ (r) $3p - 3q$

Exercise 9.5

1 (a) $8x + 21$ (b) $24 + 11p$ (c) $4y + 31$
(d) $16m + 10$ (e) $15x + 16y$ (f) $27t + 10s$
(g) $15e + 6$ (h) $4h + 12$ (i) $14x + 44y + 35z$
(j) $3p + q$ (k) $6y$ (l) $7a + 2b + 6c$
2 (a) $58r + 30$ (b) $47x - 12$
(c) $16b + 48c + 4d$ (d) $26b - 65c$
(e) $a + 7b$ (f) $35r - 31s + 4t$
(g) $4p + 13q$ (h) $5r + 20$
(i) $52x - 30y + 58z$ (j) $q - 1$
(k) $2b + 9$ (l) $9g + 15h$
(m) $12 - 16c$ (n) $15d - 64$
(o) $5p - 5q - 5r$ (p) $4x - 4y$
3 (a) $-12 - 34x$ (b) $-15 + 13m$ (c) $-10 + 10z$
(d) $-23 - 18p$ (e) $9r + 6$ (f) $-23x + 33y$
(g) $-21b + 38c$ (h) $-51d$ (i) $-21x - 6y$
(j) $-32y + 23$ (k) $-81m + 22n$ (l) $-17 + 5x$
(m) $-17p + 71q$ (n) $-26r + 34s$ (o) $21y - 4x - 3$
(p) 0 (q) $5p - 3q - 5$ (r) $17y - 8x - 12$

Exercise 9.6

1 (a) $x = 2$ (b) $p = 6$ (c) $x = 4$
(d) $x = 7$ (e) $x = 8$ (f) $x = 15$
(g) $y = 3$ (h) $y = 9$ (i) $x = 5$
(j) $x = 3$ (k) $z = 15$ (l) $x = 19$
(m) $x = -6$ (n) $x = 0$ (o) $c = -3$
2 (a) $x = 1$ (b) $y = 2$ (c) $x = 3$
(d) $x = -2$ (e) $x = 4$ (f) $a = 0$
(g) $x = 2$ (h) $y = 3$ (i) $a = 1$
(j) $p = 2$ (k) $x = 2$ (l) $x = 9$
3 (a) $x = 9$ (b) $x = 4$ (c) $s = 13$
(d) $x = 2$ (e) $x = -50$ (f) $y = -2$
(g) $x = 2$ (h) $g = 9$ (i) $x = 1$
(j) $y = 19$ (k) $x = -1$ (l) -2
4 (a) $y = 2$ (b) $x = 4$ (c) $y = -13$
(d) $y = 3$ (e) $z = -3$ (f) $m = -2$
(g) $x = 4$ (h) $a = -4$ (i) $s = -1$
5 (a) $x = \frac{1}{2}$ (b) $c = -4\frac{1}{2}$ (c) $a = \frac{1}{3}$
(d) $t = \frac{2}{3}$ (e) $x = \frac{1}{4}$ (f) $x = -\frac{1}{3}$
(g) $x = -1\frac{1}{2}$ (h) $x = -\frac{1}{5}$ (i) $x = 8\frac{2}{3}$
(j) $a = -1$ (k) $x = 3\frac{4}{5}$ (l) $x = -6\frac{1}{3}$

Exercise 9.7

1 (a) $x = 4$ (b) $y = 8$ (c) $m = 3$
(d) $s = 2$ (e) $m = -1$ (f) $x = 3$
(g) $x = 2$ (h) $y = 6$ (i) $y = -2$
(j) $t = 2$ (k) $z = 3$ (l) $r = 2$
2 (a) $c = 2$ (b) $x = 1$ (c) $x = -10$
(d) $d = 4$ (e) $x = 2$ (f) $y = 4$
(g) $x = 3$ (h) $m = 4$ (i) $x = 3$
(j) $f = 3$ (k) $x = 2$ (l) $l = -2$
3 (a) $x = \frac{1}{2}$ (b) $p = \frac{4}{5}$ (c) $y = 2\frac{1}{2}$
(d) $x = \frac{4}{5}$ (e) $x = \frac{7}{9}$ (f) $t = 10$

Exercise 9.8

1 (a) $y = 12$ (b) $x = 4$ (c) $z = -6$
(d) $y = 20$ (e) $x = -30$ (f) $x = 50$
(g) $y = 6$ (h) $z = 8$ (i) $x = 12$
2 (a) $x = 10$ (b) $z = -12$ (c) $s = 20$
(d) $f = -6$ (e) $y = -5$ (f) $x = 20$
(g) $x = 11$ (h) $y = 1$ (i) $x = -12$
(j) $y = -10$ (k) $m = \frac{8}{11}$ (l) $y = \frac{3}{5}$

Exercise 9.9

1 (a) 8 (b) 10 (c) 5 (d) 4
2 (a) $2(x + 4)$ (b) $3(y + 7)$ (c) $4(y + 4)$ (d) $5(m - 7)$
(e) $4(2t + 9)$ (f) $5(2t - 7)$ (g) $10(2f + 5)$ (h) $4(3s + 4t - 5)$

3 (a) $2(2r + s - 4)$ **(b)** $8(2x + 3)$
(c) $5(6x + 3y - 5)$ **(d)** $9(2m + n)$
(e) $4(5t + 4u - 9)$ **(f)** $3(1 - 7g)$
(g) $6(x + 5y)$ **(h)** $4(x + 8y - 9z)$
(i) $9(2m - 3n + 9)$ **(j)** $20f - 17g$
(k) $7(4r + 7s - 3)$ **(l)** $2(3f - 4g)$
(m) $15(2r + 3s - 1)$ **(n)** $6(3m + 6n - 7)$
(o) $-5(f + 2g)$

4 (a) $5(2m - 5n - 11)$ **(b)** $4(5d + 7e - 3)$
(c) $11(r - 3s + 7)$ **(d)** $20(2x - 3y)$
(e) $100(3f + 7g - 6)$ **(f)** $13(x - 2y + 3)$
(g) $8(2m + 3n)$ **(h)** $2(12x + 18y - 1)$
(i) $3(4b + 3c - 6)$ **(j)** $7(6m - 7n + 11p)$
(k) $17(x + 3y)$ **(l)** $2(2g + 3h - 5i)$
(m) $8(2f - 3g)$ **(n)** $10(2x + 5y)$
(o) $35(2s + t)$ **(p)** $25(2x + y - 3)$
(q) $8(4r + 5s)$ **(r)** $11(3x - 5y + 8z)$

Exercise 9.10

1 $3(x + 5) = 27, x = 4$ **2** $3y + 11 = 38, y = 9$
3 $2x + 7x = 45, x = 5$ **4** $15 + 4x = 55, x = 10$
5 $\dfrac{5x}{2} = 10, x = 4$ **6** $18y = 36, y = 2$
7 $4(2y + 7) = 52, y = 3$ **8** $\dfrac{9x}{2} = -9, x = -2$

9 (a) $x = 5$ cm   **(b)** $x = 6$ cm   **(c)** $x = 15$ cm
(d) $x = 4\frac{1}{2}$ cm   **(e)** $x = 6$ m

Exercise 9.11

1 (a) $x > 1$ **(b)** $x < 5$ **(c)** $y \leqslant 5$
(d) $x \geqslant 1$ **(e)** $y > 2$ **(f)** $y < 9$
(g) $y \leqslant 2$ **(h)** $p < \frac{1}{4}, x > 4$ **(i)** $y \geqslant 1$
(j) $v < 5$ **(k)** $t \leqslant 4 \cdot 8$ **(l)** $p < \frac{1}{4}$
2 (a) $n < 4$ **(b)** $n \geqslant \frac{7}{8}, x \geqslant 5$ **(c)** $x > 1$
(d) $x \leqslant 1$ **(e)** $p \geqslant 5$ **(f)** $x \leqslant 1$
(g) $x > 1$ **(h)** $x < 4\frac{1}{2}$ **(i)** $x > 2\frac{4}{5}$
(j) $t \leqslant \frac{4}{7}$ **(k)** $n \geqslant \frac{7}{8}$ **(l)** $x < 6\frac{3}{4}$

Review exercise 9

1 (a) $7m$ **(b)** $8p$ **(c)** $2m + 8n$
2 (a) $x = 2$ **(b)** $n = 6$ **(c)** $p = 2$
3 (a) $12y + 8$
(b) $21r - 14s + 7t$
(c) $-20f - 12g + 4h$
4 (a) $11p + 14q$ **(b)** $11x - 14y$ **(c)** $m - 3n$
5 (a) $y = 3$ **(b)** $x = 8$ **(c)** $p = 2$
6 (a) $x = 7$ **(b)** $y = -2$ **(c)** $s = 10$
7 (a) $x = 5$ **(b)** $x = -2$ **(c)** $x = 12$
8 (a) $2(4x + 5y)$
(b) $6(3m - 7n)$
(c) $3(3f - 5g + 7h)$
9 (a) $2(x + 11) = 50, x = 14$
(b) $5y + 2y = -63, y = -9$
10 (a) $p > 2$
(b) $m > 3$
(c) $x \geqslant \frac{1}{2}$

Exercise 10.1

1 (a) (i)

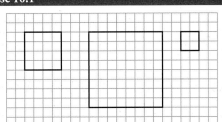

(ii)

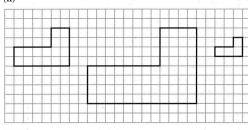

(iii)

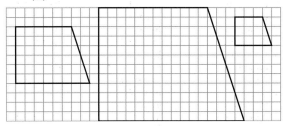

2 (a)

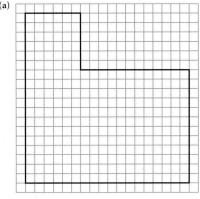

(b)

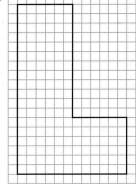

(c)

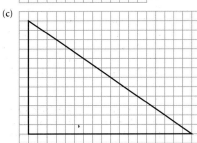

3 (a)   **(b)**   **(c)**

4 (a)

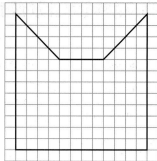

(b)

(c)

(d)

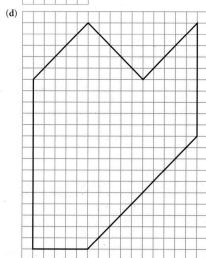

(e)

(f)

5 (a) 6 cm, 8 cm

(b) $2\frac{1}{2}$ cm, 4 cm

(c) 8 cm, 3 cm, 10 cm, 4 cm

6 (a) $\frac{1}{2}$ **(b)** 2   **(c)** 3
(d) 5   **(e)** 4   **(f)** $\frac{1}{3}$
(g) $\frac{1}{4}$ **(h)** $\frac{2}{3}$ **(i)** $\frac{1}{2}$

7 (a) 3   **(b)** 5   **(c)** $\frac{1}{4}$ **(d)** $\frac{1}{10}$ **(e)** $\frac{1}{4}$
8 (a) Enlarge   **(b)** Enlarge
  (c) Reduce   **(d)** Enlarge
  (e) Reduce   **(f)** Enlarge

Exercise 10.2

1 (a) scale factor 3 and **(c)** scale factor $\frac{1}{5}$
2 (a) scale factor $\frac{3}{10}$ **(b)** scale factor $\frac{7}{2}$
  (d) scale factor $\frac{3}{10}$ **(f)** scale factor $\frac{5}{8}$
3 (a) 1·5   **(b)** $\frac{2}{7}$ **(c)** 2·5

Exercise 10.3

1 (a) (i) 4   **(ii)** 8
  (b) (i) $\frac{1}{5}$ **(ii)** 2
  (c) (i) $3\frac{1}{2}$ **(ii)** 35
  (d) (i) $2\frac{1}{2}$ **(ii)** 12·5
2 (a) 6   **(b)** 72   **(c)** 6·5 cm   **(d)** 20
3 (a) (i) 6 cm   **(b) (i)** 8 cm   **(c) (i)** 5 cm
   (ii) $\frac{1}{9}$ **(ii)** $\frac{1}{12}$ **(ii)** $\frac{1}{13}$
   (iii) 4 cm   **(iii)** 6 cm   **(iii)** 7 cm
   (iv) 36 cm   **(iv)** 72 cm   **(iv)** 91 cm
  (d) (i) 4 cm   **(e) (i)** 7 cm
   (ii) $\frac{1}{15}$ **(ii)** $\frac{1}{11}$
   (iii) 6 cm   **(iii)** 5 cm
   (iv) 90 cm   **(iv)** 55 cm

Review exercise 10

1 (a) Enlarge   **(b)** Enlarge
  (c) Reduce   **(d)** Reduce
2 (a)   **(b)**

  (ii)

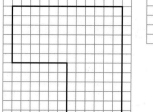

(iii)

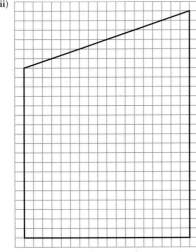

3 (a) 4   **(b)** $\frac{1}{3}$

4 (a) $\frac{24}{8} = \frac{30}{10}$ **(b)** $\frac{18}{12} = \frac{3}{2}$

5 (a) 2, 20 cm   **(b)** $\frac{1}{5}$, 6 cm

Chapter 11

Exercise 11.1

1 Pupils' own answers
2 **(a)** 9 cm
  (b) 15 cm
  (c) 60 mm
3 **(a)** 30 mm
  (b) 15 mm
  (c) 7 cm

Exercise 11.2

1

Item	Circumference (c)	Diameter (d)	c ÷ d calculator	c ÷ d rounded
Zig zog	132	42	3·142 857 1	3·14
Holo	110	35	3·142 857 1	3·14
Licorice Roll	42·4	13·5	3·140 740 7	3·14
Fruit tube	60·6	19·3	3·139 896 3	3·14
Choc button	89·4	28·5	3·136 842 1	3·14
Minty patty	182	58	3·137 931	3·14

2 More accurately, the circumference of a circle is 3·14 times the diameter.
3 China 480 AD
  (a) $\frac{4}{1} - \frac{4}{3} + \frac{4}{5} - \frac{4}{7} + \frac{4}{9} - \frac{4}{11} + \frac{4}{13} - \frac{4}{15} + \frac{4}{17} - \frac{4}{19}$
  (b) (i) 3·08   **(ii)** 3·14

Exercise 11.3

1 **(a)** 28·3 mm   **(b)** 94·2 cm   **(c)** 1570 mm   **(d)** 135 cm
2 **(a)** 37·7 cm   **(b)** 59·7 cm   **(c)** 72·3 cm
3 **(a)** 101 cm   **(b)** 126 cm   **(c)** 84·8 cm
4 383 m
5 40 074 km
6 **(a)** 113 cm, 251 cm
  (b) 370 cm
7 **(a)** 220 cm   **(b)** 154 cm   **(c)** 264 cm   **(d)** 363 cm
8 **(a)** 88 cm   **(b)** 22 cm   **(c)** 132 cm   **(d)** 154 cm

Exercise 11.4

1 **(a)** 195 cm   **(b)** 9750 cm
2 25·9 m
3 309 cm
4 **(a)** 77·3 cm   **(b)** 38·6 cm   **(c)** 19·3 cm
5 141 m
6 **(a)** 514 m   **(b)** 513 m
7 **(a)** 15·9 cm   **(b)** 2·5 cm   **(c)** 12·1 cm
8 **(a)** 192 m   **(b)** 104 times
9 2 510 000 times
10 **(a)** 4·71 m   **(b)** 1·57 m   **(c)** 141 m   **(d)** 90
11 Length = 23·6 cm, breadth = 10 cm
12 47 m
13 6·28 m

Exercise 11.5

1 **(a)** 15·9 cm   **(b)** 43·6 cm   **(c)** 31·2 cm
2 **(a)** 63·7 cm   **(b)** 10·0 cm   **(c)** 1·91 cm
3 44·6 cm
4 British = 4·11 cm   American = 4·27 cm
5 32 cm
6 8·594 km
7 **(a)** 22·3 cm   **(b)** 0·66 cm
8 **(a)** 6·37 cm   **(b)** 4·77 cm

Exercise 11.6

1

Radius (r)	r^2	Area (A)
2	4	12
3	9	27
4	6	48
5	25	75
6	36	108

  (e) The area of a circle is about $3 \times r^2$.
2 **(a)** 147 cm^2 **(b)** 300 cm^2 **(c)** 108 cm^2

Exercise 11.7

1 **(a)** 1260 cm^2 **(b)** 314 cm^2 **(c)** 12·5 mm^2 **(d)** 50·2 cm^2
2 **(a)** 14 500 cm^2 **(b)** 2290 cm^2 **(c)** 1760 cm^2
3 **(a)** 804 cm^2 **(b)** 2550 m^2 **(c)** 290 cm^2
4 707 cm^2
5 5940 cm^2

Exercise 11.8

1 **(a)** 7·07 m^2 **(b)** 6·79 m^2
2 **(a)** 50·3 m^2 **(b)** 5·03 kg
3 **(a)** 5660 cm^2 **(b)** 20 800 cm^2
4 2870 cm^2
5 **(b) (i)** 254 cm^2 **(ii)** 254 cm^2 **(iii)** 254 cm^2
6 1·54 m^2
7 He will not double the area. Area multiplies by 4.

Exercise 11.9

1 **(a)** 23·6 cm   **(b)** 5·5 cm   **(c)** 168 mm   **(d)** 6·28 cm
  (e) 12·8 cm   **(f)** 12·6 cm   **(g)** 27·3 cm   **(h)** 33·0 mm
2 **(a)** 7·85 cm   **(b)** 23·6 cm
3 **(a)** 6·14 m   **(b)** 1070 cm

Exercise 11.10

1 **(a)** 756 cm^2 **(b)** 1640 cm^2 **(c)** 2210 cm^2 **(d)** 251 cm^2
2 28·3 square inches.
3 13·1 cm^2
4 15·8 cm^2 4·19 cm^2 6·93 cm^2 18·1 cm^2
5 120 m^2
6 **(a)** 87·4 m^2 **(b)** 40·2 m^2 **(c)** 47·2 m^2
7 **(a)** 78·5 m^2 **(b)** 704 m^2

Review exercise 11

1 (a) 50·2 cm   (b) 120 cm   (c) 75·4 cm   (d) 565·2 mm
2 (a) 74 500 mm² (b) 254 cm²   (c) 129 cm²   (d) 1662 mm²
3 5·4 cm
4 4·8 cm
5 (a) Perimeter = 157 cm   (b) area = 1197 cm²
6 (a) 1390 cm   (b) 48 400 cm²
7 363 cm
8 15 100 cm²
9 (a) 119 mm   (b) 10·3 cm   (c) 52·9 cm
10 (a) 10·1 m²   (b) 5·81 cm²   (c) 136 000 m²
11 6·54 m²

Chapter 12

Exercise 12.1

1 (a) 3 hrs 42 mins   (b) 3 hrs 18 mins
   (c) 4 hrs 54 mins   (d) 10 hrs 12 mins
   (e) 1 hr 18 mins   (f) 5 hrs 42 mins
   (g) 1 hr 36 mins   (h) 3 hrs 50 mins
2 (a) 2·25 hrs   (b) 4·5 hrs   (c) 0·3 hrs   (d) 1·75 hrs
   (e) 1·1 hrs   (f) 2·7 hrs   (g) 1·4 hrs   (h) 3·9 hrs

Exercise 12.2

1 12 mph
2 240 miles
3 14 hrs 30 mins
4 (a) 56 km/h   (b) 34 km/h   (c) 72 km/h
   (d) 52 km/h   (e) 30 km/h   (f) 70 km/h
5 (a) 3 hrs   (b) 4 hrs
   (c) 2 hrs 30 mins   (d) 1 hr 30 mins
   (e) 1 hr 45 mins   (f) 48 mins
   (g) 2 hrs 12 mins   (h) 1 hr 12 mins
6 528 km
7 Cardiff–Birmingham   106 miles
   Birmingham–Nottingham   52½ miles
   Nottingham–Leeds   72 miles
   Leeds–Newcastle   92 miles
   Newcastle–Edinburgh   105 miles
8 (a) 40 miles per hour   (b) 44 miles per hour
9 No, the journey takes 4 hrs 55 mins which is too long.
10 598·5 miles

Exercise 12.3

1 (a) 1000 m/min   (b) 3000 m/min
   (c) 9000 m/min   (d) 5500 m/min
2 (a) 8⅓ m/s   (b) 11⅔ m/s
   (c) 20 m/s   (d) 7·5 m/s
3 (a) 43·2 km/h   (b) 64·8 km/h
   (c) 100·8 km/h   (d) 259·2 km/h
4 (a) 700 m/min   (b) 5 m/s
   (c) 250 m/min   (d) 133⅓ m/min
5 (a) 22 m   (b) 56 m
   (c) 100 m   (d) 258 m

Exercise 12.4

1 (a) (i) 25 miles   (ii) 11 km
   (b) 16 minutes
   (c) 2 miles
   (d) 10 minutes

Exercise 12.4

2 (a) (i) 30 miles   (ii) 30 miles   (iii) 40 miles
   (b) Achnasheen to Kyle of Lochalsh
   (c) 30 miles
   (d) 2 hrs 20 mins

Exercise 12.5

1 (a) 30 miles   (b) 30 minutes   (c) 60 mph
2 (a) 15 miles   (b) 20 minutes   (c) 45 mph
3 (a) 65 miles   (b) 80 minutes   (c) 48·75 mph
4 (a)

From	To	Distance miles	Time mins	Speed mph
Glasgow	Stirling	25	40	37·5
Stirling	Perth	40	40	60

   (b) 48·75 mph
5 (a) 120 miles   (b) 20 minutes
   (c) M74 to Penrith   (d) Speed up
   (e) 5 miles   (f) slow through traffic
   (g) (i) 210 miles   (ii) 4 hrs
   (h) 52·5 mph
6 (a) (i) 56·5 mph   (ii) 68·6 mph
   (b) No
   (c) 5.05 pm

Exercise 12.6

1 (a) 146 miles   (b) 433 miles   (c) 245 miles   (d) 394 miles
2 (a) 48 mph   (b) 52 mph   (c) 51 mph
3 (a) 45 mins
   (b) 2 hrs 24 mins
   (c) 6 hrs 27 mins
4

Aberdeen						
245	Carlisle					
105	141	Edinburgh				
171	199	144	Fort William			
148	97	44	102	Glasgow		
106	264	156	65	167	Inverness	
211	60	106	250	150	262	Newcastle
86	159	42	102	62	114	148	Perth

Review exercise 12

1 51 mph
2 No, he took 2 hrs 19 mins
3 (a) 3 km/h
   (b) 3 hrs 40 mins
4 (a) 7.58 am
   (b) Yes, average speed was 53·3 km/h
5 213 metres
6 2·5 m/s
7 (a) 45 minutes   (b) 3 hours
   (c) 10 miles, 1 hour   (d) 2 hrs 45 mins
   (e) 31 mph
8 (a) 11 miles
   (b) 6 miles

Chapter 13

Exercise 13.1

1 (a) (b)

Triangle	Area of square A	Area of square B	Area of square C
P	1	1	2
Q	1	4	5
R	2	2	4
S	1	9	10

   (c) Area of C = Area of A + Area of B.

2 (a)

Triangle	Area of square A	Area of square B	Area of square C
T	5	8	9
V	2	10	16

(b) Area A + Area B ≠ Area C

(c) They are not right angled triangles.

Exercise 13.2

1 (b) 25 cm²
(d) 25 cm²
(e) They are the same
(f) A square – all sides equal and all angles 90°
(g) 5 cm   (h) 5 cm
2 (a) 100 cm²   (b) 169 cm²   (c) 225 cm²
3 (a) 9 cm²   (b) 81 cm²   (c) 1600 mm²

Exercise 13.3

1 (a) r (b) s (c) y (d) a (e) i
2 (a) AC   (b) DF   (c) IG   (d) KM

Exercise 13.4

1 (a) 15 cm   (b) 13 cm   (c) 7·5 cm
(d) 25 cm   (e) 2·5 cm   (f) 17 cm
2 (a) 5·2 m   (b) 3·9 m   (c) 3·25 m
3 (a) 6·4 m   (b) 9·2 cm   (c) 6·5 cm   (d) 9·4 cm
4 6·4 cm
5 (a) 20 inches   (b) 30 inches   (c) 22·5 inches   (d) 40 inches
6 5·22 m
7 90 metres
8 (a) 1·82 m
(b) 7·28 m²
(c) No, the felt costs £36.40 which is £1.40 too much.
9 11·18 metres

Exercise 13.5

1 (a) 8 cm   (b) 12 cm   (c) 6 cm
(d) 2 cm   (e) 7·5 cm   (f) 4·8 cm
2 (a) 2 m   (b) 1·2 m   (c) 1·5 m
3 (a) 3·3 cm   (b) 8·9 cm   (c) 10 cm   (d) 5·1 cm
4 (a) 1·3 m   (b) 1·05 m   (b) 3·3 m
5 1·55 m
6 3·74 m

Exercise 13.6

1 3·5 cm
2 50 km
3 640 m
4 10·5 m
5 40 m
6 (a) 4·5 cm   (b) 18 cm²
7 27·2 cm
8 Red rectangle
9 5 units
10 (a)   (b) 13   (c) 15   (d) 13
11 7·1 cm
12 Yes, as the diagonal is 2·69 which is less than 2·7.
13 (a)

Number	1	2	3	4	5	6	7	8	9	10	11	12	13	14	15
Square number	1	4	9	16	25	36	49	64	81	100	121	144	169	196	225
Number	16	17	18	19	20	21	22	23	24	25	26	27	28	29	30
Square number	256	289	324	361	400	441	484	529	576	625	676	729	784	841	900

(b) 3, 4, 5;   6, 8, 10;   10, 24, 26;   9, 12, 15;   12, 16, 20;   15, 20, 25; 18, 24, 30;   8, 15, 17;   7, 24, 25

Exercise 13.7

1 (b) as $25^2 = 7^2 + 24^2$, (d) as $17^2 = 15^2 + 8^2$
2 Yes, $4·5^2 = 2·7^2 + 3·6^2$
3 Yes, $30^2 = 18^2 + 24^2$
4 No, $11^2 \neq 8^2 + 8^2$
5 Yes, $3^2 + 4^2 = 5^2$

Review exercise 13

1 (a) 10 cm   (b) 6·5 cm   (c) 8·5 cm
2 (a) 12 cm   (b) 2·5 cm   (c) 15 cm
3 (a) 6·4 cm   (b) 10 cm   (c) 3·3 cm   (d) 9·4 cm
4 2·80 m
5 640 m
6 (a) 18 cm   (b) 9 cm
7 (a) 9·5 cm   (b) 28·5 cm²
8 3·26 m
9 (a) Yes, $6·25^2 = 3·75^2 + 5^2$ (b) No, $40^2 \neq 36^2 + 15^2$
10 Yes, $3·75^2 = 3^2 + 2·25^2$

Chapter 14

Exercise 14.1

1 (a) $\frac{1}{6}$ (b) $\frac{1}{2}$ (c) $\frac{1}{3}$ (d) $\frac{1}{2}$
2 (a) $\frac{1}{40}$ (b) $\frac{1}{250}$
3 (a) $\frac{1}{7}$ (b) $\frac{2}{7}$ (c) $\frac{5}{7}$ (d) $\frac{2}{7}$ (e) $\frac{5}{7}$
4 (a) $\frac{1}{6}$ (b) $\frac{1}{3}$ (c) $\frac{1}{2}$ (d) 0
5 (a) $\frac{2}{11}$ (b) $\frac{1}{11}$ (c) $\frac{4}{11}$ (d) $\frac{7}{11}$
6 (a) $\frac{1}{3}$ (b) $\frac{2}{3}$
7 (a) $\frac{1}{3}$ (b) $\frac{2}{7}$ (c) $\frac{16}{21}$
8 (a) $\frac{8}{25}$ (b) $\frac{1}{2}$ (c) $\frac{1}{2}$
9 (a) $\frac{1}{10}$ (b) $\frac{1}{4}$ (c) $\frac{1}{40}$
10 (a) $\frac{1}{6}$ (b) $\frac{1}{4}$ (c) $\frac{5}{12}$ (d) $\frac{5}{12}$ (e) $\frac{1}{6}$
11 (a) $\frac{1}{2}$ (b) $\frac{3}{13}$ (c) $\frac{1}{26}$ (d) $\frac{1}{13}$
(e) $\frac{1}{4}$ (f) $\frac{5}{52}$ (g) $\frac{5}{13}$ (h) $\frac{1}{52}$
12 (a) RTA, RAT, TAR, TRA, ART, ATR
(b) (i) $\frac{1}{6}$ (ii) $\frac{1}{2}$ (iii) $\frac{1}{6}$
13 (a) 345, 354, 534, 543, 435, 453
(b) (i) $\frac{1}{3}$ (ii) $\frac{1}{3}$ (iii) $\frac{1}{3}$ (iv) $\frac{2}{3}$ (v) $\frac{1}{3}$ (vi) 0
14 (a) 1257   1275   1527   1572   1725   1752   2157   2175   2517
2571   2715   2751   5127   5172   5217   5271   5712   5721
7125   7152   7215   7251   7512   7521
(b) (i) $\frac{1}{2}$ (ii) $\frac{3}{4}$ (iii) $\frac{1}{4}$ (iv) $\frac{1}{4}$ (v) $\frac{1}{6}$ (vi) 0

Exercise 14.2

1 (a) $\frac{3}{5}$ (b) $\frac{33}{50}$ (c) $\frac{1}{10}$
2 (a) $\frac{2}{5}$ (b) $\frac{1}{12}$ (c) $\frac{2}{15}$
3 (a) $\frac{1}{25}$ (b) $\frac{1}{5}$ (c) $\frac{6}{25}$
4 (a)

	1	2	3	4	5	6
1	2	3	4	5	6	7
2	3	4	5	6	7	8
3	4	5	6	7	8	9
4	5	6	7	8	9	10
5	6	7	8	9	10	11
6	7	8	9	10	11	12

(b) (i) $\frac{1}{36}$ (ii) $\frac{1}{6}$ (iii) $\frac{1}{2}$ (iv) $\frac{1}{6}$ (v) $\frac{7}{12}$ (vi) $\frac{7}{36}$

Exercise 14.3

1 (a) $\frac{3}{4}$ (b) $\frac{2}{7}$
2 (a) $\frac{1}{5}$ (b) $\frac{1}{7}$
3 (a) $\frac{7}{9}$ (b) $\frac{8}{35}$
4 (a) $\frac{12}{33}$ (b) $\frac{1}{8}$
5 (a) $\frac{5}{8}$ (b) $\frac{2}{5}$
6 (a) $\frac{1}{26}$ (b) $\frac{13}{51}$
7 (a) $\frac{3}{8}$ (b) $\frac{3}{5}$

8 (a) $\frac{3}{5}$ **(b)** $\frac{3}{5}$ **(c)** $\frac{5}{9}$

9 (a) $\frac{1}{16}$

  (b) (i) $\frac{1}{3}$ **(ii)** $\frac{4}{15}$ **(iii)** 0

10 (a) $\frac{2}{3}$ **(b)** $\frac{5}{8}$ **(c)** $\frac{3}{4}$

Exercise 14.4

1 120

2 125

3 5

4 (a) 40   **(b)** 250   **(c)** 50   **(d)** 25

5 (a) $\frac{2}{5}$ **(b)** 16

6 4

7 (a) 65   **(b)** 5   **(c)** 10   **(d)** 30

  (e) 5   **(f)** 50   **(g)** 5

8 (a) (i) $\frac{61}{200}$ **(ii)** $\frac{3}{8}$ **(iii)** $\frac{22}{25}$

  (b) (i) 6   **(ii)** 10   **(iii)** 34

Review exercise 14

1 (a) $\frac{1}{6}$ **(b)** $\frac{1}{2}$ **(c)** $\frac{1}{3}$ **(d)** $\frac{5}{6}$

2 (a) $\frac{5}{18}$ **(b)** $\frac{1}{6}$ **(c)** $\frac{5}{9}$ **(d)** $\frac{5}{9}$

3 (a) $\frac{11}{20}$ **(b)** $\frac{3}{10}$ **(c)** $\frac{1}{8}$

4 (a) $\frac{3}{7}$ **(b)** $\frac{2}{5}$

5 (a) 25   **(b)** 25   **(c)** 5

6 (a) (i) $\frac{23}{180}$ **(ii)** $\frac{17}{45}$ **(iii)** $\frac{3}{5}$

  (b) (i) 80   **(ii)** 50   **(iii)** 70

Chapter 15

Exercise 15.1

1 (a) (i)

x	0	2	5
y	3	5	8

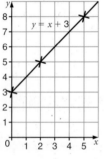

  (ii)

x	0	3	5
y	1	10	16

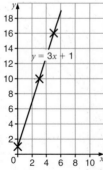

2 (a) A(1, 4)   B(3, 12)   C(5, 20)

  (b) P(0, 5)   Q(2, 9)   R(4, 13)

  (c) K(2, 6)   L(5, 9)   M(7, 11)

  (d) S(0, 1)   T(1, 6)   U(6, 31)

3 (a)

x	0	1	2	3	4	5
y	1	2	3	4	5	6

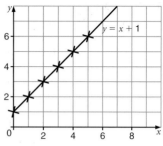

(b)

x	0	1	2	3	4	5
y	0	1	2	3	4	5

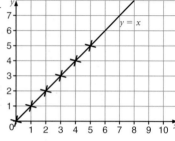

(c)

x	0	1	2	3	4	5
y	2	3	4	5	6	7

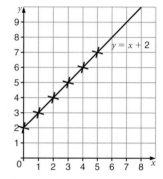

(d)

x	0	1	2	3	4	5
y	5	6	7	8	9	10

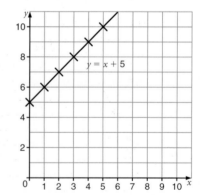

(e)

x	0	1	2	3	4	5
y	2	5	8	11	14	17

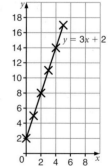

(f)

x	0	1	2	3	4	5
y	1	3	5	7	9	11

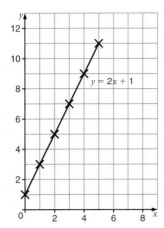

$y = 2x + 1$

(g)

x	0	1	2	3	4	5
y	0	3	6	9	12	15

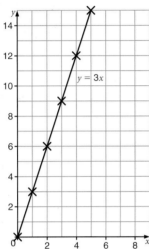

$y = 3x$

(h)

x	0	1	2	3	4	5
y	4	6	8	10	12	14

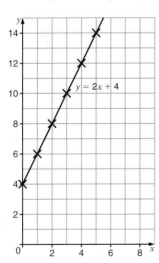

$y = 2x + 4$

Exercise 15.2

1 (a)

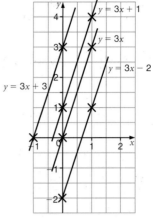

$y = 3x + 1$
$y = 3x$
$y = 3x - 2$
$y = 3x + 3$

(c) (i) They are parallel
   (ii) The same, 3

2 The lines in each family are parallel.
The x-coefficient is
  (a) 1   (b) 4   (c) 2

Exercise 15.3

1 (a) (i) 5   (ii) 5
  (b) (i) 3   (ii) 3
  (c) (i) 8   (ii) 8
  (d) (i) 3   (ii) 3
  (e) (i) 8   (ii) 8
  (f) (i) 1   (ii) 1
  (g) (i) $\frac{1}{2}$ (ii) $\frac{1}{2}$
  (h) (i) 1   (ii) 1

2 (b) and (d)   (f) and (h)   (c) and (e)

3 $y = 2x$ $y = x + 8$ $y = 5x - 5$ $y = 10x$
  $y = 2x - 6$ $y = x + 10$ $y = 5x - 7$ $y = 10x + 3$
  $y = 3x$ $y = 6x - 12$ $y = 4x + 6$ $y = 9x$
  $y = 3x - 8$ $y = 6x + 10$ $y = 4x - 7$ $y = 9x + 3$

4 $y = 10x, y = 10x + 3$ – largest gradient

Exercise 15.4

1 (a)

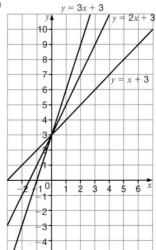

$y = 3x + 3$
$y = 2x + 3$
$y = x + 3$

(c) They are the same
(d) $(0, 3)$

2 (a)

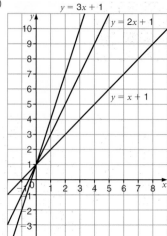

(b) They are the same
(c) $(0, 1)$

3 (a)

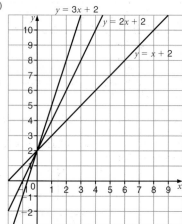

(b)

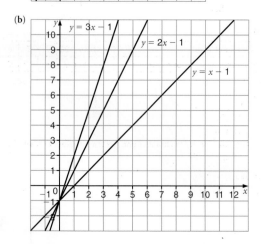

(c)

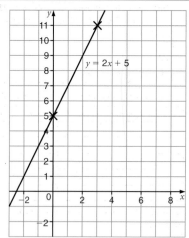

Exercise 15.5

1 (a) $(0, 7)$ (b) $(0, 5)$ (c) $(0, -7)$ (d) $(0, -9)$
2 (a) 9   (b) 7   (c) -4 (d) 1
   (e) -1 (f) -9 (g) 8   (h) 0
3 (a) (i) 2, (ii) 3   (b) (i) 4, (ii) 9   (c) (i) 1, (ii) 5
   (d) (i) 3, (ii) 1   (e) (i) 7, (ii) -2 (f) (i) 10, (ii) -3
   (g) (i) 8, (ii) -11 (h) (i) 1, (ii) -1 (i) (i) 1, (ii) $-\frac{1}{2}$
   (j) (i) 5, (ii) 0   (k) (i) $\frac{1}{4}$, (ii) 1   (l) (i) 12, (ii) $-\frac{5}{8}$
4 (a) $y = 2x + 4$ (b) $y = 7x + 3$ (c) $y = 5x + 8$ (d) $y = x + 9$
   (e) $y = 3x - 6$ (f) $y = 4x - 2$ (g) $y = 9x - 9$ (h) $y = x - 5$
5 (a) $y = 6x + 2$ (b) $y = 8x + 7$ (c) $y = 3x$ (d) $y = x + 6$
   (e) $y = x$ (f) $y = 10x - 2$ (g) $y = 5x - 12$ (h) $y = -3$
6 $y = 9x + 7$

Review exercise 15

1 (i)

x	0	3	5
y	5	11	15

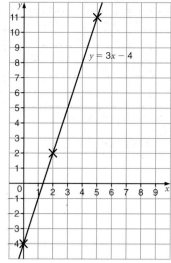

(ii)

x	0	2	5
y	-4	2	11

2 (a) A(1, 3)   B(4, 12)   C(9, 27)
  (b) P(0, −3)   Q(2, 7)   R(10, 47)
3 (a) 6   (b) 9   (c) −2   (d) −8
4 $y = 2x − 7$ $y = −x + 12$ $y = 7x$ $y = x$
  $y = 2x + 12$ $y = −x + 9$ $y = 7x − 2$ $y = x − 9$
5 (a) (0, 3)   (b) (0, 9)   (c) (0, 0)   (d) (0, −8)
6 (a) $y = 7x + 2$ (b) $y = 5x$ (c) 2   (d) $y = 2x + 4$

Chapter 16

Exercise 16.1

1 (a) 21, 23
  (b) 24, 26
2 (b) Craig 19 years, Seamus 12 years Andrew 8 years
  (c) 3 years
3 (a)

Sum of odd numbers	Total
1	1 or 1^2
1 + 3	4 or 2^2
1 + 3 + 5	9 or 3^2
1 + 3 + 5 + 7	16 or 4^2
1 + 3 + 5 + 7 + 9	25 or 5^2
1 + 3 + 5 + 7 + 9 + 11	36 or 6^2

  (b) Square numbers
  (c) (i) 49   (ii) 100   (iii) 400
  (d) (i)   sum of first 5 odd number = 25 or 5^2
      (ii) sum of first ten odd numbers = 100 or 10^2
      (iii) sum of first fifteen odd numbers = 225 or 15^2
      (iv) sum of first fifty odd numbers = 2500 or 50^2
4 1 £93·40
  2 £40 per kg
  3 £436
  4 £11·80 per 10 cm height
  5 Assuming can height 10 cm and diameter 6·5 cm,
    9 piles of coins fit round can, giving total £106·20
5

Number of dots on boundary	Area of shape in cm²
4	2
5	$2\frac{1}{2}$
6	3
7	$3\frac{1}{2}$
8	4

  (c) Area = $\frac{1}{2} ×$ number of dots on boundary
  (d) 8 cm²
6 (a)

Shape	Number of dots on boundary (b)	Number of dots inside (i)	$\frac{1}{2}b + i$	Area (A) in square units
A	8	1	5	4
B	12	2	8	7
C	10	4	9	8
D	8	3	7	6
E	12	0	6	5

    (iii) The last column is one less
    (iv) $A = \frac{1}{2}b + i − 1$.
  (b) F = 14, G = 6, H = 11, I = 10
  (c) J = 16, K = 15, L = 18

7 (a)

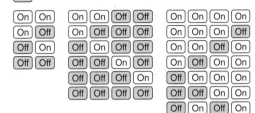

  (b)

  (c)

Number of lamps in a row	1	2	3	4
Number of possible arrangements	2	4	8	16

  (d) (i) $32 = 2^5$ (ii) $1024 = 2^{10}$
8 (a) 16   (b) 15   (c) 256
9 (a) 36   (b) 3   (c) 4
10 (a) Morris's van, Model T, Ford pop, Red Rod, Barracuda Model Y,
       Big boots, Funny car, Dragster
   (b) Model Y, Big boots
   (c) 6. Morris's van Model T, Ford pop, red rod, Barracuda Model Y
       or Big boots
   (d) Model Y and Big boots cannot be loaded with the two longest
       cars as there is not enough space.
11 (a) (i)   (ii)
       1 box   6 boxes
   (b)

Number of roads	1	2	3	4	5	6
Maximum number of control boxes	0	1	3	6	10	15

   (c) 10
   (d) 28
   (e) (i)   3
       (ii) 3, 6
       (iii) 4, 10
       (iv) Multiply by the number one less than number of roads then
             divide, $\frac{R(R − 1)}{2}$
   (f) 190
   (g) $\frac{n(n − 1)}{2}$

Index